RICHARD MATHESON'S

The Twilight Zone Scripts

Volume Two

D1479252

RICHARD MATHESON'S

The Twilight Zone Scripts

Volume Two

EDITED BY STANLEY WIATER

EDGE BOOKS

■ *2002* ■

Davie County Public Library
Mocksville, North Carolina

RICHARD MATHESON'S "THE TWILIGHT ZONE SCRIPTS"
(VOLUME TWO)

ISBN 1-887368-52-3

Original scripts copyright © 2002 by RXR, Inc.

Accompanying text and interview material
copyright © 2002 by ShadoWind, Inc.

Cover Illustration by Marcelo M. Martinez
Design by Michael Bayouth

"The Twilight Zone" is a registered trademark of CBS, Inc.

This book is a work of fiction. Names, characters, places and
incidents are either the products of the author's imagination or are
used fictitiously. Any resemblance to actual events or locations or
persons, living or dead, is entirely coincidental.

Manufactured in the United States of America
All Rights Reserved

FIRST EDITION
Trade Paperback Edition

1 2 3 4 5 6 7 8 9 10

EDGE BOOKS
An imprint of Gauntlet Press
Gauntlet Publications
309 Powell Road, Springfield, PA 19064
Phone: (610) 328-5476
Email: info@gauntletpress.com
Website: http://www.gauntletpress.com

TABLE
OF
CONTENTS

ACKNOWLEDGEMENTS

I want to thank my interviewer Stanley Wiater not only for his outstanding work in that respect but for being directly instrumental in getting this book published.

—R.M.

* * *

I would like to thank Marc Scott Zicree, who first found most of the ingredients refined for this particular recipe.

Richard Matheson for graciously allowing me to add my layer of "frosting" to his wondrous run of fourteen "cakes."

Of course, my eternal gratitude to Rod Serling for creating the series—and then giving Richard Matheson the opportunity to write these classic scripts.

And Richard Chizmar, for simply doing the right thing.

—S.W.

To Rod Serling
for creating *The Twilight Zone* and making
my years of writing for the show so pleasant
and fulfilling.

To Carol Serling
for being the lovely person she is and
giving me her blessing for this
collection of my scripts.

To Buck Houghton
with many thanks for his help and kindness
during those enjoyable years.

To Marc Zicree
for his most excellent book about
The Twilight Zone experience.

To Herb Hirschman and Bert Granet
for enhancing my last two years on the show.

To all the talented and creative people who
worked on *The Twilight Zone* and
left me with a wonderful
legacy of lasting shows.

And, finally, to my dear and talented friend
throughout those halcyon days:
Charles Beaumont.

Submitted For Your Approval:

RICHARD MATHESON'S

The Twilight Zone Scripts

"Rod Serling, one of television's most famous playwrights, brings you an extraordinary dramatic series described by the author as: 'The land that lies between science and superstition, between the pit of man's fears and the summit of his knowledge. You will find the bizarre, but the believable; the different, the shocking that is yet understandable. It's tales must be shown; they cannot be told. And each carries with it it's own special surprise.'"

— original CBS advertisement for the series, which premiered October 2, 1959

* * *

"*The Twilight Zone* is a wondrous land of the very different. No luggage is required for the trip. All that the audience need bring is imagination."

— Rod Serling, "Seeking Far Horizons" (TV Guide, 1959)

* * *

"Rod Serling freely admitted that he was unabashedly a great devotee of tales of horror, fantasy, and the supernatural. He grew up reading Poe and Lovecraft, so that when CBS gave the green light to the new series, he sought out the master fantasy storytellers of the day...

"Several years later, when an Emmy Award was presented to Rod for the series, he said, 'Come on over, fellahs, we'll carve it up like a turkey.' He was really speaking to two 'fellahs:' Richard Matheson

and Charles Beaumont. In collaboration, the three of them produced over ninety-nine percent of the work for the early years of *The Twilight Zone.*"
    — Carol Serling, "Preface" to
The Twilight Zone: The Original Stories

*   *   *

"What Serling was—in addition to being one of the greatest television writers of all time—a canny producer who brought individuals with their own talents and visions into his playroom, and let them run loose. Over time the series seems to be a homogenous whole, but look closely and you'll see that there were at least three very distinct subgenres of *Twilight Zone* stories—humanistic parables like 'Eye of the Beholder" and 'Changing of the Guard,' most of them written by Serling; darker, moodier pieces like 'The Jungle' and 'Shadowplay,' hallmarks of [Charles] Beaumont's writing; and inventive, plot-driven stories which, as Marc Scott Zicree has put it, are so involving that you have to keep watching to find out *what happens next*, and those were and are the domain of Richard Matheson."
    — "Introduction" by Alan Brennert to *New Stories from The Twilight Zone* edited by Martin H. Greenberg

*   *   *

"Many film critics are in the habit of analyzing films in a way that suggests the films sprang fully-formed from the minds of their directors, totally ignoring the writers' contribution. The *auteur* theory in regard to directors may be perfectly valid in some cases but it can equally apply to writers, and often with much more justification. One example of this is the work of Richard Matheson...one of the major contributors to the excellent television fantasy series *The Twilight Zone*.
    — John Brosnan, *The Horror People*

*   *   *

"*The Twilight Zone* staged some of the best nervous breakdowns in TV history, two of them occurring just before CBS pulled the plug

on the show. Richard Matheson's classic "Nightmare at 20,000 feet" (10/11/63) plays on a half-dozen barely articulated anxieties (fear of flying, of madness, of betrayal by a spouse), as William Shatner—who had already demonstrated a flare for obsessive-compulsive behavior as the superstitious honeymooner in "Nick of Time" (11/18/60)—hallucinates a gremlin on the wing of a jetliner. Once seen, this show can never be forgotten; Shatner's freak-out displays a range (and a knack for comedy) that he seems to have lost on his first *Star Trek*."
    — from "America's Twilight Zone" by J. Hoberman

* * *

"Matheson's skill in creating empathy lends special strength to his work. Capturing our credibility with believable characters helps make their predicaments seem equally plausible. Thus convinced, his reading or viewing audience becomes ensnared as Matheson whipsaws them between the heights of hysteria and the depths of dread. The secret weapon he employs is his own sensitivity to the fears and innermost imaginings which are common to us all."
    — Robert Bloch

* * *

"Although it shared conceptual concerns with and adapted stories from the cream of the science fiction field, *The Twilight Zone* cannot be wholly considered a science fiction television series. It wasn't horror either—yet it's shock endings are among the most horrific ever filmed for television (or motion pictures). And it would be unfair to pass the series off as pure fantasy, for it was grounded in a reality far more real and true for its day—and ours."
    — "Introduction" to *Visions from the Twilight Zone* by Arlen Schumer

* * *

"Richard Matheson is almost too good to be true. He is what every horror-and-supernatural writer should be, and few are. For example, he lives in a remote area of the San Fernando Valley. Big, black furry tarantulas so frequently saunter in and out of his house that they are regarded as pets. He is an enormous man, luxuriantly bearded and pale-eyed, like a seer of old. He has a deep and abiding belief in psychic phenomena, in ghosts and mediums, gremlins and poltergeists, in all things arcane, outre, occult, in everything super-,para-, preter-, extra- or un-natural. Of course, the image is somewhat spoiled by his easy charm, his ready laugh, his wit, and the Midwestern twang of his speech. But nobody's perfect."

— Ray Russell

*   *   *

"Matheson is and has always has been a writer's writer. His influence, a singularly compelling voice that runs through the contemporary history of science fiction, terror and horror literature, is better left for assessment by scholars and critics. For now it is enough to say that his courage, his measured understatement and his refusal to court fashion by accommodating popular trends exemplify an integrity that is unsurpassed in the commercial arena. His novels are relentless in their intensity, written in the cold sweat of absolute conviction; his screenplays are models of structural economy, tightly suspenseful without sacrificing larger meanings, and his short stories are tours de force, demonstrating the strength of obsessive narrative freed from stylistic indulgence ... He is the very best of the best, an archetype of what a career is supposed to be all about."

— Dennis Etchison

*   *   *

"Some well-known actors appeared on *Twilight Zone*, but it was the stories rather than the performances that made the show work. Serling's original opening narration to the show set the scene appropriately. The opening: 'There is a fifth dimension beyond that which is known to man. It is a dimension as vast as space and as timeless as infinity. It is the middle ground between light and darkness,

between science and superstition, and it lies between the pit of man's fears and the summit of his knowledge. This is the dimension of imagination. It is an area we call *The Twilight Zone*.'"
— Tim Brooks and Earle Marsh, *The Complete Directory to Prime Time Network and Cable TV Shows*

* * *

"With this rather purple invocation—which did not sound purple at all in Rod Serling's measured and almost matter-of-fact delivery— viewers were invited to enter a queerly boundless other world...and enter they did. *The Twilight Zone* ran on CBS from October of 1959 through the summer of 1965—from the torpor of the Eisenhower administration to LBJ's escalation of American involvement in Vietnam, the first of the long hot summers in American cities, and the advent of the Beatles.

"Of all the dramatic programs which have ever run on American TV, it is the one which comes closest to defying any overall analysis."
— Stephen King, *Danse Macabre*

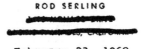

ROD SERLING

~~██████████~~
~~██████████~~, CALIFORNIA

February 23, 1968

Mr. Richard Matheson
P. O. Box 81
Woodland Hills, California 91364

Dear Dick,

        Occasionally down the Pike walks a guy with
sensitivity and a decent regard for the feelings of his
colleague. And that's you doing the walking, old friend.

        Your letter simply supported that which I've
thought about you for lo, these many years -- that you
were twenty cuts above the average -- certainly, in talent --
but most especially as a human being. It was gracious of
you, Dick, to feel concerned about re-writing my script.
It was uncommonly decent of you to take the time and trouble
to indicate that concern via the letter.

        Have no further concerns, and don't sweat this.
We both know it happens all the time. We both know that
sometimes it can serve as an abrasive to a relationship.
But I think you and I are old enough friends to know that
it's not the kind of thing that will in any way hurt our
relationship. I think we mutually respect each other too
much to allow anything like this to render our friendship
any damage.

        So go with God with the script, do all and any-
thing you can to improve, to change, or as you say, to start
from scratch on it. I hope it gets you an Oscar and a million
dollars. Both rewards couldn't accrue to a nicer guy. And
I mean that.

                                Warm regards,

                                Rod Serling

RS/ml

"This letter was in reference to a movie that George Pal was going to do called, I think, *The Last Revolution*. Rod had done a script, and I was offered a rewrite on it. This was at a time when the Writer's Guild did not require it, but now it's a rule that when you rewrite somebody's script, you just automatically have to tell them. But back then, that was not the case."

"I felt uneasy about it, and wrote him a letter explaining everything, and this was his response. Which I think is a very good example of how generous and thoughtful and kind that he was."

—Richard Matheson

PROLOGUE

Richard Matheson was born on February 20, 1926, in Allendale, New Jersey. By the summer of 1959, he was already an accomplished and successful writer before ever hearing of *The Twilight Zone*. (At that point in his career he had published no less than six novels and three collections of short stories.) Along with other established writers, he was invited to a private screening of the show's pilot episode. With him was his close friend and sometime collaborator, Charles Beaumont (1929-1967), with whom they both happened to share the same agent.

"Charles Beaumont and I had joined an agency called Adams, Ray, and Rosenberg, and all of a sudden we were inundated with telephone calls and appointments and meetings," Matheson recalls. "One of the calls was to go see the pilot for *The Twilight Zone*. I don't recall exactly who was there, but to my recollection neither Rod Serling nor producer Buck Houghton were present. But the fact that they were showing us the pilot indicated their interest."

Serling had already been frustrated in finding previously published stories that would fit *The Twilight Zone* format. Beyond that, there were simply few, if any, television writers who were experienced in the fantasy, science fiction, and horror genres. And an earlier "open call" for submissions—more than 14,000 received, not a single script useable—had already proven an unmitigated disaster.

"I believe Rod had in mind—as I believe Gene Roddenberry had in mind later with *Star Trek*—to use all the top writers in the fantasy and science fiction field to write for the show. And in both cases, as I understand it, they didn't have much success in that area. There were only a few people who ever worked out." (Matheson, incidentally, later also went on to write for *Star Trek*.)

Indeed, Matheson believes his name may first have been brought to Serling's attention because the show had purchased two of his short stories in that initial search for appropriate fantasy material. The first story purchased was "Disappearing Act"—filmed as "And When the Sky was Opened"—and the second was "Third from the Sun." (The latter being Matheson's second published story, by the way.) However, it was Rod Serling who then did the script adaptations for the first season—not Matheson.

"He may have bought the stories before I even saw the pilot. But I think that if I had known I was going to be working on the show, I would have tried to do the scripts myself. At the time he was starting out, I knew he was reading through a massive amount of material. He must have picked out those two stories. I'm just guessing, but maybe that was why Chuck Beaumont and I were called in to look at the pilot. To see if we could do original scripts as well."

Matheson also feels that, even though he had not yet written for television, Serling was probably also aware that Matheson had adapted his own 1956 novel, *The Shrinking Man,* into the successful motion picture *The Incredible Shrinking Man.*

Whatever the initial reason for their being sought out, both Matheson and Beaumont were quickly hired to write original scripts—or adapt their own published stories for the new show. Though no one knew it at the time, these two writers—after Serling of course—would be responsible for the greatest number of scripts produced for the series' five season run. Quite simply, almost no one else seemed able to have the particular knack for creating a story that was uniquely *The Twilight Zone.* (Ray Bradbury, a world-famous fantasy writer even then, managed only a single produced episode.)

"I think there's a number of reasons for that," Matheson notes. "One is that both Chuck Beaumont and I were very visual writers. So when you read our stories, you can see them in your mind. And so we were able to adapt to the screenplay format very easily, because a screenplay of course is strictly visual. Even the adaptations of our own stories were not that difficult because the stories were written in a similar way."

And if that weren't enough, both writers instinctively wrote in a manner which readily fit the special format most desired by the producers of the show. "For one thing, both Chuck Beaumont and I wrote stories that tried to grab the reader immediately. Which fit into the *Twilight Zone* pattern of having that little teaser at the beginning. Our stories usually had a surprise ending. If not, they had an ironic ending that was still completely appropriate for *Twilight Zone*."

Although Beaumont and Matheson agreed to sometimes collaborate on scripts for other television series (*Have Gun Will Travel, Wanted: Dead or Alive, Philip Marlowe*) they decided from the outset *not* to collaborate on *The Twilight Zone*. "There was no need to, because that was our field," Matheson explains. "The other fields—westerns, detective—we were really not that familiar with, although I did six *Lawman* scripts on my own." (In fact he won a Writers Guild of America Award for a script he wrote for *Lawman*.) "But this was the area of expertise that we both had, so it would have been crazy for us to collaborate on *The Twilight Zone*."

Since both men had established reputations as writers of the fantastic in prose, they were anxious to bring their imaginations to a new medium for which, in Serling's words: "No luggage is required. All the audience need bring is their imagination."

Or as Matheson simply now believes, "We were ideal for *The Twilight Zone*."

* * *

In an interview for a definitive PBS documentary entitled *Rod Serling: Submitted For Your Approval*, Matheson stated that part of the continuing appeal of the series was because each episode could be considered a "miniature film noir" in many ways: "They were filmed in black and white to begin with, and much of the lighting was a noir type of lighting. There were so many dark fantasy ideas, and so many dark science fiction ideas, the series had the feeling of being composed of mini-film noirs. At one point the network wanted Serling to do the series in color, but that would have ruined it."

Without taking anything away from the many great episodes penned by Serling himself, it was an open secret at the time that many stories were meant to specifically comment on topical social issues. From his years of writing original, award-winning plays for television, Serling was accustomed to his stories Saying Something Important. Yet for Matheson (and Beaumont, for that matter) this was never a concern. Truthfully, this may be one of the reasons their episodes have not dated to the degree many of Serling's highly topical scripts have.

"Rod was very deep into that, and said so in his public commentary" admits Matheson. "I don't think I wrote any episodes that had any kind of social commentary in them, but he was very much involved in that sort of thing. And that's why so many of his *Twilight Zones* incorporated that kind of thinking. Whereas Chuck and I were the entertainment gadflies. The story was what mattered."

Matheson had no obvious political or social axe to grind. "And I never had any overall attitude or approach to my scripts. I just went at them one at a time, and did each one as honestly and as capably as I could. If there was any similarity or pattern to them, then that was just inevitable because I was the one who did them."

To this day, he feels the primary reason why the series is endlessly rerun is simply because of the stories that were told: "I'm convinced that the reason it's lasted so long is because the *stories* are interesting. That's why they transcend time. Every once in a while you get caught in a chronological boo-boo, like in my "Steel," but beyond that, most of the stories just transcend the effects of time. They're stories about *people*—with intriguing ideas."

*   *   *

Over the years, Richard Matheson has pointed out in numerous interviews and studies the flaws and missed opportunities he still sees in the episodes he's written. It's almost appeared at times that he has disliked more episodes than he would care to mention by name. Even so, there's no denying many of his tales are regarded amongst the series' all-time most memorable—and terrifying. In truth, Matheson himself has grown increasingly less critical of his fourteen episodes with the passing of time. And he does not necessarily see this as coming from the blurry perspective of growing nostalgia. But rather from his lifelong convictions as the original—and usually sole—creator of a story who now must find himself working in a highly collaborative medium.

"I've always had this 'problem'—I don't know if it's only a problem of mine—but when I write a script, I see it *precisely* in my head. Then, when it appears on television or the screen it couldn't possibly—or almost never—be exactly what I've seen in my brain. Once in a blue moon that happens, and then it's astonishing. But most of the time the results vary. As it would have to be—because other people are doing their work; interpreting your script in their own way. So very often I've had a sense of disappointment in what I saw.

"But then, after a while, I lose that feeling of 'Well, it should reflect my script *exactly*.' I begin to look at the collaborative effort for what it is, and then I begin to appreciate it more. Of course, the closer the finished episode came to what I originally visualized in mind, the more I liked it. But after that need to see my brainstorm directly reflected faded, then I could look at each episode on its own terms, and appreciate it for the values given to it by the other people involved."

Just as we now can appreciate these classic scripts before they were interpreted by anyone other than their original storyteller, Richard Matheson...

Mute

"Mute" would the first of two compelling scripts that Matheson would write in a one-hour format for the fourth season of the series's run. Serling himself was reportedly not thrilled about expanding to an hour, but the network assumed it might increase the viewership—and the always mediocre ratings. "I don't know whose idea it was to go an hour, whether it was CBS or Rod's. I was not unhappy with my two one-hour episodes. But it wasn't *The Twilight Zone* structure anymore, and wisely, they went back to the half-hour for the final season."

"Mute" is based on a memorable novelette that Matheson wrote in 1962 (for Charles Beaumont's anthology, *The Fiend In You*), which was later reprinted in *Shock II* and finally in *Collected Stories*. The most obvious change in its being transformed from story to script was that the title character was now a telepathic little girl rather than a telepathic little boy. The story deals sincerely and rationally with the paranormal, a theme Matheson has always taken extremely seriously.

"I wrote 'Mute' in a deliberately professional way. Most stories I get an inspiration, and sort of dash it off before I redo it in another draft. This one I did very methodically. I don't know why they changed the character from a little boy and made him into a little girl. I know I wrote the script that way, but it must have been after their suggestion I do so. Maybe they thought there would be more sympathy for the character if it was a little girl."

Regardless, to many fans the story is, ultimately, quite downbeat. Even to this editor, "Mute" would appear to be a prime example of yet another inevitable "unhappy ending."

Of course, the author/scriptwriter begs to differ.

"I never thought of it having an unhappy ending. It's true her parents were kind to her, but she was more or less like a test case to them. Whereas with the people she was going to live with now— although she may have lost her telepathic ability—she was going to be in a loving home. Marc Zicree didn't think that was a happy ending either. But I think it is. Better to grow up in a loving home than to have a sixth sense. There have been too many miserable people who have been psychic."

<u>MUTE</u>

<u>PERFORMANCE</u> <u>DATE</u>: 1/31/63

<u>PRODUCER</u>: HERBERT HIRSCHMAN

<u>DIRECTOR</u>: STUART ROSENBERG

<u>CAST</u>:

ILSE NIELSEN: ANN JILLIAN

HARRY WHEELER: FRANK OVERTON

CORA WHEELER: BARBARA BAXLEY

MISS FRANK: IRENE DAILEY

PROF. KARL WERNER: OSCAR BEREGI

FRAU NIELSEN: CLAUDIA BRYER

FRAU MARIA WERNER: EVA SORENY

TOM POULTER: PERCY HELTON

FADE IN:

1.   EST. SHOT - HEIDELBERG - LATE NIGHT

Featuring the University, quiet and deserted.
TITLE: Heidelberg, Germany, 1952

                                        LAP DISSOLVE TO:

2.   EXT. HEIDELBERG STREET

Angle on one particular building; the Heidelberg equivalent of
a small apartment house. One of the upper windows shows
illumination.

                                        LAP DISSOLVE TO:

3.   EXT. WINDOW

In the livingroom of the flat, four couples are seated around a
large, circular table. None of them are talking. They all watch
one of the men- HOLGER NIELSEN - who is writing quickly
on a sheet of paper, puffing on a pipe.

                                        LAP DISSOLVE TO:

4.   INT. LIVING ROOM - CLOSE ON HOLGER NIELSEN'S
     HANDS

As he writes with great rapidity. CAMERA PANS UP to
show his face, his expression one of restrained excitement.
CAMERA PANS TO FANNY NIELSEN, Holger's wife.
She watches her husband with a tense elation almost equal to
his own. O.S., the SOUND of Holger's RAPID WRITING
continues as the CAMERA PANS TO HERR AND FRAU
KALDAR who are watching with approval. CAMERA PANS
TO PROFESSOR KARL WERNER and his wife. FRAU
WERNER is pregnant.

                                        (CONTINUED)

4.   CONTINUED

She and her husband exchange a look, hers somewhat uneasy.
Professor Werner gives her a reassuring smile and puts his hand
on hers; the smile she returns is an unconvincing one.
CAMERA PANS TO the last couple, THE ELKENBERGS,
observing with interest. CAMERA PANS
BACK TO the Nielsens as Holger finishes, puts down his pen
with a hard, precise movement and looks up, smiling tightly,
triumphantly.

                         HOLGER
           So.

He puts down his pipe carelessly and picks up the sheet of
paper; Fanny puts the pipe in an ash tray. Holger begins to read
what he has written and, as he does, the CAMERA DRAWS
BACK SLOWLY until all four couples are in view. (Holger,
while Scandinavian in appearance, is an American, therefore,
has no accent.)

                         HOLGER
           The undersigned, having accepted the fol-
           lowing propositions: A: That, prior to the
           inception of language, man communicated
           by telepathic means. And - B: That this
           ability not only still exists but can be rede-
           veloped to its former effectiveness; do,
           here by, agree to the following precepts.

5.   TIGHT TWO SHOT - HOLGER AND FANNY NIELSEN

                         HOLGER
                        (reading)
           One: That we shall, henceforth, dedicate our
           professional and private lives to the study of mental
           telepathy and whatever extra-sensory functions may
           be supplemental to it.

6.   SERIES OF SHOTS

Showing each of the other couples as they listen to Holger
reading. Only Frau Werner - and, to a lesser degree, her
husband - displays anything but enthusiasm.

> HOLGER'S VOICE
> Two: That the findings of this study
> will be applied not only to ourselves
> but to all our children, born and unborn.
> Three: That each family unit shall reside
> in a location appropriate to this study and
> shall conduct its affairs in a manner cal-
> culated to prevent the interference of
> society. Four: That monthly correspon-
> dence shall be exchanged until such time
> as the coordination of a mutual system of
> procedure shall make it possible for all
> four units to incorporate; at which time,
> they will establish a joint colony in which
> communication of every sort shall be,
> exclusively, mental.

7.   FULL SHOT - ALL - ANGLE ON HOLGER AND FANNY

Holger looks up from the paper.

> HOLGER
> There are sure to be other details, of
> course - but for now this should
> suffice to get us started.
> (beat)
> Comments?

There is a momentary lull; then:

(CONTINUED)

7.   CONTINUED

                    ELKENBERG
                  (with an accent)
              More than sufficient, I think.

                      KALDER
                 (nodding; with an accent)
              Most specific.

                      HOLGER
                  (looking at Werner)
          Karl?

                      WERNER
          (almost non-committally; with an accent)
          It is what we agreed upon.

Holger cocks his head a trifle, directing a wry smile at Werner.

                      HOLGER
          That sounds very close to disapproval.

                      WERNER
          No, no; not at all. I will be pleased to sign.

                      HOLGER
          You're certain now? This must not be
          entered into except with absolute
          assurance.

                   FRAU WERNER
          He is assured, Holger. His apparent
          uncertainty is - only a sympathetic reflec-
          tion of my own.

                              (CONTINUED)

7.   CONTINUED

> HOLGER
> (genuinely concerned)
> You are still uncertain?

> FRAU WERNER
> Not of the general concept, Holger; I agree
> with it - believe in it.   It is - that I yet wonder:
> Have we the right to impose this - study
> on our children?
> (touching her stomach)
> Even those unborn?

> HOLGER
> (not understanding)
> Impose, Maria?   You speak as though
> we harm our children.   It is not rather
> that we hope to bestow, upon them,
> a gift beyond price?

> FRAU WERNER
> Of course that is our hope, but - we offer
> them no choice in the matter.   Is that just?

There is silence; then Fanny Nielsen speaks, gently but firmly.

> FANNY
> I am, also a mother, Maria; devoted to the
> welfare of my child.   Yet, I am convinced;
> it is just.

8.   CLOSE SHOT - HOLGER NIELSEN

> HOLGER
> (quietly; intensely)
> It is more than just.   It is inevitable.
> (beat)
> Destiny demands it.

9.   FULL SHOT - ALL

There is a brief suspension of SOUND and movement before
Holger Nielsen picks up the pen and signs the paper. He looks
at his wife and they exchange a smile of pride. She takes the
paper and pen and adds her signature, then passes them to Frau
Kalder who, also signs. As her husband signs, she turns to Fanny.

                    FRAU KALDER
                      (softly)
          Have you and Holger decided definitely
          not to remain in Europe?

Herr Kalder, having signed, passes the paper to Professor
Werner who also signs.

                       FANNY
          Yes. There's a house in Pennsylvania which
          was left to Holger by an uncle. We plan to
          live in it.

Professor Werner passes the paper to his wife who hesitates;
Holger Nielsen observing her indecision.

                    FRAU KALDER
                      (nodding)
          Excellent. What town is this?

                       FANNY
          German Corners.

                    FRAU KALDER
                    (smiling back)
     Ah.

Frau Werner signs and, quickly, passes the paper to the
Elkenbergs; Professor Werner takes her hand and smiles at her.
As the Elkenbergs sign, CAMERA PANS TOWARD the
bedroom door.

                                   (CONTINUED)

9.   CONTINUED

> FANNY'S VOICE
> It's small - secluded - very pleasant. . .

By now, her voice has faded and the CAMERA HAS
REACHED ROD SERLING, who is standing in the bedroom
doorway.

> SERLING
> What you have witnessed is the
> curtain raiser to a most extraordinary
> play: To wit, the signing of a pact, the
> commencement of a project. The play
> itself will be performed almost entirely
> off-stage; for its characters and actions
> are important only as they serve to pre-
> pare the elements of the final scenes -
> which are to be enacted a decade hence -
> and with a different cast.

10.   INT. BEDROOM - ANGLE ON DOOR

Ilse Nielsen's crib rail in f.g. Serling turns and enters the bed
room, moving to the crib.

> SERLING
> The main character of these final scenes
> lies sleeping in her crib, unaware of the
> singular drama in which she is to be
> involved.

CAMERA PANS DOWN to reveal the baby ILSE NIELSEN,
two years old and beautifully asleep.

> SERLING'S VOICE
> Her Name is Ilse; the daughter of professor
> and Mrs. Nielsen; age - two.

(CONTINUED)

10.   CONTINUED

SERLING'S VOICE (CONT'D)
Ten years from this moment, Ilse Nielsen
is to know the desolating terror of living
simultaneously in the world - and in the
Twilight Zone.

FADE OUT:
FIRST COMMERCIAL

FADE IN:

11.   EXT. SIDE OF HIGHWAY - CLOSE ON SIGN NIGHT

Approximately two o'clock in the morning. TITLE: <u>1962</u>.
TITLE FADES and, after several moments, a TRUCK passes
on the o.s. highway, its headlights illuminating the sign which
reads: <u>German Corners</u> - <u>Pop</u>. <u>2,124</u>. Now a CAR passes o.s.
lighting up the sign once more before the CAMERA PANS
RIGHT to reveal a somnolent little community hacked up
against the night-shrouded hills.

LAP DISSOLVE TO:

12.   FULL SHOT - GERMAN CORNERS

Houses darkened; its population stilled in sleep. CAMERA
PANS ACROSS the peaceful town, STOPPING as a particular
section of the distant slopes is revealed in b.g. Abruptly, a
tiny blaze flares into visibility there.

13.   INT. WHEELER BEDROOM - CLOSE ON TELEPHONE

RINGING in the darkness. O.s., HARRY WHEELER grunts
awake and, groaning sleepily, reaches INTO FRAME to lift
the receiver.

(CONTINUED)

13.   CONTINUED

CAMERA PANS with his hand as he carries the
receiver to his ear, grunts inquiringly into the mouthpiece.

                    VOICE ON PHONE
                    (Germanic; agitated)
          Sheriff?

                         WHEELER
                         (groggily)
          Uh?

                    VOICE ON PHONE
          This is Bernard Klaus!
          The Nielsen house is burning.

                         WHEELER
                    (twitching and opening his eyes)
          What?

                    VOICE ON PHONE
                    (exaggeratedly)
          There is a <u>fire</u> at the Nielsen house <u>Big</u>
          fire! <u>Hurry</u>!

                         WHEELER
                         (alert now)
          <u>Right</u> <u>away</u>.

CAMERA DRAWS BACK as he hangs up the receiver
quickly, flings aside the covers and, sitting up, switches on the
table lamp between his bed and Cora's. Hastily, he dials a
three-digit number.

14.   ANOTHER ANGLE - INCLUDING CORA WHEELER

Pushing up on an elbow, looking at Harry in sleep alarm.

> CORA
> Harry? What - ?

> WHEELER
> (cutting her off)
> Max? Harry. There's a fire at the Nielsen house.
> Call the volunteers and get the truck out.
> I'll be there in ten or fifteen minutes.
> (beat)
> Got it?

He listens for another moment, then hangs up and reaches down for his boots, Cora watching him concernedly. As he jerks on his right boot, he exchanges a look with her.

> CORA
> Did it just start?

> WHEELER
> (grimly)
> I hope so.
> (reaching for the other boot)
> If it didn't. . .

> CORA
> (distressed)
> It's so far out.

Wheeler has his boots on now. Jolting to his feet, he hurries OUT OF FRAME. CAMERA MOVES IN on Cora Wheeler's face as she watches him begin to dress.

(CONTINUED)

14.   CONTINUED

>   CORA
>   (pained)
>   The girl.
>   (during DISSOLVE)
>   That lovely girl. . .

                                    DISSOLVE TO:

15.   EXT. NIELSEN HOUSE - FULL SHOT - NIGHT

Standing in a wood-ringed clearing; already lost, the fire a
leaping crackling inferno. O.s., the grinding labor of a
TRUCK ENGINE is heard, then the smoother sound of a CAR.

16.   ANGLE ON FIRE TRUCK AND SHERIFF'S CAR

As they speed up the dirt road and across the clearing, jerking
to a stop in close f.g. Wheeler, wearing his sheriff's uniform
and hat, jumps out of his car as the others debark in haste
from the truck, the o.s. fire reflecting on them. There are four
men in addition to Wheeler; his deputy MAX EDERMAN,
postal clerk TOM POULTER and TWO UNIDENTIFIED
TOWNSMEN. Wheeler runs into CLOSE-UP, wincing at the
sight of the fire.

17.   POV SHOT - BURNING HOUSE

Obviously beyond help; a night-lashing sheet of flame.

18.   FULL SHOT - ALL - WHEELER FEATURED

Ederman runs up beside him.

>   EDERMAN
>   We'll never put that out!

                                    (CONTINUED)

18.   CONTINUED

Wheeler's expression indicates that he already knows this. He
turns to the three men on the truck, shouting to be heard above
the fire's ROAR.

                    WHEELER
            Never mind the house!
            Keep the woods from catching!
                    (to Ederman)
            Let's check the back!

He starts forward, running OUT OF FRAME. Ederman
follows as the three men start to unload shovels and uncoil the
truck's hose.

19.   MOVING SHOT - WHEELER AND EDERMAN

Sprinting around the side of the burning house, faces distorted
by grimaces, arms raised to ward off the singeing buffet of heat.
CAMERA WITHDRAWS until they reach the rear of the
house and stop, looking at -

20.   REAR OF NIELSEN HOUSE - THEIR POV

No way in. Fire gouts from the doorway and every window.

21.   WHEELER AND EDERMAN

Looking at the house with sickened expressions.

                    EDERMAN
            They're done for!
                    (pause)
            Poor kid. . .

22.   MOVING SHOT - TOM POULTER

Moving around the border of the clearing, battering out sparks
and tiny blazes with the flat of a shovel. CAMERA STOPS
and, as he turns into CLOSE SHOT, Tom sees something o.s.,
reacts in startlement. Keeping his eyes on the o.s. sight, he
averts his face enough to summon Wheeler.

                    POULTER
    Harry!
                    (beat)
    Over here!

          POULTER (CONT'D)
    He keeps staring at the sight. In several
    moments, Wheeler rushes INTO FRAME
    and stops beside him, breathing hard,
    reacting as he sees -

23.   ILSE NIELSEN - THEIR POV

Curled up on the ground, in her nightgown. She might be
asleep. She might, also, be dead.

24.   FULL SHOT - ALL

Wheeler and Poulter approach the motionless girl and look
down at her uneasily. Even at this distance, firelight makes
vision possible.

                    POULTER
        You think she's - ?

Wheeler doesn't answer. He starts to kneel beside Ilse.

25.   CLOSE SHOT - ILSE AND WHEELER

Wheeler kneeling beside her, looking at her.

> POULTER'S VOICE
> She burned?

> WHEELER
> (curious)
> No.

He turns her over - to see that her eyes are open wide. He recoils a bit, then smiles with relief.

> WHEELER
> You're <u>alive</u>.
> (pause; leaning over)
> You all right?

26.   CLOSE SHOT - ILSE

Gazing up at Wheeler with a blank expression.

27.   ILSE, WHEELER AND POULTER

> POULTER
> (tightly)
> She's in shock, Harry.

> WHEELER
> (disturbed)
> Get a blanket on her.

He picks her up and starts toward his car. CAMERA MOVES with him, HOLDING CLOSE on Ilse's face as she stares across Wheeler's shoulder, dazed, uncomprehending.

28.   MOVING SHOT - HOUSE - ILSE'S POV

Part of the roof starting to crumble.

29.   CLOSE-UP - ILSE

Staring mutely at the o.s. house, the firelight reflecting on her immobile features.

30.   INT. WHEELER'S CAR

Outside, Wheeler approaches, carrying Ilse. Poulter opens the door and Wheeler sets Ilse on the front seat, reaches into the back and, unfolding a blanket, puts it over her, tucks it in around her body. Ilse makes no move or sign of recognition, only staring at the house.

31.   EXT. CAR - WHEELER AND POULTER

As Wheeler straightens up, both of them looking in at Ilse.

> POULTER
> Bad off. Can't talk nor cry nor nothin'.

> WHEELER
> (confused)
> She isn't burned though.
> (looking at the house)
> How could she get out of that house
> without being burned?

He looks back toward Ilse.

32.   POV SHOT - ILSE

Sitting in the car, staring at the o.s. house, the firelight glinting on her numbed expression. . .

DISSOLVE TO:

33.   INT. WHEELER LIVING ROOM - CLOSE ON CORA -
      NIGHT

About three a.m.; still dark outside; Cora standing by the
window in her robe, gazing out worriedly.

34.   ANGLE FROM FRONT HALLWAY

Cora reacts as the o.s. sound of Wheeler's CAR is heard.
CAMERA PANNING with her, she moves to the front door
and opens it as the car is BRAKED outside.

35.   POV SHOT - CAR

Harry gets out and moves around quickly to the other side,
pulls open the door.

36.   CLOSE ON CORA

Catching her breath as she sees Harry lifting Ilse from the car.
CAMERA PULLS BACK as Harry comes up the porch steps
and INTO FRAME, carrying Ilse who is heavily asleep.

37.   INT. FRONT HALLWAY

Harry enters, carrying Ilse, and Cora shuts the door, looking at
the girl with an expression of pitying distress. They both
speak softly.

                          CORA
            Is she hurt?

                        WHEELER
            Not physically.
                 (as Cora looks startled)
            I think she's in shock.
            We'd better put her to bed.

He starts for the staircase.

38.   ANGLE FROM STAIRCASE

Railing in f.g. Harry comes toward the stairs, carrying Ilse,
Cora following.

                    WHEELER
          We'll have to use Sally's -
                 (breaks off; tightly)
          - the other bedroom, Cora.

She doesn't answer, looking suddenly disturbed. Wheeler
starts up the stairs.

39.   DOWN ANGLE SHOT

From second-floor landing. Wheeler ascending the stairs with
Ilse, Cora behind him.

                    WHEELER
          Cora?

                    CORA
                 (overlapping, tightly)
          All right, Harry.

40.   INT. SALLY'S ROOM - ANGLE ON DOOR

In the hall, FOOTSTEPS are heard. Then Wheeler opens the
door and switches on the light, moves OUT OF FRAME,
carrying Ilse. Cora remains by the door, looking into the
room with a strained expression.

41.   POV SHOT - SALLY'S ROOM

Clearly that of a young girl; kept in spotless condition. Harry
stops by the bed and looks back inquiringly at the o.s. Cora.

42.   CORA

Bracing herself against the renewed intrusion of grief.

                    CORA
        I'm sorry.

She hurries across the room, CAMERA MOVING with her
and, hastily, draws back the bedcovers. Harry puts Ilse on the
bed and Cora covers her up. CAMERA MOVES IN
excluding Harry from the scene. O.s., his departing FOOT
STEPS are heard - but not by Cora.

                CORA (CONT'D)
                (stroking Ilse's hair)
        Poor darling.

She straightens up, looking down at Ilse.

                CORA (CONT'D)
        She looks a little like - Sally, doesn't she?

She turns as she finishes the sentence, her voice trailing off
when she sees that Harry is gone. She looks back to Ilse for a
few moments; then, with a trembling inhalation, turns away
and moves OUT OF FRAME for the door. CAMERA PANS
DOWN and HOLDS on Ilse's sleeping face. The light is
switched off, the other o.s. door SHUTS.

43.   INT. KITCHEN - ANGLE ON DINING ROOM - DOOR
       WAY

Wheeler at the table, pouring coffee into a thermos bottle.
O.S. Cora descends the stairs and pushes open the door, walks
toward Harry.

                            (CONTINUED)

43.   CONTINUED

                    CORA
You want something to eat?

                  WHEELER
No; I've got to get right back.
                  (beat)
Thought I'd take some coffee to the boys.

                    CORA
               (a hesitating beat)
Are her - parents. . .?

                  WHEELER
        (starting to cork and cap the bottle)
No way of knowing. We haven't been
able to get near the house yet; it's burning
too hard.

                    CORA
               (glancing upward)
But - ?

                  WHEELER
Tom Poulter found her outside.

                    CORA
Outside?

                  WHEELER
We don't know how she got there.
                  (pause)
I expect her folks are dead though;
it's an awful fire.

(CONTINUED)

43.   CONTINUED

                    CORA
          The poor child.

                    WHEELER
          Something wrong with her. I know she
          isn't deaf or dumb - or retarded or anything
          but -
                    (beat)
          - before she fell asleep, I tried to get her to talk.
          She never said a word. Not a word.

44.   CLOSE SHOT - WHEELER

       Going to the door; looking back.

                    WHEELER
          I don't think she knows how to talk.
          I don't think her parents ever taught her.

45.   CORA WHEELER

       Disturbed by this information. The o.s. door OPENS,
       SHUTS. She stares at it.

                              DISSOLVE TO:

46.   INT. SALLY'S ROOM - CLOSE ON WINDOW - NIGHT

       About forty-five minutes later; still dark. A wind has risen
       and the leaves on the tree outside are rustling, the shade is
       flapping. CAMERA PANS ACROSS the room to an ECU of
       Ilse's sleeping face. The tree boughs trembling outside make
       shadow movements on her face. As the o.s. shade FLAPS with
       particular loudness, her eyes jump open and she stares up at
       the ceiling.
                              (CONTINUED)

46.   CONTINUED

After several moments she tries to reach her mother, calling
out in thought, the sound of her mind voice echoing and
re-echoing each time with less volume until the sound has faded.

>   ILSE'S MIND VOICE
>   Mother?
>   (pause)
>   Mother?

There is no reply. Ilse's face tightens with concentration.

>   ILSE'S MIND VOICE (CONT'D)
>   Mother?
>   (pause)
>   Where are you, Mother?

The frantic mind call echoes off into the distance but is not
answered. Ilse's expression becomes one of impending alarm.

>   ILSE'S MIND VOICE (CONT'D)
>   (frightened; uncertain)
>   Are. . .you - near me, Father?

No answer, Ilse's lower lip begins to tremble and she digs her
teeth into it; concentrates again. The face of Fanny Nielsen
appears SUPERIMPOSED over her forehead. After a
moment or so, it begins to drift away. Ilse's face tenses and
the face comes back; then, despite her concentration, slowly
disappears. Ilse makes a faint noise in her throat, one of
rising dread. She concentrates again and the face of Holger
Nielsen appears, SUPERIMPOSED on her forehead. Like the
face of Ilse's mother, Holger's face also drifts away into the
darkness. Ilse makes a tiny, sobbing noise.

(CONTINUED)

46.   CONTINUED

ILSE'S MIND VOICE (CONT'D)
(crying out in desperation)
Mother! Father! Where are you?

The cry echoes away. There is no reply. Sucking in a
convulsive breath, Ilse presses her head down tightly, closes her
eyes and concentrates with all her might. CAMERA PANS
DOWN to her left hand which is outside the covers. Slowly,
tautly, her fingers draw in, talon-like, nails scratching at the sheet.

47.   ECU - ILSE'S FACE

Growing more and more rigid as she concentrates, a tracery of
lines and ridges scarring her brow. We see what she is seeing
in her mind, the CAMERA traveling rapidly through the
woods, shoving through the clumps of bushes, past tree
branches. Suddenly, the CAMERA STOPS at the edge of the
clearing and we see the blackened smoking tangle of the
Nielsen house. The fire is almost out. A zoom takes us to the
two townsmen shooting streams of water onto the remaining
flames. The only sound is that of Ilse's labored breathing.

Suddenly the CAMERA WHIP PANS to the left to show
Wheeler breaking in the panes of a French door with an axe,
Ederman watching him. Ilse's face grows even tighter and the
picture in her forehead ZOOMS TO A CLOSE SHOT of
Wheeler and Ederman as they kick open the French doors and
enter the house. CAMERA FOLLOWS as they move across
the living room, wincing at the heat from still-glowing
timbers, the reeking smoke of smoldering rugs and upholstery.
They look around, then Wheeler points at the o.s. bedroom.
CAMERA WHIP PANS to reveal the bedroom doorway, then
ZOOMS toward it, ENTERS the bedroom and PANS to reveal
the bed covered with debris, a great beam fallen across it.

(CONTINUED)

47.   CONTINUED

CAMERA ZOOMS IN on the lifeless hand of Fanny Nielsen
sticking out from underneath the beam edge. Ilse makes a
hideous, wheezing sound and the mental picture vanishes,
leaving only her stricken face as she sits up suddenly, CAMERA
DRAWING BACK. She tries to scramble from the bed; the
blankets catch her legs. She crashes to the floor, rears up in a
tangle of sheets, her face in momentary CLOSE-UP, then twists
away and falls against the table, knocking the lamp to the floor.
O.s., in the hallway, there are hurried FOOTSTEPS and the door
is opened, light falls across her. Scrabbling around, Ilse gapes
toward the doorway like a trapped animal. Cora rushes across
the room and INTO FRAME, Ilse shrinking from her in dread.
Cora kneels beside her.

                    CORA
         What is it, Ilse?

She tries to touch Ilse but the girl recoils with a strangled gasp,
bumping against the side of the bed.

48.   CORA

Looking at Ilse in fearful concern.

                    CORA
         Darling, what is it?
              (beat)
         I'm not going to hurt you.
              (beat)
         Ilse, what's the matter?

49.   CLOSE SHOT - ILSE

Staring at cora, her face a mask of horror.

                              (CONTINUED)

49.   CONTINUED

                        ILSE'S MIND VOICE
                (rising in volume; no echo effect)
                They're dead. They're <u>dead</u>.
                They're <u>dead</u>! They're <u>DEAD</u>!

50.   INT. WHEELER'S BEDROOM - CLOSE ON PHOTOGRAPH

The face of the late Sally Wheeler; a girl about Ilse's age, pretty,
smiling. CAMERA WITHDRAWS to show Cora sitting on her
bed looking at it. Wheeler, back in his pajamas, ENTERS
FRAME and sits on his bed with an exhausted groan, lies
on his side. Cora looks at him.

                            CORA
                How did the fire start, Harry?

                          WHEELER
                We're not positive but - apparently
                the Professor was smoking his pipe in bed;
                fell asleep.

                            CORA
                          (pause)
                And there was - nothing left to - ?

                          WHEELER
                        (cutting in)
                Everything was <u>burned</u>, Cora; I told you.

                            CORA
                      (pause; worriedly)
                There's no way of getting in touch with
                Ilse's relatives, then.

                                        (CONTINUED)

50.   CONTINUED

>   WHEELER
>   (rubbing his face; tiredly)
> Tom Poulter says the Nielsens get three let-
> ters from Europe the end of every month.
> Maybe they're from relatives. We'll wait
> till the next batch arrives - write to the three
> addresses.
>   CORA
>   (hesitantly)
> What are we going to do with the girl until then?

>   WHEELER
>   (awkwardly)
> We'll have to keep her here.
>   (defensively)
> It'll only be a week or so, Cora.

She doesn't respond and he averts his eyes from her steady gaze.

>   WHEELER (CONT'D)
> Unless the girl can tell us something.

>   CORA
>   (dully)
> No.

>   WHEELER
>   (looking back at her)
> You don't think she can talk either?

>   CORA
>   (quietly; distress)
> I tried everything I could to get her to but. . .

50.   CONTINUED

She shakes her head. Wheeler grunts, nodding.

                    WHEELER
          That explains it.

                    CORA
          What?

                    WHEELER
          Those times Miss Frank and I tried to talk
          the Nielsens into putting the girl in
          school.
                    (pauses; grimly)
          The answer was always no. Now I know
          why.

                    CORA
          Maybe there is something physically wrong
          with her, Harry.

                    WHEELER
          The Nielsens would have told us if there
          was, Cora.

                    CORA
          Not if they wanted to keep it a secret.

                    WHEELER
                    (sighs)
          Well. . .We can have Doc Steiger check
          her over but I don't think he'll find
          anything.

(CONTINUED)

50.   CONTINUED

                    CORA
                 (distraught)
But - they were educated people, Harry.
Why wouldn't they teach their own daughter
to talk?

                   WHEELER
They were strange people too, Cora.
Hardly spoke a word themselves.
                (a little stiffly)
As if they were too good to bother talking
to us.
                (closing his eyes)
It might not be a bad idea to put her into
school while we're waiting for those letters.
                (turns on his back; sighs)
Teach her how to talk, at least.

                    CORA
                 (uneasily)
          Not right away.

51.   INT. SALLY'S ROOM - MED. SHOT - ILSE

Lying on her back, staring at the ceiling. As Wheeler's o.s.
VOICE speaks on, CAMERA MOVES IN on her face until it
fills the screen. Bit by bit, an uncertain dread takes over her
expression. She doesn't know what the words mean but she
senses, clearly, the danger which threatens her.

               WHEELER'S VOICE
Why not? She's got to learn sooner or
later, doesn't she?
                              (CONTINUED)

51.   CONTINUED

                    CORA'S VOICE
            She just lost her parents, Harry.

                    WHEELER'S VOICE
                        (grudgingly)
            All right; I didn't mean tomorrow or
            the next day.
                        (pause)
            It's a crime though; a girl her age not being
            educated. Not even knowing how to talk.
            Her father a professor too. Keeping his own
            child in ignorance.
                        (pause)
            Well, something's going to have to be done
            about it.
                        (beat)
            Somebody's going to have to undo what
                her parents did to her.

                                    FADE OUT:

                    END ACT ONE

    FADE IN:

52.   INT. WHEELER DINING ROOM - CLOSE UP - ILSE -
       NIGHT

    Face tautly held, her eyes on Wheeler. We can hear his VOICE
    o.s. - but not the words he speaks. Only the pure sound of it is
    audible; pulsing, throbbing, rising and falling in pitch and in
                volume; an endless, garbled din.

53.   CLOSE ON WHEELER'S FACE - ILSE'S POV

Lips moving as he talks. No words; just the sound as Ilse hears it - a harsh, rhythmless beat, jarring and grating. Now he stops.

54.   CLOSE SHOT -ILSE

Relaxing slowly; drawing in a wavering breath. She starts to raise her fork, to eat a little food, but, before it reaches her mouth, Cora Wheeler starts to TALK o.s. No words; just pounding, disconcerting noise. Ilse stiffens again, looking at her.

55.   POV SHOT - CORA

As Ilse sees and hears her; her lips moving, the senseless waves of sound pouring from her.

56.   CLOSE-UP - ILSE

Suffering mutely as the SOUND of Cora's talking assaults the delicate balance of her awareness. She bites her lower lip and sits rigidly in the chair, face a mask of repressed anguish.

ILSE'S MIND VOICE
(echoing)
Please don't talk.
(pause; pleading)
Please - don't - TALK!

57.   ILSE, CORA AND WHEELER

Ilse sitting in f.g., back to CAMERA; Cora and Wheeler in the b.g.

CORA
(in mid-sentence)
- can't understand it, he said.

(CONTINUED)

57.   CONTINUED

> CORA (CONT'D)
> There's nothing wrong with her;
> he checked everything. He said there
> isn't a reason in the world why she
> shouldn't be able to talk.

> WHEELER
> I told you that when she first -

As he has spoken he has glanced toward Ilse and, seeing her
expression, he breaks off, gestures with his head toward her.
Cora looks in that direction.

58.   ILSE

Watching them fearfully.

59.   CORA AND WHEELER

Wheeler's reaction one of weary disgust, Cora's one of renewed
compassion.

> CORA
> What did they do to her?
>   (beat; gently)
> What is it, Ilse?

60.   CLOSE ON ILSE

Staring at Cora. Cora's VOICE, as she continues talking,
becomes the unpleasant clash of sound again. Abruptly, Ilse
shuts her eyes. The sound of Wheeler's VOICE is heard o.s.,
clearly angry. Silence then. In several moments, one of Cora's
hands reaches down INTO FRAME. Just before it touches
Ilse's shoulder, Ilse twitches and her eyes pop open; she looks
up startledly at Cora.

61.   POV SHOT - CORA

Looking down at Ilse with a tender smile.

CORA'S THOUGHT VOICE
Don't be afraid of us, Ilse.

62.   ILSE AND CORA

Ilse's lips quiver and she almost smiles in relief as Cora helps
her to her feet and starts to lead her toward the o.s. hall.
CAMERA MOVES IN on Ilse's face and, as it does, Cora
starts to TALK again, her speech changing from understandable
words to pure sound.

CORA
You mustn't be afraid of us, Ilse. We won't -

Now her voice is sound again and Ilse's face grows fixed into a
suffering grimace. Suddenly, unable to bear the torment any
longer, she twists away from Cora and rushes almost blindly for
the hall, bumping into Wheeler and knocking the glass of water
from his hands.

WHEELER
Oh, for - !

63.   CLOSE-UP - WHEELER - ILSE'S POV

Lips moving as he speaks to her in anger, the sound of his voice
thunderous.

64.   ILSE

Panicked by the noise of Wheeler's VOICE she stumbles back
from him, bumps into the sideboard, whirls with a frightened
gasp and lunges for the hallway.

65.   ANGLE FROM HALLWAY - THE THREE

Ilse in f.g., fleeing toward the stairs and OUT OF FRAME;
Cora and Wheeler in b.g., watching her go. Now Cora starts
after her.

                    WHEELER
          Cora!
               (as she stops and looks at him)
          Leave her be.

                    CORA
          Harry, I can't just -

                    WHEELER
               (interrupting)
          She's been with us over a week now, Cora.
          What's the use? There's just no way of getting
          through to her.

                    CORA
               (pauses, quietly)

She starts into the hallway and OUT OF FRAME. With a wary
exhalation, Wheeler starts mopping at the table.

66.   INT. SALLY'S ROOM - CLOSE ON ILSE

Looking through the window, breathing with some effort, her
expression that of someone who has just escaped a terrible fate
- but knows that escape is only temporary. In the b.g. the door
is opened and Cora ENTERS. Ilse tightens again, bracing her
self for more suffering as Cora crosses the room and stops
beside her.

                    CORA
          Ilse?

                                        (CONTINUED)

66.   CONTINUED

Ilse winces slightly, doesn't move. Cora puts an arm around the
girl's shoulders.

CORA (CONT'D)
Can't you tell me what's - ?

She breaks off again as Ilse tightens more.

CORA (CONT'D)
(sadly)
Didn't they _ever_ talk to you?

Again, Ilse reacts to the sound of Cora's voice; again, Cora gazes
at her in silence, trying hard to understand. CAMERA MOVES
IN SLOWLY on Ilse's face.

CORA (CONT'D)
Try to talk Ilse. Try.
(pause)
Say your name at least.
(beat, hopefully)
Ilse. Ilse.

Ilse's face is in CLOSE-UP now and Cora's Voice becomes
pure sound as she repeats Ilse's name two more times. Cora
stops as she shuts her eyes, grimacing, shuddering.

67.   ILSE AND CORA

CORA
If only I could make you understand.
(beat)
Take away your fear.

(CONTINUED)

67. CONTINUED

She gazes at Ilse for a few more moments, then turns away
with a surrendering sigh and starts toward the door, changing
direction and moving to the bed where she begins to smooth
the wrinkles on the spread.

68. REVERSE SHOT

Ilse in b.g., turned away; Cora in f.g., smoothing the bed spread.
Now, she straightens up, looking at the bed, her expression
becoming one of grief.

69. ILSE

Looking through the window. Abruptly, she hears a faint,
pitiful SOBBING and, tightening, she starts to turn.

70. CORA AND ILSE

Cora in f.g., looking down at the bed; not making a sound.
In the b.g., Ilse completes her turn and looks at Cora with a
perplexed expression.

71. ILSE

Looking at Cora, hearing the SOBBING.

72. CORA - ILSE'S POV

CAMERA MOVES IN on the back of her head.
The SOBBING is within her head.

73. ECU - ILSE

On her forehead, SUPERIMPOSED, we see what she is picking
up from Cora's mind; a SHOT of Cora in the kitchen, wearing a
summer dress. She looks o.s. and moves to the back door,
opens it.

                                                    (CONTINUED)

73. CONTINUED

CLOSE SHOT of TWO MEN standing on the porch, one of
them holding the blanket-covered body of Sally Wheeler in
his arms, one of Sally's hands visible, hanging down limply.
The man, holding her, speaks and we hear a dim, remembered
echo of his voice.

                    MAN'S VOICE
           She was swimming in the lake,
           Mrs. Wheeler and. . .

74. CLOSE-UP - CORA

Looking at the bed, eyes glistening with tears about to fall.
After several moments, she starts and looks down to her right,
reacts. CAMERA PANS DOWN to reveal Ilse standing by
Cora's side, looking up at her, both sorrow and sympathy
written on her face. CAMERA DOWN PANS to Cora's hand.
Ilse's hand moves slowly INTO FRAME and, very timidly,
takes hold of Cora's fingers. Cora SOBS.

75. CORA AND ILSE

Cora starts to cry and sits weakly on the bed; then, convulsively,
pulls Ilse to herself and holds her tightly, CAMERA MOVING
IN CLOSE on them. Ilse stays with her, somewhat frightened
by this display of emotion but sensing Cora's need for her.
After a short while, Cora draws back and stares at Ilse, curious
and not a little awed.

                    CORA
           It's almost as if. . .you understand.

Ilse's lips falter; she very nearly smiles.

                                   DISSOLVE TO:

76.   INT. KITCHEN - CLOSE ON ILSE - MORNING

Sitting at the table, eating a bowl of cereal.

77.   ILSE, WHEELER AND CORA

Ilse in b.g., Wheeler and Cora in f.g., Wheeler donning his hat and jacket. Finished, he pecks at Cora's cheek.

                    WHEELER
         See you at lunch.

                     CORA
                   (smiling)
         Goodbye, dear.

He moves for the door.

78.   CLOSE ON ILSE

Looking around suddenly. CAMERA PULLS BACK FAST to show what she is staring at - the telephone. After a moment, it starts to RING.

79.   FULL SHOT - ALL

Wheeler stops at the door and waits as Cora moves across the room and answers the phone, Ilse, watching her intently.

                     CORA
         Hello?
                   (listens)
         Yes, he is.

She holds out the receiver for Wheeler and he starts toward her.

80.   CLOSE ON ILSE

Watching Wheeler; tensely excited by something.

81.   ANOTHER SCALE

Ilse in f.g. starts for the table. In the b.g. Wheeler takes the
receiver from Cora and she starts for the table.

Ilse turns back hurriedly and starts eating cereal, remaining
vividly alert. Cora sits and smiles at her. Ilse's returned smile
is fleeting and distracted.

> WHEELER
> Yeah?
>> (listens)
> Okay, Tom. Be right over.
>> (hangs up, turns; satisfied)
> The three letters are in.

> CORA
>> (stiffening)
> Oh?

> WHEELER
> Be back in a while.

He moves OUT OF FRAME and leaves the house. Ilse,
repressing her excitement with effort, glances at Cora and
allows herself a moment of sympathetic curiosity over Cora's
bleak expression. Then she glances toward the telephone,
turns back to the table and eats, smiling faintly to herself.

> ILSE'S THOUGHT VOICE
>> (no echo effect)
> Now they'll come and get me; take me to
> the other children who are the way I am.

(CONTINUED)

81.   CONTINUED

Cora sits staring into her coffee. Ilse looks at her again, then
goes on eating glancing once again at Cora, but not really
understanding Cora's sorrow.

DISSOLVE TO:

82.   INT. KITCHEN - ILSE AND CORA - DAY

At the sink, Cora washing, Ilse drying. Suddenly, Ilse looks
toward the back door even though there is no sound from that
direction. After a few moments, Wheeler's FOOTSTEPS are
heard on the back porch and the door is OPENED. Cora turns
quickly.

83.   ANOTHER ANGLE - INCLUDING WHEELER

He shuts the door and hangs up his hat and jacket. Ilse winces
as they start to talk but remains despite this, looking at Wheeler.

CORA
You have them?

WHEELER
What, the letters?

CORA
(tensely)
You said -

WHEELER
(turning)
We can't have the letters, Cora; it's against
the law. Tom's got to send them back.
All he let me do was copy the return addresses.

(CONTINUED)

83.   CONTINUED

                           CORA
          Oh.

                          WHEELER
          I'm going to -

He breaks off, noticing Ilse staring at him; hurriedly she averts
her eyes. Frowning, he turns back to Cora.

                     WHEELER (CONT'D)
          I'm going to write to them now.

Cora starts to say something, then doesn't. She goes on
washing dishes as Wheeler gets a pen and paper from a drawer
and sits down at the table, prepares to write. Cora notices that
Ilse is observing him closely and touches her on the shoulder.
Caught off-guard, Ilse starts and glances over. Cora manages a
smile and points toward the dining room, Ilse looks reluctant to
leave but does so, glancing at Wheeler as she moves across the
kitchen. After she has gone, Cora draws in a long breath and
speaks.

                           CORA
          I suppose you -
                    (as he looks over)
          - have to write to them.

                          WHEELER
                    (Not understanding)
          What do you mean?

                           CORA
                    (pause)
          Nothing.

She returns to the dishes and, after looking at her curiously for
several moments, Wheeler starts to write the first letter.

84.   REVERSE ANGLE

Wheeler in f.g., writing the letter. In the b.g., Cora turns from
the sink and looks at him. She starts to speak; then says nothing,
stares at him indecisively. Finally, she gets two mugs from a
cupboard, pours coffee into them from the pot on the stove and
carries them to the table sets one down in front of Wheeler.

                    WHEELER
                  (glancing up)
         Oh; thanks.

She smiles at him briefly, then sits down with her own mug of
coffee and watches him write. Finally, she must speak.

                     CORA
         What are you telling them?

                    WHEELER
               (drinking some coffee)
         Oh. . .just about the fire; the Nielsens dying.
         Asking them if they're related to the girl - or
         know where any of her relatives are.

He puts down the mug and goes back to writing. After a
moment or so, Cora speaks:

                     CORA
         What if - ?

                    WHEELER
                   (writing)
         Mmm?

                     CORA
                (getting it said)
         What if her relatives don't do any better
         with her than her parents did?

                              (CONTINUED)

84.   CONTINUED

                    WHEELER
                  (looking up)
       That's none of our business, Cora.

                      CORA
                    (flaring)
     The welfare of a child is everybody's business!

                    WHEELER
       We're not in a position to decide for her.

85.   CLOSE SHOT - CORA

                      CORA
                    (bitterly)
       No, of course not. Our position is to
       send her away - get rid of her.
                  (pause; miserably)
       And maybe she'll never talk, Harry.
       Maybe she'll be terrified of shadows
       all her life. Maybe -

                 WHEELER'S VOICE
                  (cutting in)
       Cora.

86.   CORA AND WHEELER

                    WHEELER
                (sympathetically)
       I know how you feel. Sally gone.
       Another child in the house.
                     (firmly)
       But she's not our child, Cora.
       We have no rights where she's concerned.
       And there's something wrong with her.

                                        (CONTINUED)

86.   CONTINUED

CORA
Is that why you want to get rid of her?

He looks at her disapprovingly. Cora sits motionless, staring
at him. Then, as he starts to write again, she closes her eyes
and presses her lips together, despairing in silence. CAMERA
MOVES IN on the letter Wheeler is writing. After a moment,
SUPERIMPOSED on it, Ilse's face APPEARS. Then the letter
FADES OUT and Ilse's face fills the screen as she stands by the
window in Sally's room, her expression exultant.

ILSE'S THOUGHT VOICE
Now they'll come and get me.

DISSOLVE TO:

87.   INT. KITCHEN - CLOSE ON TABLE - LATER

A sealed envelope lies on the table addressed to Elkenberg in
Sweden. Another sealed envelope is dropped on top of it, this
one addressed to Professor Kalder at some address in
Switzerland.

88.   WHEELER

Licks the flap of the last envelope and seals it. Standing, he
puts on his jacket and hat, picks up the letters and walks
toward the dining room.

89.   FRONT HALLWAY - ANGLE FROM STAIRS

Wheeler enters from the dining room and moves down the hall
way, CAMERA PANNING with him, STOPPING as he goes
out the front doorway. After several moments, Cora's hand
ENTERS THE FRAME from above, descending to the bannister
railing.

90.   CORA

On the stairs, motionless, listening. O.s., Wheeler's FOOT
STEPS fade. Cora moves.

91.   EXT. FRONT PORCH

CAMERA SHOOTING THROUGH the curtained window of
the front door. Cora moves to the door, looks out.

92.   POV SHOT - WHEELER

As he slides the three letters under a clip on top of the mailbox,
then gets into his car and drives away.

93.   CORA

Waiting. O.s., the CAR is driven off. Cora keeps looking at
the mailbox.

94.   CLOSE SHOT - THE THREE LETTERS

After the sound of the CAR has faded away, the o.s. front door
is OPENED and Cora's FOOTSTEPS move across the porch,
down its steps, along the gravel path. They stop.

95.   UP ANGLE SHOT - CORA AND THE LETTERS

The letters in f.g.; Cora in b.g., looking down at them.
Abruptly, she grabs them and turns back for the house.

96.   INT. SALLY'S ROOM - DOWN ANGLE SHOT - CORA

Down below, hurrying up the path toward the house.
CAMERA DRAWS BACK to reveal Ilse watching her. Cora
disappears and, in a moment, the front door SHUTS. Ilse turns
into CLOSE-UP her expression one of alarm.

(CONTINUED)

96.   CONTINUED

SUPERIMPOSED on her forehead we see Cora walking
across the dining room and into the kitchen. CUT TO
kitchen; Cora moving to the cellar door and opening it.
The picture vanishes and, gasping Ilse rushes for the door.

97.   INT. CELLAR - UP ANGLE SHOT

Cora above, switching on the cellar light and hurrying down
the steps. CAMERA PANS with her as she moves to the
furnace and, opening the door, throws in the letters, then stands
motionless, watching them begin to burn, firelight glinting on
her frightened yet, somehow, elated expression. Now Ilse's
running FOOTSTEPS can be heard above and Cora whirls to see -

98.   ILSE - CORA'S POV

Lunging into the kitchen doorway and stopping, looking down
at Cora.

99.   CLOSE-UP ILSE

Trembling; horrified.

100. DOWN ANGLE SHOT - ILSE AND CORA

Ilse in f.g., back to CAMERA; Cora below, looking up at her
with something akin to fear. Abruptly, Ilse whirls into
CLOSE-UP and rushes OUT OF FRAME. Cora stands
motionless, looking up.

101. CLOSE SHOT - CORA

Awed; confused; not wanting to believe that Ilse knows what
she has done but unable to rid herself of the notion. Up above,
the front door SLAMS and Cora catches her breath, rushes
OUT OF FRAME.

(CONTINUED)

101. CONTINUED

CAMERA PANS to open furnace doorway, HOLDS on the
burning letters. After a moment, Ilse's contorted face is
SUPERIMPOSED on them. The SHOT of the burning
letters contracts until it is on her forehead, then is gone as she
rushes down the street, away from the Wheeler house,
CAMERA PULLING AHEAD of her. In the b.g., Cora runs
out on to the front porch, sees her flight.

                    CORA
          Ilse!

Ilse runs OUT OF FRAME, Cora starting after her.

102. SERIES OF SHOTS

Showing Ilse's panic-driven flight through German Corners;
Cora's pursuit of her; Ilse pushing past some people, colliding
with others. Finally, as she reaches Main Street, she loses
breath and strength and staggers to a panting halt against a
lightpole, slumps down beside it. CAMERA MOVES IN until
her face is in CLOSE-UP.

               ILSE'S THOUGHT VOICE
                    (no echo)
          They'll never find me now. Never. Never.

Suddenly, she looks around, face twisted by fear. MORE
SHOTS rapidly alternated between Ilse and what she sees; the
townspeople moving in on her, Cora among them.

103. ECU - ILSE

               ILSE'S THOUGHT VOICE
               (an anguishedly echoing cry)
          Oh, please! Help me!

                                        (CONTINUED)

103. CONTINUED

CAMERA STARTS TO BOOM UP from her until, at FADE
OUT, she is a small, pathetic figure surrounded by the
menacing albeit well-meaning residents of German Corners.

ILSE'S THOUGHT VOICE
I'm here! Ilse Nielsen! Here! HERE!!
(beat; weakening)
Help - me - please -

FADE OUT:

END ACT TWO

FADE IN:

104. INT. SALLY'S ROOM - CLOSE SHOT - DAY

Lying on the bed, looking apathetically at the ceiling.
CAMERA MOVES IN on her face and, after several
moments, she frowns, disturbed, and turns her head, looking,
toward the window. A few seconds later, she starts to get up,
even more disturbed. CAMERA PULLS BACK as she rises
from the bed and moves toward the window.

105. CLOSE ON WINDOW

Ilse comes up to it, draws aside the curtains and looks down at
the street.

106. POV SHOT - STREET

Nothing. A quiet, Sunday afternoon.

107. ILSE

Not comforted, she leans forward and peers along the street,
reacting with uncertain dread as she catches sight of -

108. MISS EDNA FRANK - ILSE'S POV

Approaching down the street, wearing her Sunday best.

109. MOVING SHOT - MISS FRANK

Walking along the sidewalk with short, resolute strides, a gaunt, middle-aged virgin who has not known a caress of love since childhood.

110. INT. SALLY'S ROOM - DOWN ANGLE SHOT

Ilse in f.g., looking down at Miss Frank who turns in at the gate and moves toward the house. Catching her breath, Ilse lets the curtain fall back into place and turns into CLOSE-UP, much alarmed.

111. INT. LIVING ROOM - CORA AND WHEELER

Cora sewing; Wheeler, his feet propped on an ottoman, halfway through the Sunday paper, a pile of discarded sections by his chair. O.s., the doorbell RINGS and Cora looks in that direction.

CORA
Now who would that be?

WHEELER
(reading)
Probably Miss Frank.

Cora looks startled, Wheeler continues to read the newspaper, then looks up at her.

WHEELER
Aren't you even going to let her in?
(pause; lightly)
Yes, Cora; I asked her to come.

(CONTINUED)

111. CONTINUED

She looks at him a moment or so longer, then, putting aside her sewing, rises and moves toward the hallway.

112. INT. FRONT HALLWAY

Cora comes through the living room arch, walks to the door and opens it. Miss Frank smiles tightly.

> MISS FRANK
> Mrs. Wheeler.

> CORA
> (smiling with effort)
> Good afternoon Miss Frank.
> (stepping aside)
> Won't you come in?

> MISS FRANK
> Thank you.

She enters and Cora shuts the door, gestures toward the living room, managing another smile. Miss Frank goes into the living room.

> WHEELER'S VOICE
> Afternoon, Miss Frank.

> MISS FRANK'S VOICE
> Sheriff.

Cora is about to follow Miss Frank in when something catches the corners of her eyes and she looks up at the second-floor landing; reacts.

113. POV SHOT - ILSE

Standing at the head of the stairs, looking down at her.

                    WHEELER'S VOICE
              Glad you could come.

                    MISS FRANK'S VOICE
              I felt it was my duty.

114. CLOSE SHOT - ILSE

Looking at Cora questioningly; almost pleadingly.

                    ILSE'S THOUGHT VOICE
              Don't put me in school. Please.

115. CLOSE SHOT - CORA

Looking up at Ilse; very upset but with no comfort to offer.

                    WHEELER'S VOICE
              Won't you sit down?

                    MISS FRANK'S VOICE
              Thank you.

116. ILSE

Turning away and going back toward her room, defeated.

117. CORA, WHEELER, AND MISS FRANK

Cora in close f.g. looking up worriedly. In b.g., in the livingroom,
Wheeler sits down; Miss Frank has already seated herself.

                              (CONTINUED)

117. CONTINUED

>   WHEELER
>   (looking toward her)
>   Cora?

Cora starts. She composes herself and enters the room.

118. INT. LIVING ROOM - THE THREE

Cora returns to her place and sits, a smile frozen on her lips.

>   WHEELER
>   Like I explained to you the other day
>   Miss Frank, I wrote to these people in
>   Europe four, five weeks ago but we just
>   haven't gotten an answer. We don't
>   know exactly what we're going to do
>   with the girl; but until we decide, I feel
>   she ought to start getting some education.

>   MISS FRANK
>   (forcefully)
>   She most certainly should.
>   (beat)
>   It was positively criminal of her parents
>   not to have started her education years ago.
>   (a resentful grunt)
>   The smugness of them. The insufferable
>   disdain.
>   (imitating Holger Nielsen)
>   We do not wish our daughter in your
>   school.
>   (hisses briefly)
>   Just like that.

Her eyes narrow and she imparts the following with a rather
mysterious air.

>   (CONTINUED)

118. CONTINUED

MISS FRANK
In many ways, that fire may have been
the blessing of her life.

CORA
Miss Frank!

MISS FRANK
I'm not just referring to her lack of
education, Mrs. Wheeler.

CORA
But to call the hideous death of Ilse's
parents a blessing. . .

MISS FRANK
(withdrawn)
I'm sure I didn't mean it that way,
Mrs. Wheeler.

WHEELER
What do you mean, you weren't just
referring to her lack of education?

MISS FRANK
I'd rather not discuss it at this time,
Sheriff; except to say that I believe I
know why Ilse doesn't speak -

CORA
(stunned)
You know?

(CONTINUED)

118. CONTINUED

                    MISS FRANK
                    (continuing)
          - and know how very much she <u>needs</u> to
          be educated.

                    CORA
                    (breaking in)
          Why doesn't she speak?

                    MISS FRANK
          I can't go into details right now,
          Mrs. Wheeler. I shall at some later date
          - after I've had an opportunity to
          question Ilse.

                    CORA
          Question?

                    MISS FRANK
          The first thing she must learn to do of
          course, is <u>talk</u>.
                    (ending the conversation)
          If I may see her now.

Cora stares at her but doesn't move. Wheeler, noting this,
pushes up from his chair, grimacing.

                    WHEELER
          I'll get her.

Cora tightens as he starts across the room.

                    MISS FRANK
          Tomorrow morning would be -

She breaks off as Cora rises quickly.

                                        (CONTINUED)

118. CONTINUED

> CORA
>
> Harry.

119. INT. FRONT HALLWAY

Harry stops and looks around suspiciously as Cora ENTERS FRAME.

> CORA
> (whispering)
> I'd like to talk to you before -

> WHEELER
> (cutting her off under his breath)
> Cora, if it's about the girl going to school -

> CORA
>
> Not here, Harry.

CAMERA PANS as she moves down the hallway to the dining room door, drawing Wheeler with her.

120. INT. DINING ROOM

Cora and Wheeler ENTER, Wheeler stopping just inside the doorway. They still talk guardedly.

> WHEELER
> Cora, we've waited long enough; those people obviously aren't going to answer. The girl has got to go to school.

> CORA
> (afraid; weakly)
> No, Harry.

(CONTINUED)

120. CONTINUED

> WHEELER
> (aggravated)
> What do you <u>mean</u>, no? Why shouldn't
> she?

> CORA
> I - don't know. It's just that -

> WHEELER
> (cutting in)
> Well I <u>do</u>. She starts tomorrow morning.

He turns for the hallway but Cora grabs his arm.

> CORA
> She'll be so frightened, Harry.

> WHEELER
> All right, she'll be frightened - a day,
> maybe two days. Then she'll get over it;
> start to <u>learn</u>.

> CORA
> But <u>she</u> <u>isn't</u> <u>ignorant</u>. I-I swear she
> understands me sometimes. With<u>out</u> talking.

Wheeler leaves the room. After a moment or so, she follows him.

121. INT. LIVINGROOM ANGLE TOWARD HALLWAY

Miss Frank in f.g. Wheeler, goes up the stairs and, after a few
seconds, Cora appears, stopping outside the archway. She and
Miss Frank look at each other - one, all love, the other, loveless.

> CORA
> She's. . .very shy, Miss Frank.

Miss Frank regards her dispassionately; says nothing.

> CORA
> She'll need understanding.

(CONTINUED)

121. CONTINUED

                              MISS FRANK
                               (crisply)
                    She shall receive it, Mrs. Wheeler.

        Cora tries to smile with little success. Now she turns toward
        the stairs.

122. CORA

        Looking up at -

123. ILSE AND WHEELER

        Coming down the stairs, Wheeler looking stern, Ilse as if she
        knows that she is descending to her doom. CAMERA
        DRAWS BACK until Cora is included IN FRAME. She puts
        an arm around Ilse's shoulders, gives her an encouraging smile.

124. INT. LIVINGROOM - ANGLE ON ARCH

        As Wheeler, Cora and Ilse start into the livingroom, Ilse
        freezes in her tracks. CAMERA ZOOMS IN on her suddenly
        stricken face as she stares at -

125. MISS FRANK - ILSE'S POV

        CAMERA MOVES TOWARD her quickly as she looks at Ilse
        with a chilly little smile. Eerie SOUND EFFECTS indicate
        the state of Miss Frank's mind - winds and strange cries,
        animal noises; all increasing in volume as the CAMERA
        MOVES so close to her that her dark eyes fill the screen.

126. ECU - ILSE

        Staring at Miss Frank in dumb horror, the hideous cacophony
        of NOISES rushing over her, they stop abruptly at the SOUND
        of Miss Frank's voice - no words - as she says "Come here, child."

127. FULL SHOT - ALL

Miss Frank in b.g., hand extended toward Ilse.

> MISS FRANK
> (trying to sound pleasant)
> Come <u>here</u>, Ilse.

It is Wheeler who nudges Ilse. She moves forward, staring at Miss Frank; Cora moves beside her.

128. MOVING SHOT - ILSE

Approaching Miss Frank slowly, terrified. She stops by Miss Frank's hand and looks at it almost with revulsion.

> ILSE'S THOUGHT VOICE
> (faintly)
> Don't touch me.

129. ILSE AND MISS FRANK

Miss Frank in f.g., back to CAMERA. She takes hold of Ilse's hand and CAMERA MOVES IN on Ilse as the diabolic NOISES rage again. Ilse stares at Miss Frank as though at the Medusa; she looks as though she might faint.

130. REVERSE SHOT

Miss Frank vaguely senses the import of Ilse's dread and drops her hand. Ilse shudders and leans weakly against Cora, looking belately at Miss Frank. CAMERA MOVES IN on Miss Frank's face; she is suspicious and wary but attempts, none-the-less, to look pleasant.

> MISS FRANK
> <u>Well</u>. I think we're going to get along
> just fine, you and I.

131. CLOSE-UP - ILSE

Her expression hopeless, lost.

> ILSE'S THOUGHT VOICE
> (feebly)
> No.
> (beat)
> Not <u>her</u>.

DISSOLVE TO:

132. EXT. SCHOOL YARD - DOWN ANGLE SHOT - ILSE AND CORA - DAY

Some distance below, walking toward the school, Cora holding Ilse's right hand. Ilse holds a sack lunch in her left hand.

133. MOVING SHOT - ILSE AND CORA

Ilse staring toward the school with increasing uneasiness. CAMERA MOVES IN CLOSE on her face and we begin to hear what she is mentally picking up as she approaches the classroom; dozens of strangely hollow VOICES making noises of anger, humor, jealousy, etc.; speaking words and inchoate phrases; all melded together into a virtually incomprehensible pattern of sound.

134. POV SHOT - SCHOOL - ANGLE ON DOOR

As the CAMERA MOVES TOWARD the door, the SOUND gets louder, a disquieting amalgram of words and noises, all of them human yet, somehow, not human.

135. ILSE AND CORA

No sounds but that of their footsteps as they go up the few steps to the door and Cora opens it.

136. INT. CLASS ROOM - CLOSE ON DOOR

Cora and Ilse stand there, looking in. CAMERA ZOOMS IN
on Ilse and she shudders violently as if a tangible force is
striking her; the vast current of unharnessed child mentally, a
shapeless din of words and noises. Ilse clings to Cora's hand,
pressing close against her, eyes wide, quickened breath falling
from her lips. Her shocked gaze moves around the room.

137. POV PAN SHOT - CHILDREN

Staring at Ilse. Not one of them is talking but the distorted
sound waves of words, phrases and emotional noises pour out
from them in a snarled, undisciplined network. (They are all
seven to nine years of age.) CAMERA STOPS on Miss
Frank's approaching down the aisle, a tight smile on her lips.

138. ILSE, CORA AND MISS FRANK

We do not hear the noises but know, from the strained
expression on Ilse's face, that they continue unabated.

                    MISS FRANK
          Good morning, Mrs. Wheeler. We were
          just about to start.

                      CORA
                    (uneasily)
          I. . .do hope everything will be all right.
                  (turning to Ilse)
          Ilse's -

Seeing the expression on Ilse's face, she breaks off and looks
at the child with sympathy.

                  CORA (CONT'D)
          Oh, Ilse. Don't be afraid, dear.

                                        (CONTINUED)

138. CONTINUED

Miss Frank puts her hand on Ilse's shoulder and Ilse stiffens at
her touch. Miss Frank notices but veils her reaction.

MISS FRANK
Now you just leave her here, Mrs. Wheeler.
She'll be right at home in no time.

CORA
(uncertainly)
But. . .shouldn't I stay with her a little while?

MISS FRANK
(overlapping; with false patience)
As long as you're here, she'll be upset,
Mrs. Wheeler. She can't begin to adjust
until she's alone with us. Believe me, it's
the only way.

CORA
Yes. . .Well -
(backing off; smiling at Ilse)
- Goodbye, dear. I'll come and get
you after school. Don't be afraid now.

Ilse tries to move after her but Miss Frank restrains her.
As Ilse's struggles grow stronger and she sobs, Cora hesitates.

MISS FRANK
She's going to be just fine now Mrs.
Wheeler. We'll take good care of her.

Forcing a smile, Cora nods, moves for the door again.

139. CLOSE ON ILSE

Making faint noises of dread as she watches Cora's departure.

140. POV SHOT - CORA

Opening the door and leaving. The door shuts.

141. ILSE

Reacting with terror, tears welling to her eyes. Suddenly, she
looks around with a gasp as Miss Frank starts turning her. We
hear the sound of Miss Frank saying "Now."

142. ILSE AND MISS FRANK

                         MISS FRANK
          Come along.

Ilse hangs back as Miss Frank leads her toward the front of the
class, all the children staring at her.

143. MOVING SHOT - ILSE

Hearing the strange conglomerate SOUND of the children's
minds again; looking around in dazed alarm.

144. SERIES OF SHOTS - ILSE AND THE CHILDREN

As she looks at them. None of them speak but we can hear the
sounds of their thinking; whispered phrases; giggles; a word
intelligible here and there: "Funny -" "Wonder -" "What's the -"
Snickers; grunts; all manner of incomprehensible noises.

145. ILSE AND MISS FRANK

Ilse moving woodenly by Miss Frank's side, threading a path
of consciousness through the living undergrowth of young,
untrained minds.

146. ANOTHER ANGLE

As they reach the front of the class, Miss Frank turns Ilse so
that she faces the children.

> MISS FRANK
> Class, this is Ilse Nielsen. We're going
> to have to be very patient with her
> because her parents never taught her how
> to speak. She doesn't understand a word
> of English.
> (pause)
> We're going to help her learn though,
> aren't we?

Scatterings of "Yes, Miss Frank" throughout the room.

147. CLOSE SHOT - MISS FRANK AND ILSE

> MISS FRANK
> We're going to work with her until
> she's just like everybody else.
> (beat)
> Aren't we, class?

> CHILDREN'S VOICES
> (from various points)
> Yes, Miss Frank.

> MISS FRANK
> Now, Ilse. . .

Ilse continues to stare at the class and Miss Frank grasps her
firmly by the shoulder, making her turn with a gasp.

> MISS FRANK
> (continued)
> Can you say your name, Ilse? Ilse?

(CONTINUED)

147. CONTINUED

> MISS FRANK (CONT'D)
> Ilse Nielsen?
>> (pause)
> Try to <u>say</u> it, child. Your <u>name</u>. Ilse. Ilse.

148. CLOSE ON ILSE

Miss Frank's fingers digging into her shoulder; hurting her.
We hear the SOUND of Miss Frank's VOICE as she repeats
Ilse's name. Ilse's face starts to tense as if she is about to cry
and the hand releases her.

149. UP ANGLE SHOT - MISS FRANK

Looking down at Ilse with a harsh, imperious expression.

> MISS FRANK
>> (flatly)
> You'll learn.

150. DOWN ANGLE SHOT - ILSE AND MISS FRANK

CAMERA SHOOTING OVER Miss Frank's shoulder, Ilse
looking up at her with fear-ridden eyes.

> CUT TO:

151. INT. CLASSROOM - MOVING SHOT - DAY

The children have their readers open in front of them; one, a
BOY, is standing in the middle aisle, reading aloud. In the ____,
sits Ilse, staring at him, both resisting and confused.
CAMERA MOVING TOWARD her.

> (CONTINUED)

151. CONTINUED

                        BOY
                    (laboriously)
        This is a boat. A boat sails on the -
        the o-shing.

                MISS FRANK'S VOICE
        O-cean.

                        BOY
        O-shin. The man who - men who live
        and work on the boat are called s. . .ailors.

CAMERA IS CLOSE on Ilse now and, as the boy continues
READING o.s., we hear only what Ilse hears, the sound of his
voice, not the words. ILSE watches him for several moments,
then looks down at the reader on her desk.

152. INSERT - READER PAGE

A picture of a boat; it, the words describing it.

153. CLOSE-UP - ILSE

Looking down at the book, then up at the boy; at the book
again; at the boy. O.s., the sound of the boy's VOICE fades.

                ILSE'S THOUGHT VOICE
        He's trying to tell about the boat.
                    (pause; confusedly)
        But the boat isn't words. It isn't words.
                    (pause)
        Why don't they learn the way Father
        taught me?

CAMERA MOVING IN on her face until it fills the screen
and we see, SUPERIMPOSED on her forehead, the
remembrance of her own method of studying.

                                        (CONTINUED)

153. CONTINUED

She sits at a table across from her father and he holds up
pictures for her, gazing at her as she looks at the pictures,
one by one; when she nods, he puts a picture face down and
shows Ilse the next one.

We see, now, the picture of a boat he shows to Ilse. He gazes
at her, she at the picture; and the picture comes to life and Ilse
sees exactly what a boat is; what it looks like, how it moves
and functions; every sight and sound of its actuality. She
smiles both in her memory and in her presence in the classroom.
Her father shows her another picture; that of a forest. Ilse sees
and hears a real forest.

154. MISS FRANK

Eyes narrowing as she catches sight of Ilse's distracted state.

155. POV SHOT - ILSE

At her desk, obviously not with the class; smiling dreamily as
she recalls the beauty of learning without the encumbrance of
words.

156. CLOSE ON ILSE

As she remembers; her recollections SUPERIMPOSED on her
forehead. After a few moments, a shadow falls across her and
she twitches, looking up and focusing her eyes on -

157. MISS FRANK - ILSE'S POV

Looming overhead, a hard expression on her face.

MISS FRANK
You must pay attention, Ilse.

158. CLOSE ON ILSE

Cringing, staring up at Miss Frank, hearing, as we do, only the
<u>sound</u> of Miss Frank's voice as she says "If you do not pay
attention, you will never learn." Then, "<u>Get</u> up, Ilse."

159. ILSE AND MISS FRANK

As Ilse only stares, Miss Frank; takes hold of her arm and
pulls her upward slowly, brutally.

> MISS FRANK
> I said: Get <u>up</u>, Ilse.

Ilse makes a sound of pain and rises to her feet. Miss Frank
leads her to the front of the classroom and turns her.

> MISS FRANK (CONT'D)
> (continuing)
> Now. We'll try again.
> (with sadistic kindness)
> Say your name, Ilse. Your <u>name</u>. Your
> name is Ilse; Ilse Nielsen. Do you under-
> stand?
> (beat)
> No, you do not. I will <u>help</u> you to under-
> stand then. I will say your name for you.
> Your name is Ilse. Ilse.
> (prodding, Ilse's chest with each syllable)
> <u>Il</u>-<u>se</u>.

160. CLOSE ON ILSE

Miss Frank's thin finger prodding her cruelly with each
syllable as she repeats Ilse's name again and again, only the
SOUND of it audible.

161. ILSE AND MISS FRANK

Miss Frank turns to the class.

>   MISS FRANK
>   Tell her what her name is, class.
>   On the count of three; one - two - three -
>   (prodding Ilse's chest again)
>   Il-<u>se</u>. Il-<u>se</u>.

>   CLASS VOICE
>   (simultaneously with Miss Frank)
>   Il-<u>se</u>. Il-<u>se</u>.

CAMERA MOVES IN on Ilse's face until the voices of
Miss Frank and the children coalesce into one, loud
bludgeoning SOUND, repeated and repeated. CAMERA
KEEPS MOVING IN until Ilse's mute, suffering eyes
fill the screen.

162. INT. CLASSROOM - CLOSE ON WALL CLOCK

Three o'clock. O.s., we hear the FOOTSTEPS of the
departing children.

163. ANGLE ON DOOR

Miss Frank standing there, the children passing her as they exit.
Ilse starts to pass but Miss Frank takes hold of her arm and
holds her back. Ilse looks up at her in alarm, but Miss Frank
does not return the look, gazing straight ahead. Ilse looks
through the doorway desperately.

164. POV SHOT - PARENTS AND CHILDREN

Among them, standing by the road, Cora Wheeler.

165. ILSE AND MISS FRANK

Ilse tries to pull loose, then has to stop, grimacing, as
Miss Frank digs her fingers into her arm. Miss Frank
continues looking straight ahead until the last of the children
have gone; she then looks down at Ilse.

> MISS FRANK
> I want you to know that you aren't
> fooling me, Ilse. I know exactly what
> you are. I know because my father tried
> to force me into being the same thing
> when I was your age.

166. CLOSE ON ILSE

Hearing the SOUND of Miss Frank's voice, not understanding
what Miss Frank is saying or thinking; confused, frightened.

167. ILSE AND MISS FRANK

> MISS FRANK
> - and, after many years of concentrated
> effort, I was able to overcome the
> sickness which my father had forced on
> me. As I am going to help you overcome
> it, Ilse.
> (pause; sharply)
> It's true, isn't it? They were trying to
> make you into a medium. Trying to
> distort your innocent mind so that you
> could communicate with the dead.

168. MISS FRANK

> MISS FRANK
> You've been trained to be a medium haven't you?

(CONTINUED)

168. CONTINUED

Her eyes narrow. Suddenly, she thinks the words.

>   MISS FRANK'S THOUGHT VOICE
>   You've been trained to be a medium
>   haven't you?

169. CLOSE ON ILSE

Stiffening as she gets the thought.

>   MISS FRANK'S THOUGHT VOICE
>   Haven't you?

Ilse shakes her head rapidly.

>   ILSE'S THOUGHT VOICE
>   (echoing)
>   No! It isn't true! That's not what
>   they were training me for!

170. ILSE AND MISS FRANK

Miss Frank smiling in cold triumph as Ilse shakes her head.

>   MISS FRANK
>   You understand me. You know what
>   I'm thinking. That proves it, Ilse.
>   Don't you see? You've proven it to me.

She leans over and pulls Ilse's face close to hers, her eyes
glittering vengefully.

>   MISS FRANK'S THOUGHT VOICE
>   You-are-a-medium.

171. CLOSE-UP - ILSE

> ILSE'S THOUGHT VOICE
> No. I'm <u>not</u>, you're wrong!
> I'm <u>not</u> a medium!

Suddenly, Miss Frank's head jerks loose and Ilse turns toward the doorway as FOOTSTEPS sound.

172. ILSE, MISS FRANK AND CORA

Cora enters the doorway, stops and looks at them.
Miss Frank smiles quickly.

> MISS FRANK
> Mrs. Wheeler.

> CORA
> I wondered what -

She breaks off as Ilse rushes to her side and clings to her.

> CORA (CONT'D)
> Ilse. . .
> (to Miss Frank)
> Was it - bad?

> MISS FRANK
> (smiling tightly)
> Not at all. She's coming along nicely.
> Oh, she's still a little timid, of course;
> but she's learning.
> She's most definitely, learning.

> CORA
> (gratefully)
> I'm so glad.

(CONTINUED)

172. CONTINUED

                    MISS FRANK
We'll see her in the morning then.

                    CORA
    Yes.
               (to Ilse)
    Come along, dear. Goodbye, Miss Frank.

They leave and Miss Frank moves to the doorway to watch.

173. MOVING SHOT - ILSE AND MISS FRANK

Ilse in f.g., next to Cora, CAMERA DRAWING AHEAD of her.
In the b.g., Miss Frank watches from the schoolhouse doorway.

         MISS FRANK'S THOUGHT VOICE
         See you tomorrow, Ilse.

Ilse stiffens, starts to turn, then looks intently to the front, face
rigid as she listens to Miss Frank's thought voice.

         MISS FRANK'S THOUGHT VOICE
               (gently cruel)
         And the next day. And the next day.

As she moves from the school, Ilse, losing her resistance, leans
tiredly against Cora and, on her face, we see her recognition of
the fact that she is caught in a losing battle.

         MISS FRANK'S THOUGHT VOICE
         And the next day. And the next day.
         And the next day.

                              FADE OUT:

          END ACT THREE

FADE IN:

174. EXT. GERMAN CORNERS - MAIN STREET - DAY

> Four months later; May. A bus stops at the curb and a couple
> debarks, approaches CAMERA. As they stop in f.g. we see
> that they are the Werners - Karl and Maria - ten years older but
> not much dissimilar in appearance to what they were in 1952.
> A MAN passes by and Werner speaks to him.

                    WERNER
     Please?

                     MAN
                  (stopping)
     Mmn?

                    WERNER
     Where might we find authority?

                     MAN
                (not understanding)
     Authority?

                    WERNER
     Yes; uh, how do you say it?
     The constable? - The - ?

                     MAN
     - sheriff?

                    WERNER
                  (smiling)
     Ah. Yes; the sheriff.

                                        (CONTINUED)

174. CONTINUED

                        MAN
                    (pointing)
        Down one block on the other side.
        Can't miss it.

                        WERNER
        Thank you.

                        MAN
                    (moving off)
        Welcome.

The Werners look at each other, exchange a rather melancholy
smile and, as she takes his arm, they start along the street,
CAMERA PULLING AHEAD of them.

                        MARIA
                    (unhappily)
        I feel so guilty, Karl.

                        WERNER
                    (gesturing sadly)
        What could we do? We simply could
        not get away sooner; we have our own
        responsibility to the project.

                        MARIA
        I know. . .but almost six months since
        we last heard from Holger and Fanny.

                        WERNER
        If only they hadn't chosen such a
        far-removed location, for their work.

                        MARIA
        They are Americans, Karl. We could not have
        expected them to reside in Europe.

                                    (CONTINUED)

174. CONTINUED

                    WERNER
          (looking around distractedly)
    Ja.

                    MARIA
          (pause uneasily)
    You still think that - something bad
    has happened to them?

                    WERNER
    Why else would they fail to write?

                    MARIA
    I hope you are wrong.
          (beat)
    That lovely child. . .

                    WERNER
          (tightly)
    And such a talent. Their progress with
    her has been phenomenal. It is as if
    she was born telepathic. I think that,
    of all the children, she has the most
    potential.

                    MARIA
          (pause; hopefully)
    Perhaps they were forced to move like the
    Elkenbergs; to avoid prying.

                    WERNER
    Let us hope so.
          (pointing)
    There it is.

They start across the street, CAMERA HOLDING as they
approach the Sheriff's office.

175. INT. WHEELER KITCHEN - CLOSE ON CORA

Stirring cake batter. O.s., the telephone RINGS. CAMERA
MOVING with her, Cora puts down the stirring spoon and
walks to the phone, cleaning off her hands with a dish towel.
She reaches the phone and picks up the receiver, her face in
CLOSE-UP now.

> CORA
>
> Hello?

> WHEELER'S VOICE
> It is me, Cora.

> CORA
> Yes, dear.
> (as he says nothing)
> What is it, Harry?
> (pause)
> Harry?

> WHEELER'S VOICE
> The ones from Germany are here, Cora.

She stiffens with shock. There is a momentary silence.

> WHEELER'S VOICE
> Did you hear me?

> CORA
> (swallows)
> Yes.

> WHEELER'S VOICE
> I'm. . .going to have to bring them
> to the house.

(CONTINUED)

175. CONTINUED

Cora draws in a deep breath and lets it waver out between her parted lips.

WHEELER'S VOICE

We'll be over in a little while.

CORA
(feebly)

All right.

She hangs up after he does and stares at the telephone. Abruptly, she closes her eyes.

CORA

No.

(almost a sob)

No. . .

DISSOLVE TO:

176. INT. LIVING ROOM - ANGLE ON WINDOW - LATER

Cora stands before it, motionless, looking out.

177. CLOSE-UP - CORA

Face drained of expression. In a moment, o.s., we hear the sound of Wheeler's CAR approaching down the street. Cora tightens, looking at it.

178. POV SHOT - WHEELER'S CAR

Pulling up to the curb and stopping.

179. INT. CAR - WHEELER AND THE WERNERS

> WHEELER
> (tense with worry)
> If only we'd heard from you; but there
> was never a word.
> (beat)
> Under the circumstances. . .you can
> understand why we felt at liberty to. . .
> start adoption proceedings.

> WERNER
> We understand completely, Sheriff.
> As I said, however, we received no letters.

> WHEELER
> (shaking his head)
> - just don't understand it.
> (pause; bracing himself)
> Well.

He opens the door and gets out. Werner opens the opposite
door and starts out.

180. EXT. CAR

As Werner debarks and helps out Maria. CAMERA DRAWS
AHEAD of them as they walk beside Wheeler up the path.
They look at each other.

> MARIA'S THOUGHT VOICE
> Holger and Fanny dead. I still can't
> believe it. How horrible.

> WERNER'S THOUGHT VOICE
> More horrible, the thought of Ilse exposed
> to people who do not understand.
> Pray heaven we are in time to save her.

181. ANGLE FROM PORCH

As they come up onto the porch and Cora opens the door.

182. INT. FRONT HALLWAY - ALL

Wheeler gestures tensely and the Werners go inside; he follows.

> WHEELER
> (gesturing)
> Cora, this is Professor Werner;
> Mrs. Werner. My wife.

> CORA
> (tightly; trying to smile)
> How do you do?

> WERNER AND MARIA
> Mrs. Wheeler.

> CORA
> (drawing in breath)
> Won't you come in?

They start for the living room.

> WHEELER
> Cora, they say they never received
> those letters I wrote.

> CORA
> (startled)
> Oh?

183. INT. LIVING ROOM - ALL

As they enter.

> CORA
> (strained)
> That's odd.
> (to the Werners)
> Won't you sit down?

> WERNER
> (smiling)
> Thank you.

184. THE WERNERS

As they sit on the sofa.

> WERNER'S THOUGHT VOICE
> She <u>burned</u> those letters, Maria.

> MARIA'S THOUGHT VOICE
> Yes, I know.
> (beat)
> How terribly she suffers.

185. CORA AND WHEELER - CORA FEATURED

Sitting in a chair, looking at the Werners, her expression taut, repressed.

> CORA
> You. . . came a long way - Frau Werner.

186. THE WERNERS

> MARIA
> (smiling)
> Yes, we did.
> (her THOUGHT VOICE)
> Are we going to tell them anything about Ilse?

> WERNER'S THOUGHT VOICE
> Not unless we have to.
> (his VOICE)
> May we see Ilse?

187. CORA AND WHEELER - CORA FEATURED

> CORA
> I'll be going to get her out of school in a little while.

188. THE WERNERS

Looking pained.

> WERNER
> (dully)
> School.
> (his THOUGHT VOICE: whispering)
> God in Heaven. . .school!

189. INT. CLASSROOM - CLOSE ON MISS FRANK

> MISS FRANK
> Ilse Nielsen - stand.

190. ILSE

Rising and standing beside her desk. She looks tired; almost defeated.

(CONTINUED)

190. CONTINUED

> MISS FRANK'S VOICE
> Come forward.

Ilse moves to the front of the room, CAMERA DRAWING AHEAD of her, STOPPING when Miss Frank is included. Ilse stops and looks at her.

191. ILSA AND MISS FRANK

> MISS FRANK
> Face the class.
>> (as Ilse does)
> Straighten up. Shoulders back.
>> (as Ilse does this)
> What is your name?

Ilse's lips twitch; there is a dry, rattling in her throat.

> MISS FRANK
>> (continuing)
> Your name.

192. CLOSE SHOT - ILSE

Lips moving tentatively as if she is trying to speak.

> MISS FRANK'S VOICE
> What is your name?

A choking, spastic-like noise sounds in Ilse's throat.

193. ILSE AND MISS FRANK

Miss Frank turning to the class.

(CONTINUED)

193. CONTINUED

> MISS FRANK
> Class; we will do again what we've
> been doing for the past few weeks.
> On the count of three - <u>think</u> -
> of Ilse's name. Don't say it aloud;
> just <u>think</u> it: Ilse, Ilse, Ilse. Ready now?
>
> One - two - three.

194. ILSE

Stiffening with resistance as the concentrated THOUGHT
VOICES of the children speak her name.

> CHILDREN'S THOUGHT VOICES
> Ilse! Ilse! Ilse!

195. CLASS - ILSE'S POV

Sitting quietly in their seats, looking at Ilse.

> CHILDREN'S THOUGHT VOICES
> Ilse! Ilse! Ilse!

196. ECU - ILSE

Trembling, mouth ajar, lips twitching, the name tearing at her
mind.

> CHILDREN'S THOUGHT VOICES
> Ilse! Ilse! Ilse! Ilse! Ilse! Ilse!

197. INT. LIVING ROOM - WHEELER AND THE WERNERS

Wheeler in f.g., looking out the window. In b.g., the Werners
are sitting on the sofa. On the table in front of them, sit coffee
cups, coffee pot, creamer, sugar dish, a plate of cookies.

198. THE WERNERS

Werner finishes his coffee and puts down the cup. A few
moments pass.

> WHEELER'S VOICE
> Here they come.

They look around, then Werner stands, looking toward the
hallway.

199. THREE SHOT - WHEELER AND THE WERNERS

All of them looking toward the front hallway.

200. CLOSE ON ARCH TO HALLWAY

O.s., FOOTSTEPS are heard on the porch. The o.s. door is
OPENED, CLOSED. Cora leads Ilse into the arch and they
stop, Ilse starting as she sees the Werners; the sight of them
has caught her completely by surprise.

> CORA
> Ilse, this is Professor and Frau Werner.

201. THE WERNERS

Looking at Ilse, Maria with a tender little smile, her husband
with an intent expression.

> WERNER'S THOUGHT VOICE
> Ilse. You remember us. Our children
> are the ones who are just like you. Werner.
> Germany.

202. CLOSE-UP - ILSE

Faint recognition in her eyes; but, in her mind, only confused
uncertainty. We hear, very faintly, the disassociated <u>sound</u> of
Werner's thought message; no words. Ilse gapes at him, dread
starting to rise in her.

203. THE WERNERS

Looking at Ilse. CAMERA MOVES IN on Werner who is
beginning to show signs of alarm.

> WERNER'S THOUGHT VOICE
> <u>Ilse</u>. You remember. The Elkenbergs,
> the Kalders, us, your father and your
> mother. Heidelberg, ten years ago.
> The <u>project</u> on telepathy.

204. ECU - ILSE

An expression of uncomprehending dismay on her face. She
can only sense the vaguest fragments of Werner's message.

> WERNER'S THOUGHT VOICE
> (barely audible)
> . . .here. . .Germany. . .you. . .

205. WHEELER AND THE WERNERS

> WHEELER
> The Werners are here from Germany, Ilse.
> They were friends of your parents.

CAMERA MOVES IN on Werner as his thought voice drowns
out Wheeler's.

(CONTINUED)

205. CONTINUED

                    WERNER'S THOUGHT VOICE
                         (desperately)
         Ilse! Think!
                          (beat)
         Where is your mind, Ilse! Your mind!
                          (beat)
         Hear me, Ilse!

He stiffens and suddenly is still as, o.s., Ilse SOBS wrackingly.

206. WHEELER AND THE WERNERS

Staring at Ilse in shock as her terrible SOBS continue.

207. CORA

Looking down at Ilse, stunned. CAMERA PANS DOWN to
Ilse who is looking at Werner and sobbing in wretched despair,
not knowing how to sob, the sound strange and, somehow,
terrible. Now she speaks - and the sound of her voice is
unfinished, like that of a puppet; thin, wavering, brittle.

                            ILSE
         My. . .name. . .is - Ilse.

She shakes with a violent, sobbing breath.

                        ILSE (CONT'D)
         My. . .name - is - Ilse.

208. WHEELER AND THE WERNERS

Staring at her, the Werners deeply pained, Wheeler not
knowing whether to be pleased or disturbed.

                        ILSE'S VOICE
         My - name is - Ilse.

209. CORA

Looking at Ilse.

ILSE'S VOICE
My name is - Ilse.

210. ECU - ILSE

ILSE
(tormented unable to stop)
My name is Ilse. My name is Ilse.
My name is Ilse. My name is Ilse.

211. THE WERNERS

ILSE'S VOICE
(babbling on)
My name is Ilse! My name is Ilse!

CORA'S VOICE
(overlapping)
Ilse!

212. ILSE AND CORA

Cora beside her, holding her in her arms, trying to turn Ilse's
face to hers.

ILSE
My name is Ilse, my name is Ilse,
my name is Ilse,my name is - !

CORA
Ilse, don't!
(turning Ilse's face)
Don't!

(CONTINUED)

212. CONTINUED

Suddenly, Ilse begins to cry heartbrokenly, clinging to Cora
who kisses her cheeks and throat passionately, starting to cry
herself.

> CORA
> (continuing; brokenly)
> <u>Shhh</u>; Ilse. Don't cry. Don't cry.
> I'm with you. <u>I'm</u> <u>with</u> <u>you</u>.

Suddenly, she turns on the Werners.

> CORA
> (continuing)
> You can't take her from me: you <u>can't</u>.

> WHEELER'S VOICE
> Cora -

> CORA
> No, I won't let them!
> (to the Werners)
> I <u>love</u> her! And she loves me!
> She <u>needs</u> me!
> (beat)
> <u>You</u> <u>have</u> <u>no</u> <u>right</u>, <u>no</u> <u>right</u>!!!

213. WHEELER AND THE WERNERS

Looking at Cora and Ilse.

> WHEELER
> Cora, in the name of . . .

He cannot finish, staring at her in great distress. The Werners
stand motionless, saying nothing. O.s., we hear Ilse's crying.

                                             DISSOLVE TO:

214. EXT. MAIN STREET - LATER - DAY

The Sheriff's car pulls up to the curb and stops.

215. INT. CAR - WHEELER AND THE WERNERS

                    WHEELER
                   (awkwardly)
        Look, I. . .apologize again for both
        my wife and myself. We - well, we thought -

                    WERNER
                   (overlapping)
        We understand. Naturally, you would
        both think that we had come to take Ilse
        back with us.
                   (glancing at Maria)
        However, as I've said, we have no
        legal power to demand her - being no relation.

Wheeler nods and smiles awkwardly. He takes Werner's
extended hand.

                    WERNER
        Goodbye, Sheriff.

                    WHEELER
        Goodbye. Good luck.

216. EXT. CAR

Professor Werner gets out with his wife.

                    WHEELER
        And thanks again.
                   (beat)
        Your bus should be here in five or ten minutes.

                                      (CONTINUED)

216. CONTINUED

They smile and nod and Wheeler drives off. They walk
toward the bench by the bus station.

                    WERNER
        I hope we have not made a mistake
        letting them keep her even though we
        <u>have</u> the legal right to -

                    MARIA
                (cutting in)
        I don't think so, Karl. To take her to
        the other children now. . . it would be too
        terrible for her. The facility is gone.
        Even with work, it might not return.

                    WERNER
                (sighs)
        I suppose.
                (pause; grimly)
        All those years Holger and Fanny spent
        on her - <u>wasted</u>.

                    MARIA
        Wasted, Karl? If they had not made her
        mind so receptive, how could they have
        led her from the burning house even
        though they, themselves, were trapped?

                    WERNER
        We can only <u>assume</u> this to be the case,
        Maria. Though, I don't see how else she
        could have gotten out.
                (sighs again)
        Ah, but the loss; the <u>loss</u>.
                (shaking his head)
        It isn't <u>right</u>.

                                    (CONTINUED)

216. CONTINUED

They reach the bench and sit down.

>   MARIA
> There is no right or wrong to it, Karl.
> They all meant well. No one wanted to
> do anything but help her.

>   WERNER
> But to lose <u>everything</u>.

>   MARIA
>   (smiling)
> She has not lost everything. Why do you
> think I asked for you to let her stay here?
>   (beat)
> Because she has <u>gained</u> something, Karl.

>   WERNER
>   (turning in surprise)
> Gained?

>   MARIA
> We always knew that Holger and Fanny
> did not really care for her.

>   WERNER
>   (frowning)
> <u>Maria</u>.

>   MARIA
> Oh, they were not unkind; they gave
> her what affection they had in them to give.
> But the project always came first; you
> <u>know</u> that, Karl. To them, Ilse was less a
> daughter than she was an experiment in
> flesh.

(CONTINUED)

216. CONTINUED

> MARIA (CONT'D)
> (smiles)
> She is going to be all right. For now she
> is loved. And that is so much more
> important than telepathy.
>
> (takes his arm)
> Isn't it, mein Professor?

Werner looks at her non-commitally for several moments, then smiles and takes her hand.

> WERNER
> Ja, liebchen. Much more important.

CAMERA MOVES IN on their joined hands.

> DISSOLVE TO:

217. EXT. STREET - CLOSE SHOT - ILSE'S AND CORA'S HANDS

Holding each other tightly, CAMERA PULLS AWAY and UP to reveal the two of them walking side by side, Cora looking down at Ilse with a loving smile. Ilse is still upset but she looks back at Cora and manages to smile a little in return. CAMERA KEEPS PULLING AWAY from them as they walk along the quiet, tree-lined street, not speaking, close together in silence and in understanding. O.s., somewhere, a bird sings in vernal joy.

> FADE OUT:

THE END

Death Ship

"Death Ship" is another fine example of Matheson's interest in the paradoxes of time travel—and this one has a fascinating interplanetary twist on the legend of the "Flying Dutchman" to boot.

"Both these episodes—'Mute' and 'Death Ship'—were of course based on published novelettes of mine." ("Death Ship" originally appeared in 1953, and can be found in *Collected Stories*.) "By then I was accustomed to throwing my stories in 'the hopper'— which of course they paid for—but in the beginning I preferred doing originals. Like 'Mute,' 'Death Ship' was such a long story I didn't have to invent any major new sequences. Just the scenes where the astronauts imagined they were back home again. So it was partly my published story and partly an original script."

Matheson is amused by the fact that, although the story is supposed to be taking place at some point in the far-flung future, the action is dated as taking place in—1997. He admits he had no idea either his stories or the television episodes would be forever available to the public in one form or another.

"When you're writing something from back in the Sixties, that seemed like a long time away. I set *I Am Legend*— published in 1954—in 1976! That'll teach science fiction writers to set their stories a hundred years ahead, but then of course you'll have to foresee and change the whole environment! Little did we know that we'd ever get hung-up on these things—that these *Twilight Zones* would ever last that long!"

Even though he enjoyed the challenge of writing one-hour scripts for the series, he was not really surprised that the powers that be shifted it back to a half-hour format after only one season. "I think the producers felt that it was the lesser of all the seasons simply because it did not follow the typical *Twilight Zone* pattern. I wouldn't say it was rigid, but it was always followed: you had a teaser that left the audience hanging, and then Rod would come in and talk about it. Then you'd work out the rest of the story with a first act break, a second act break, and then a zapper ending. That was the pattern."

In a situation which recalls the frustrations Serling once had in finding published stories to adapt, Matheson did not fare any better for a proposed series of his own, decades later. This was for famed producer and director Dan Curtis, with whom Matheson would work on such acclaimed projects as *Dracula, The Night Stalker,* and *Trilogy of Terror* in the Seventies and Eighties.

"Many years later, I was working with Curtis trying to put together a weekly series called *Dead of Night.* And I was reading tons of stories from *The Magazine of Fantasy and Science Fiction,* (which I think was the best of its kind at that time) and almost *never* did I run across a story that fit that pattern! So, in that sense, writing original scripts was easier because you could deliberately texture the story—structure it—to fit that pattern."

But was it due to his other writing projects that he only did two scripts for the fourth season? Besides other television series, Matheson was also involved with various feature screenplays, penning such horror classics as *House of Usher* and *The Pit and the Pendulum.* Not to mention his own novels and short stories. "No, I did as many scripts for them as I could write. Rod still had that obligation to write the majority of the episodes."

DEATH SHIP

PERFORMANCE DATE: 2/7/63

PRODUCER: HERBERT HIRSCHMAN

DIRECTOR: DON MEDFORD

CAST:

CAPT. PAUL ROSS: JACK KLUGMAN

LT. TED MASON: ROSS MARTIN

LT. MIKE CARTER: FREDRICK BEIR

RUTH: MARY WEBSTER

JEANNIE: TAMMY MARIHUGH

KRAMER: ROSS ELLIOTT

MRS. NOLAN: SARA TAFT

FADE IN:

1.   FULL SHOT - SPACE SHIP - DAY

Moving slowly over a landscape similar to that of Earth.

> SERLING'S NARRATION
> Picture of the space ship X-89 - cruising
> above the thirteenth planet of star system
> 51; the year: 1997. In a little while -
> supposedly - the ship will be landed and
> specimens taken - vegetable, mineral and,
> if any, animal. These will be brought
> back to over-populated Earth - where
> technicians will evaluate them and, if
> everything is satisfactory, stamp their
> findings with the word INHABITABLE and
> open yet another planet for colonization.
> (beat)
> These are the things that are supposed to
> happen. In actuality, they will not hap-
> pen at all - but will, instead, be superseded
> by events far more unusual, far more dis-
> tant from the realm of enlightenment.

2.   INT. CABIN - INSERT VIEWER

Table-top variety, circular, with hatch lines. In it, we see
the landscape unfolding below. On the periphery - located
at each quarter-line are four tiny screen panels on which
two sets of numbers constantly change - one longitudinal,
one latitudinal. Adjacent to the viewer is a computer
machine with various clicking dials, knobs, number banks,
graph charts being inked, lights flickering, etc. A lake is
crossed; then, as the ship moves over land again, there is a
faint glitter below.

3.   UP ANGLE SHOT - MASON

In uniform, looking down at the viewer; reacting.

                    MASON
          Captain.

FOOTSTEPS on the deck. CAPTAIN ROSS ENTERS
FRAME and looks down at the viewer.

                MASON (CONT'D)
          Something glittered.

                    ROSS
          Put in on Reverse.

Mason reaches down and flicks a switch.

4.   INSERT - VIEWER

As the lenses are switched, there is a blurring effect, then
we see the landscape as if moving away from it.

5.   UP ANGLE SHOT - MASON AND ROSS

                    MASON
          It was at two-five-five dash four-one-seven.

                    ROSS
                (grunts, pause)
          I don't see anything.

                    MASON
                (certain)
          Something glittered.

                              (CONTINUED)

5.   CONTINUED

                    ROSS
          We went over a lake, you know.

                    MASON
          I know. It wasn't that.

                    ROSS
              (grunts dubiously)
          Well. . .we'll look
              (turning away)
          But it was probably the lake.

Mason glances after Ross with slight irritation, CAMERA
DRAWING UP to show the captain moving across the
cabin toward the control board.

6.   ROSS AND MASON

     Ross coming into f.g. and slipping into a seat in front of the
     controls. In the b.g., Mason stands over the viewer, looking
     into it. Ross taps some of a large series of buttons which
     are set up in the style of an advanced typewriter keyboard.

7.   EXT. SKY - SPACE SHIP

     As it wheels around in a smooth arc and heads back in the
     opposite direction.

8.   INT. CABIN

     Mason in f.g., looking down at the viewer, pushing a switch
     to change the lens. In the b.g., Ross gets up from his seat
     and returns. He looks down disapprovingly at the viewer.

                              (CONTINUED)

8.   CONTINUED

                        ROSS
                      (grumpily)
              Probably wasting our time.

Mason only grunts, not wanting to speak, a low-pitched
excitement becoming evident on his face.

                  CARTER'S VOICE (O.S.)
              What are we turning for?

They both glance in that direction.

9.   CARTER

Comes through a doorway and starts forward, CAMERA
DRAWING AHEAD of him until Ross and Mason are
included, standing by the viewer, Mason looking down at it
again, his excitement growing. Carter looks at it.

                        CARTER
              What's up?
                      (beat, interestedly)
              Something down there?

                        ROSS
              (nods toward Mason somewhat scornfully)
              He thinks so.

                        MASON
                      (overlapping, tightly)
              There is something.

                        CARTER
              What?

                        MASON
                      (afraid to commit himself)
              I don't know.

10.   INSERT - VIEWER

The planet's landscape passing below like a slowly unrolled tapestry of wood, fields, streams.

MASON'S VOICE
We're almost there.

11.   UP ANGLE SHOT - MASON, ROSS AND CARTER

Ross looks at Mason.

ROSS
I know what you're thinking.
(beat)
Don't.

MASON
(tensely)
It's got to happen some time, doesn't it?

ROSS
Maybe.
(pause, scoffing)
You're alien-contact happy.

MASON
(resentfully)
Do you really think that man is the
only intelligent - ?

ROSS
(cutting him off)
All right, all right; not again.
(pause)
So we're going to meet another race. Great.

(CONTINUED)

11.   CONTINUED

MASON
It would be great.

Ross grunts dubiously.

MASON (CONT'D)
(cont'd; stubbornly)
It's got to happen some time.
(beat)
Why not to us?

CARTER
Man, wouldn't that be something? Another -

MASON
(cutting in)
There it is.

12.   INSERT - VIEWER

The glitter seen below again.

13.   UP ANGLE SHOT - MASON, ROSS AND CARTER

MASON
(startled)
It looks like it might be a ship.

ROSS
Hardly.

Mason switches the lens on the viewer.

14.   INSERT - VIEWER

The glitter fading behind the ship.

15.   MASON, ROSS AND CARTER

Mason looks at Ross questioningly. Ross gestures irritably
as if   to say: Don't rush me. Mason tightens, waits.

> MASON
> (appalled)
> Aren't we going to - ?

> ROSS
> (cutting him off)
> Will you - ?

He turns away abruptly and moves into close f.g., lips
pursed as he deliberates.

> CARTER
> (hopefully)
> We have to take specimens.

Ross grunts, non-committally. Carter glances at Mason
who returns it, gritting his teeth. Carter represses a smile.

> ROSS
> (doggedly)
> I don't like it.

Mason starts to say something sharp but Carter dissuades
him with a look and a hand on his arm.

(CONTINUED)

15.   CONTINUED

                              CARTER
                            (blandly)
                    Well; it's up to you, Captain.

Clearly, this strikes the proper note; Ross is the sort of man
who will make the decisions. After a few moments, he
nods, moves for the control board. Mason exhales hard,
Carter grins. Ross, slips into the seat in front of the conrols
and starts manipulating them.

16.   EXT. SKY - SPACE SHIP

As it wheels about again and heads downward for a landing.

17.   INT. SPACE SHIP - CABIN - MASON, CARTER AND
       ROSS

Mason and Carter in f.g., Ross in b.g., at the controls.

                              MASON
                         (under his breath)
                    Hard head.

                              CARTER
                    He's got to make the decisions, y'know.

                              MASON
                    It's a wonder he lets us do anything on our own.

                              CARTER
                             (dryly)
                    Does he?

They look back at the viewer.

                                                (CONTINUED)

17.   CONTINUED

> CARTER
> You really think it's a ship?

> MASON
> (tightly; excited)
> If it is - I don't see how it could possibly be from Earth.
> We've got this run all to ourselves.

> CARTER
> They might have gotten off course.

> MASON
> Not this far off.

> ROSS
> Air spring.

Mason steps over to the bulkhead and pulls a big switch.
Below them, a gigantic RUSHING noise commences.

> ROSS (CONT'D)
> Places.

The three men take seats in three foam-rubber chairs and, in
a short while the ship shudders, landing. Mason is first on
his feet, hurrying for the port.

18.   AT PORT

CAMERA SHOOTING FROM OUTSIDE as Mason comes
up and looks out. He catches his breath, reacting in shock.
Ross and Carter ENTER FRAME, react similarly as they
look out.

(CONTINUED)

18.   CONTINUED

                        CARTER
                       (unheard)
              Mother-of-God.

19.   POV SHOT - CRASHED SHIP

       What remains of a space ship after a violent crash, the body
       driven into the ground, jagged shards of super-structure
       strewn over the field.

20.   MASON, ROSS AND CARTER

       Looking through the port with sickened expressions.

                   SERLING'S NARRATION
              Picture of the crew of the space ship X-89.

21.   CLOSE PAN SHOT

       Across the stricken faces of Ross, Mason and Carter.

22.   ROD SERLING IN LIMBO - SET

                   SERLING'S NARRATION
              Captain Ross. Lieutenant Mason.
              Lieutenant Carter. Three men who, in a
              matter of minutes, will be plunged into
              the darkest, nightmare reaches - of
              the Twilight Zone.

                                        FADE OUT:

FIRST COMMERCIAL

FADE IN:

23.   INT. SPACE SHIP CABIN - MASON, ROSS AND
CARTER - DAY

Looking out through the port. Mason turns away.

MASON
(anxiously)
I'll check the atmosphere.

Ross glances at him, disapproving of the anxiety in Mason's
voice.

24.   ANOTHER ANGLE

Mason comes into f.g. and checks the atmosphere-testing appa
ratus. In the b.g., Carter continues looking through the port
as Ross starts toward Mason.

MASON
We won't need helmets.

Ross comes up beside him and double-checks the dials, pushes buttons, refines a few knob settings, Mason looking at
him. After a few moments, Ross grunts in reluctant assent
and Mason turns away.

25.   ANOTHER ANGLE

Mason moves across the cabin and opens a locker, Ross starting
after him. Taking out one of the three jumpers inside the
locker, Mason turns toward the o.s. Carter.

MASON
Mike.

26.   ANOTHER ANGLE - INCLUDING CARTER

In f.g., still at the port, looking out with that sick, awed expression of someone witnessing the aftermath of a grisly traffic accident.

                    MASON
        Mike.

Carter turns and Mason tosses him the jumper. He catches it.

                    CARTER
                    (mutedly)
        Thanks.

27.   MASON AND ROSS

Carter in the b.g., starting to don the jumper with mechanical motions, continuing to look out the port. Ross comes up to Mason and Mason holds a jumper out to him. Ross does not take it at first. Mason controls his irritation at this obvious gesture.

                    MASON
        Your jumper, Captain.

Ross looks at him appraisingly for another moment or two before taking the jumper and starting to don it.

                    ROSS
                    (critically)
        Can't get out there fast enough, can you?

                    MASON
                    (repressing anger)
        What does that mean, Captain?

                              (CONTINUED)

27.   CONTINUED

                        ROSS
                      (tensing)
          It means I don't like impetuous crew
          members; they make mistakes.

                       MASON
                      (blandly)
          Have I made mistakes, Captain?

                        ROSS
          You're on the verge.

                       MASON
          Let me know when I make them.
                       (beat)
          Captain.

          His jumper on, Mason turns for the control board.

28.   EXT. SPACE SHIP

          A bottom hatch opens and a mechanically impelled ladder
          begins to descend toward the ground.

29.   CLOSE ON LADDER

          As it stops and the three men begin to climb down - Ross
          first,   Mason next, Carter last. CAMERA DOWN PANS
          with them. They all reach the surface and look toward the
          crashed ship.

30.   POV SHOT - CRASHED SHIP

          About a hundred yards away.

31.   MASON, ROSS AND CARTER

                    CARTER
                    (mutedly)
          Lord, did they hit.

Mason starts forward.

                    ROSS
                    (quickly)
          We stay together.

Mason stops, looks around.

                    ROSS (CONT'D)
          No one takes any risk.
                    (beat; firmly)
          That's an order, Mason.

                    MASON
                    (tightly restrained)
          I understand, Captain.

They start toward the ship.

32.   POV SHOT - CRASHED SHIP

CAMERA MOVING toward it at the pace of the three men.

33.   MOVING SHOT - MASON, ROSS AND CARTER

Looking at the ship with a sense of uneasiness.

                    MASON
          It looks like -
                    (grimacing)
          - one of <u>our</u> ships.

                                        (CONTINUED)

33.   CONTINUED

                    ROSS
        Don't jump to conclusions.

                    MASON
        Well, doesn't it?

Ross presses his lips together in an obdurate refusal to
answer the question.

                    CARTER
                  (disturbed)
        From what I can see of the rockets it <u>does</u> -

                    ROSS
          (interrupting; stubbornly)
        Rocket construction could be standard
        everywhere.

                    MASON
                 (sardonically)
        You don't mean it could be from another
        race, do you?

                    ROSS
        That's enough.

34.   DOWN ANGLE SHOT - THE THREE MEN

CAMERA SHOOTING DOWN past a twisted steel plate,
showing the three men stopping at the foot of the wreckage,
gazing up at it.

35.   MASON, ROSS AND CARTER

                        MASON
                        (pained)
        It is one of ours.

                        CARTER
        How could it get so far off course?

                        ROSS
                (pointing, cutting them off)
        We'll try that opening there.
                (as they start forward)
        And stay together.

36.   ANOTHER SCALE

As the three walk up to the side of the ship where outer
plates have been violently laid open. Ross hesitates and the
other two look at him in surprise.

                        ROSS
                        (quietly)
        I don't like it.

                        MASON
                        (beat)
        We have to find out who they are, don't we?
                        (beat)
        Captain -

                        ROSS
                (cutting him off)
        All right.
                        (swallows)
        Put your gloves on.

                                    (CONTINUED)

36.   CONTINUED

They draw work gloves from the pockets of their jumpers
and, slipping them on, climb into the wreckage, Ross in the
lead followed by Mason and Carter.

37.   INT. WRECKAGE

Dark and shadowy. Ross draws a flashlight from his jumpers
and, flicking it on, points it upward. Mason and Carter do the
same.

They start climbing up through the tangle of beams and
plates, their voices hollow-sounding.

                    CARTER
          It's from Earth; there's not a doubt of it.

                    ROSS
                  (tensely)
          We don't know that.

                    CARTER
          Captain, look at the -

                    ROSS
                  (interrupting)
          We don't know it, Carter.

Carter grunts softly, unbelievingly, and Mason looks at Ross,
wondering why he is so adamant about this point.

38.   CABIN LANDING - DOWN ANGLE SHOT

Ross reaches the landing and stands on it, the other two following.
The cabin door is shut; Ross does not move for it.

                              (CONTINUED)

38.   CONTINUED

As Mason tries to open it, Ross starts to say something, then doesn't. The door will not budge.

                    MASON
No.

                    CARTER
Maybe the cabin's still pressurized?

                    MASON
Not likely.
          (tries door again)
Door frame's probably twisted.
          (beat)
Try it together.

He and Carter put both their weights to it; without success. Ross looks around uneasily, then back at his two men.

                    ROSS
If it doesn't open, we'll have to forget about it.

                    MASON
          (turning; incredulous)
Forget about it?

                    ROSS
          (firmly)
There isn't time, Mason.

                    CARTER
          (overlapping)
It's moving.

Mason turns back quickly and he and Carter heave the combined weight of their bodies against the door until, abruptly, it grates open, stopping when there is just enough of an aperture for them to pass through. Mason squeezes into the cabin.

39.   INT. CABIN

Tilted severely. As Mason enters, he plays the beam of his
flashlight toward the pilot's seat, bracing himself for what
he might see.

40.   POV SHOT - PILOT'S SEAT

Illuminated by flashlight; a duplicate of the one in the X-89.
It is empty.

41.   MASON AND CARTER

Carter just coming in. He moves his flashlight beam in the
direction Mason moves his.

42.   POV SHOT - THREE LANDING SEATS

Illuminated by the two flashlight beams, all empty.

43.   MASON, CARTER AND ROSS

The Captain just pushing in, face taut with his struggle
against apprehension.

                         CARTER
                  (nervously confused)
            Where's the crew?

Mason only grunts softly, shaking his head. They start to
move around on the tilted deck, holding on to various
fastened-down objects to keep from slipping, their boots
crunching over broken glass, kicking aside metallic debris.
They play their flashlight beams around the ruins of the cabin.

44.   MASON

Suddenly, he stops, getting an idea and turns his flashlight
beam toward the lowest point of the tilted deck.

(CONTINUED)

44.   CONTINUED

CAMERA WHIP PANS down the beam of light to reveal three bodies jammed together where the deck and bulkhead meet. Their faces are not visible.

45.   MASON, ROSS AND CARTER

Mason in f.g.

                    MASON
                    (thickly)
        Here.

CAMERA DRAWS AHEAD of him as he thuds down the incline, the other following. Mason stoops to turn over one of the bodies.

46.   CLOSE SHOT - DEAD BODY

As Mason's hands begin to turn it over.

47.   MASON, ROSS AND CARTER

Reacting in horror.

                    CARTER
                (almost whispering)
        Dear God. . .

48.   CLOSE SHOT - DEAD BODY

It has Mason's face.

49.   MASON, ROSS AND CARTER

Staring at the dead body. Abruptly, Carter looks at the other two bodies, stoops to turn them over.

                                        (CONTINUED)

49.   CONTINUED

                        ROSS
        Don't.

50.   CARTER

Turning a body BELOW FRAME, recoiling with a noise of
terrified revulsion.

51.   CLOSE SHOT - DEAD BODY

It has Carter's face.

52.   MASON, ROSS AND CARTER

Carter lunges for the third body.

                        ROSS
        Don't.

But Carter has done it. They react again.

53.   CLOSE SHOT - DEAD BODY

It has Ross's face.

54.   MASON, ROSS AND CARTER

Carter stands on shaking legs and they look down mutely at
the bodies on the deck - themselves, dead. Each man has his
flash light beam on his own dead face. CAMERA PANS
DOWN the three ribbons of light which connect the trio of
dual bodies.

55.   MASON, ROSS AND CARTER

Ross is the first to shake himself free of the sight.

                    ROSS
        Carter, try the auxiliary light system.

Carter only makes a faint, inquiring noise.

                ROSS (CONT'D)
                (letting out tension)
        The auxiliary light system!

Carter twitches, nods shakily and moves up the tilted deck.
Mason and Ross remain standing over the bodies. Ross turns
off his flashlight and draws in a deep breath, raising his eyes
deliberately.

                    MASON
                    (feebly)
        Don't understand.

                    ROSS
        It isn't what it seems.

                    MASON
                (glancing over; wearily)
        What?
                    ROSS
        Just hang on.

They start as, o.s., the emergency generator begins an initial
WHINING spin. Part of the overhead lights flicker on, go
out. The generator coughs, then begins HUMMING and the
lights go on, holding albeit flickeringly. Ross looks down
again, unable to keep his eyes away.

56.   THE DEAD BODIES

In the flickering light we see, beyond doubt, that the bodies are those of Mason, Ross and Carter.

57.   UP ANGLE SHOT - MASON AND ROSS

As Mason stoops by the duplicate body of himself and reaches down.

58.   INSERT - MASON'S HANDS

Removing a thin wallet from the breast pocket of the uniform shirt on the dead man.

59.   MASON

Opening the wallet shakily, looking at it.

60.   INSERT - WALLET

A government identification card shows the name Lieutenant Robert Mason, a photograph of him.

61.   MASON

Looking through the wallet dazedly. Now he reaches under the jumper he is wearing and removes the billfold from his own shirt pocket, compares it to the wallet he already holds. They are identical. He stares from one to the other, face stricken into blankness.

                    ROSS'S VOICE
          Put it back.

He looks around quickly.

62.   ROSS AND MASON

As Mason looks up dumbly at the Captain.

                    ROSS

Put it back.

Mason swallows, replaces the wallet in the dead man's shirt
as Carter COMES INTO FRAME and looks down at his own
corpse.

                    CARTER
                   (pause)
          I don't get it.
                   (pause; brokenly)
          What is this?

                    ROSS
          Don't let it -

                    CARTER
               (pointing; cutting in)
          That's me.
                   (too loudly)
          It's me!

                    ROSS
          Hang on!

Carter is, abruptly, silenced. He shakes his head in tight little movements, then start to stoop by his duplicate body.
Ross pulls him up.

              ROSS (CONT'D)
          That won't help.

                              (CONTINUED)

62.   CONTINUED

> ROSS (CONT'D)
> (beat)
> Get something to cover them with.
> (beat)
> Both of you.

They look at him dazedly.

> ROSS (CONT'D)
> Now.

Mason turns and moves away, glad to crowd out horror with activity. Carter backs off slowly, staring at the corpse of himself.

> ROSS (CONT'D)
> (warningly)
> Carter.

Carter grunts, turns and moves off. Ross looks down at the bodies, fighting the apparent truth before his eyes.

> ROSS (CONT'D)
> (to himself)
> It's not what it seems.

63.   INT. LOCKER

Dark for an instant. Then the door is opened and we see Mason reach in and drag out a folded tarpaulin. In the b.g. is Carter and Ross.

64.   MASON, ROSS AND CARTER

Mason returns to the captain, Carter moving with him, almost robot-like.

(CONTINUED)

64.   CONTINUED

ROSS

Cover them.

Mason shakes open the tarp and he and Carter unfold it all
the way and lower it toward the bodies.

65.   CLOSE SHOT - THE DEAD BODIES

As the tarpaulin settles over them.

66.   MASON, ROSS AND CARTER

Mason straightens up, turns away, drawing in quick breath
and moves OUT OF FRAME.

ROSS
(to Carter)
I said come away.
(as Carter fails to move)
I said come away.

CARTER
(hollowly)
That's us on the deck.
(beat; aghast)
We're dead.

Ross points o.s. with a stabbing gesture.

ROSS
(cutting in)
Our ship is where we left it! - just as we left it!
(looking around)
This ship isn't ours.
(looking down)
And those aren't ours.

(CONTINUED)

66.   CONTINUED

CARTER

But they are.

ROSS

No.
(beat; tightly)
I don't know what it is but there's a logical
explanation for this. There's a logical
explanation for everything.

He punches his own chest, winces.

ROSS (CONT'D)

This is me.

He hits Carter's chest and Carter gasps, grimacing in pain.

ROSS (CONT'D)

And this is you. We're alive.

67.   MASON

As he slumps down on the pilot's seat. O.s., the VOICES
of Ross and Carter continue, just audible.

CARTER'S VOICE

Then what is it?

ROSS'S VOICE

I don't know - but it's not what it seems;
just keep that in mind.

Mason looks around the cabin, beginning to visualize what
the last moments before the crash must have been like.
CAMERA MOVES IN on his face.

(CONTINUED)

67.   CONTINUED

> ROSS'S VOICE (CONT'D)
> Use your head. Does it make sense that -

His voice is drowned out now by Mason's imagined thoughts about the last thirty or so seconds before the crash - the screaming the shouted commands, the shriek of the failing rockets, the rushing fall; finally, the tremendous, deafening crash, the sound of which breaks off abruptly as Ross speaks.

> ROSS
> Mason.

Mason starts, looks around.

68.   MASON, ROSS AND CARTER

> ROSS
> We're leaving.

> MASON
> What?

> ROSS
> (interrupting)
> We're going back to our ship and radio the station. They'll tell us what to do.

> MASON
> (lifelessly)
> Will they?

> ROSS
> They will.

(CONTINUED)

68.   CONTINUED

Mason stands and the three men move back to the cabin
doorway. There, Carter hesitates, glancing back.

> CARTER
> Shouldn't we - ?

> ROSS
> (cutting in)
> What?

Carter is unable to answer at first, the entire insanity of the
moment sweeping over him.

> CARTER
> (weakly)
> - bury our - ?

> ROSS
> (cutting in)
> They're not ours. Now go.

Carter swallows, looks back at the bodies again. Ross
pushes him through the doorway.

> ROSS (CONT'D)
> (angrily)
> Go.

Mason also looks back, then, sucking in a tremulous breath,
leaves the cabin. Ross starts out, hesitates, looking back as
if impelled to do so.

69.   POV SHOT - THE DEAD BODIES

Motionless under the tarpaulin.

70.   CLOSE SHOT - ROSS

                        ROSS
                      (tightly)
            We're alive.
                        (beat)
            Alive.

Vengefully, he snaps off the lights and turns away. CAMERA
PULLS BACK AND DOWN until the tarpaulin-covered bodies
are in f.g., the doorway in b.g. O.s., we hear the SOUNDS of
the three men climbing downward through the twisted network
of beams. The sounds fade. There is only silence.

                                        FADE OUT:

                    END OF ACT ONE

FADE IN:

71.   SPACE SHIP CABIN - CLOSE SHOT - RADIO SPEAKER -
        DAY

Crackling with static. CAMERA DRAWS BACK TO
REVEAL the three men in front of it, Mason sitting at the controls.

                        ROSS
                  (refusing to accept)
            Try it again.

                        MASON
            Captain, I've been trying it for -

                                        (CONTINUED)

71.   CONTINUED

                    ROSS
               (cutting him off)
     Try again.

Mason starts to say something, then blows out breath and
reaches for the radio controls. He flicks a switch, fiddling
with a set of knobs as he speaks.

                    MASON
     Space Ship X-89 calling Earth Station
     Twelve-One-Seven. Space Ship X-89
     calling Earth Station Twelve-One-Seven,
     Come in Earth Station Twelve-One-Seven.

He flicks over the switch. They listen to the crackling speaker,
Ross getting more disturbed by the moment. Abruptly, he
explodes.

                    ROSS
     What is this?! It was working before!

                    MASON
     Maybe it's this planet.

                    ROSS
               (irritably)
     What are you talking about?

                    MASON
     Maybe there's an interfering field of -

                    ROSS
               (cutting in sharply)
     That's ridiculous. Try the Radionic Signal.

                              (CONTINUED)

71.   CONTINUED

                         MASON
           Captain, it's not going to -

                          ROSS
                     (interrupting)
           Will you do as I say!

Mason draws in a deep breath and lets it shudder from his
lips as he turns on the controls for the Radionic Signal
apparatus. He pushes a button and a rhythmic beeping
noise commences. He lowers the volume and lets it sound
for ten seconds, then turns it off, flicks on the loud-speaker.
Only the crackling noise is heard. Ross tightens.

                    ROSS (CONT'D)
           Again.

Mason repeats the process. There is no answering signal
through the loudspeaker.

                    ROSS (CONT'D)
                      (tensely)
           Again.

                         MASON
           Captain, if it doesn't work the first time -

                          ROSS
           (overlapping; refusing to believe)
           They didn't hear.

                         MASON
           The return signal is automatic, Captain!
           Do I have to tell you that?

                                        (CONTINUED)

71.   CONTINUED

Ross starts to flare angrily at Mason, then contains himself.
He will not let this situation overwhelm him.

                              ROSS
        All right.

He turns away, begins to pace.

                       ROSS (CONT'D)
        All right, let's go over this again. There's
        an answer here somewhere. Somewhere.

He points o.s. toward the crashed ship.

                       ROSS (CONT'D)
        Those bodies aren't ours - that much
        we're sure of.

They do not respond to this as he desires, only staring at him.

                       ROSS (CONT'D)
                         (angrily)
        Well, use your heads.
                (pointing at them and at himself)
        These are our bodies!
                (pause; to himself)
        These are our bodies.

He turns away and paces again. Mason turns off the radio
controls and the Radionic Signal apparatus.

72.   ANOTHER ANGLE - ROSS FEATURED

He paces for several moments, thinking hard; then, suddenly, turns back in excitement.

                                        (CONTINUED)

72.   CONTINUED

> ROSS
> Listen. You both remember what they
> told us once in training? About the theory
> of circumnavigating time?
> (beat)
> They said that it might be possible for
> us to leave Earth during one year and,
> when we got back - even though we
> thought it was the <u>same</u> <u>year</u> - it might
> be the year before - or the year after.
> You remember that?

> MASON
> (not getting the drift of Ross's argument)
> It was only a theory, Captain.

> ROSS
> It's more than a theory. It's what hap-
> pened to us. We went through some kind
> of time warp - right into the future.

> MASON
> (getting the point; incredulously)
> And that -
> (pointing)
> - ship over there is in the future, is that
> what you're saying?

> ROSS
> Only the probable future.

> MASON
> And what does that mean?

(CONTINUED)

72.   CONTINUED

                    ROSS
          (gesturing toward cabin)
        It means that we're not dead!

                   MASON
               (cutting in)
     It also means that we're going to be dead!

                    ROSS
            Not if we don't go up.
             (pause; quietly)
        If we don't go up, we can't crash.

                   MASON
              (thrown by this)
        But. . . our orders

                    ROSS
               (cutting in)
       They don't say to kill ourselves.
                 (pause)
       It's the only answer. We're alive now and
       the only way to make certain that we stay
       alive is not to go up. Then we can't possibly
       crash; we avoid it, prevent it.

He looks at them, his mind made up.

                ROSS (CONT'D)
     We stay.

                   MASON
                 (pause)
     Easy enough for you to decide, Captain.

                              (CONTINUED)

72.   CONTINUED

>   ROSS
>   And what does that mean, Mason?

>   MASON
>   (tautly)
>   It means that you have no one waiting for
>   you back on Earth.

>   ROSS
>   So I have no reason to go back, is that it?
>   I'll be just as happy here as I would be
>   on Earth. Is that it?

Mason recognizes the injustice of his remark but will not
back down entirely.

>   MASON
>   I think we should vote on it.

>   ROSS
>   (scornfully)
>   You do?

>   MASON
>   You're not the only one, Captain.

>   ROSS
>   I'm the only one who gives the orders.

>   MASON
>   (pause; bitterly)
>   Even where our lives are concerned, anh?

>   (CONTINUED)

72.   CONTINUED

                    ROSS
     Especially where your lives are concerned.
                 (pause; tensely)
     We stay.

                    CARTER
                 (pause; quietly)
     For how long?

                    ROSS
     I'm not setting any limit, Carter.

                    CARTER
     A month? Two months?

                    ROSS
     I'm not setting any limit.

                    CARTER
     We have enough food left for three weeks, Captain.

                    ROSS
                 (adamant)
     I've no doubt there's edible food outside.

                    MASON
     How will we know what's edible and what isn't?
     We haven't got the equipment to test it.

                    ROSS
                 (cutting in)
     We'll watch the animals.

                                    (CONTINUED)

72.   CONTINUED

MASON
I saw no animals, Captain; did you?

ROSS
There will be.

MASON
If there are they'll be a different form
of life Captain. What they could eat
might be deadly poisonous to us.

ROSS
(overlapping)
We'll worry about it when the time comes, Mason.
(beat; controlled)
Right now, there's only one thing to
consider; preserving our lives.
It may not even be necessary to stay
here permanently; we may figure
something out. But for now -
the decision is to stay.

MASON
Not our decision, Captain.

ROSS
Have you a better solution then?!

Mason fails to reply and Ross turns away, moves to the
pilot's seat and sits down, starts manipulating the controls,
reducing drain on the electrical system to the minimum.
Mason and Carter watch him for several moments, then
look at each other. With a sign, Mason gets up. walks over
to a closed wall bunk and lies down on it. CAMERA
HOLDS ON him a few moments as he stares up grimly at
the overhead.

73.   CARTER

Walks to the port and looks out.

74.   POV SHOT - CRASHED SHIP

Darkness is starting to fall. The last rays of the planet's sun
glint off the metal of the demolished ship.

75.   CARTER AND ROSS

Carter in f.g. After several moments, he walks over to some
gauges near Ross and looks at them, Ross glances over.

ROSS
(trying to convince himself as well)
Working at minimum capacity, the ship's
electrical system can hold out for months.

CARTER
(darkly)
It won't be working at minimum capacity, Captain.

ROSS
Why?

CARTER
We're going to need heat - lots of it.
(cutting off Ross's objection)
It's only twilight and, already, the outside
temperature is minus thirteen degrees.

Ross grimaces at this unwelcome information; then fights it off.

ROSS
Would you rather go up?

(CONTINUED)

75.   CONTINUED

                    ROSS (CONT'D)
        Take the risk of <u>duplicating that</u> ship over there?

                    CARTER
                    (dazedly)
        How can we duplicate it, Captain?
        How can there be two crashed ships?
        Two of me, dead? Two of you? Two of - ?

                    ROSS
                    (cutting in)
        <u>We'll</u> <u>go</u> <u>over</u> <u>it</u>. <u>Eventually</u>, <u>we'll</u> find an answer.

Carter shakes his head defeatedly and moves over to the engi
neer's seat and control board, sits down. He looks at the dials
for a few moments, then covers his eyes with one hand.
CAMERA MOVES IN CLOSE on his face.

                                    CUT TO:

76.   EXT. COUNTRY ROAD - CLOSE ON CARTER - DAY

A duplicate of the previous shot; the viewer should not, immediately,
realize that Carter is no longer in the space ship cabin except,
of course, that, now, the light is natural rather than artificial
and that the click and hum of the ship's electrical life has
ceased abruptly. Carter senses that something has changed
and lowers his hand until his eyes are uncovered. His hand
drifts downward from his face as he looks around in dazed
astonishment.

77.   POV SHOT - THE ROAD

And surrounding area.

78.   CLOSE SHOT - CARTER

Gaping at the sight, head hitching jerkily as he looks around.
After several moments, his gaze lowers and he looks down at
himself, CAMERA DRAWING BACK to reveal that he is sit
ting on a stump. Slowly, he rises to his feet, a noise of faint,
incredulous inquiry in his throat.

79.   PAN SHOT - THE ROAD AREA - CARTER'S POV

80.   CARTER

Looking around, stunned.

                    KRAMER'S VOICE
        Mike?

Carter gasps and whirls.

81.   ANOTHER ANGLE - INCLUDING KRAMER

Coming out of the underbrush in hunting clothes, carrying a
rifle.
                    KRAMER
                    (smiling)
        Hi, boy. When did you get home?

Overwhelmed by confusion, Carter doesn't know what to say,
only gaping at Kramer.

                    KRAMER
        On leave, are you?

                    CARTER
        I. . .

Kramer pats his arm affectionately.

                                        (CONTINUED)

81.   CONTINUED

> KRAMER
You're looking fit.
> (beat)
I expect Mary's mighty pleased to have you back.

> CARTER
> (stiffening)
Mary.

He turns away from Kramer and starts walking down the
road, looking ahead, hungrily.

> KRAMER
Wait a second. I'll walk you.

Carter glances back, stopping and staring at Kramer until
the other man joins him. They start walking side by side,
Carter looking around constantly, his expression clearly
reflecting his conviction that this is all a cruel dream.

> KRAMER
How long you been home?

> CARTER
I. . .just got here.

Kramer looks askance at Carter's outfit - which lacks cap
and jacket.

> KRAMER
> (grins)
You rocket boys are sure traveling
informally these days.

(CONTINUED)

81.   CONTINUED

Carter doesn't answer, still unable to adjust to the shock of
being here.

                    KRAMER
          Mary know you're coming?

                    CARTER
                  (distractedly)
          I don't - think so.

                    KRAMER
          Going to surprise her, uh?

                    CARTER
                   (weakly)
     Yes.

                    KRAMER
          How long have you got?

                    CARTER
          (terrified that all of this may end)
          I don't know.

                    KRAMER
                (a little concerned)
          You all right, Mike?

Carter cannot answer. Driven, he walks faster and Kramer
increases his pace accordingly. Suddenly, Carter jolts to a
halt, hearing -

                  MRS. NOLAN'S VOICE
          Hello, Mike.

He looks o.s. toward -

82.   MRS. NOLAN - CARTER'S POV

An old, white-haired woman in a smock, gardening in her back yard, smiling at the o.s. Carter.

                    MRS. NOLAN
            Home on furlough?

83.   CARTER AND KRAMER

Carter getting more and more alarmed with every passing moment. How long can this last?

                    CARTER
                  (anguishedly)
        I don't know.

He starts to walk again, quickly, Kramer moving alongside of him.

                    KRAMER
                  (affectionately)
        Old Mrs. Nolan. She goes on forever.
                    (pause)
        Maybe we can do some hunting while
        you're home, hanh, Mike?
                  (beat; dryly)
        Not that I ever hit anything but -

He breaks off in surprise as Carter suddenly leaves him behind, breaking into a run.

84.   MOVING SHOT - CARTER

Dashing down the road, leaving Kramer behind. Now he reacts, seeing ahead -

85.   CARTER'S HOUSE - CARTER'S POV

Standing by itself on a rise.

86.   CARTER

Running hard, desperate to be home.

                    CARTER
          Mary . . .

87.   FULL SHOT - CARTER

Running toward his house, in front of which is parked a 1997 car.

88.   INT. HALL

CAMERA SHOOTING THROUGH window beside the door, showing Carter rushing up the path, face taut with fearful eagerness. He opens the door and rushes in.

                    CARTER
          Mary!
                (looking around)
          Mary, I'm home!

He hesitates a moment, listening, then rushes into the living room.

89.   INT. LIVING ROOM

As Carter runs in and stops, looking around, a half-crazed smile on his lips.

CARTER

He listens, runs for the kitchen.

90.   INT. KITCHEN - ANGLE TOWARD DOOR

Carter shoves open the swinging door and bursts in, stops.
Seeing that the kitchen is empty, he turns, leaves.

91.   INT. LIVING ROOM - CARTER

                        CARTER
                    (starting to panic)
        Mary?

He looks into the den.

                        CARTER (CONT'D)
        Mary!

92.   INT. HALL - ANGLE TOWARD LIVING ROOM

Carter crosses the living room, running hard, and lunges
through the living room archway, stops at the foot of the
stairs, looking up.

                        CARTER
        Mary!
                    (voice breaking)
        Are you up there?

With a sobbing breath, he starts up the steps two at a time.

93.   DOWN ANGLE SHOT - FROM SECOND FLOOR
       LANDING

Carter surging upward desperately. CAMERA PANS as he
reaches the landing and runs across it to the bedroom doorway.

94.   INT. BEDROOM - ANGLE ON DOOR

As Carter opens it and starts in.

                                        (CONTINUED)

94.   CONTINUED

                          CARTER
               Mary - !

His voice cuts off suddenly as he sees -

95.   POV SHOT - MARY

Lying, face down, on the bed, motionless.

96.   CARTER

Overjoyed and apprehensive at the same time, he starts
across the room, CAMERA DRAWING AHEAD of him.
He comes up to the bed and looks down.

97.   POV SHOT - MARY

Crying almost soundlessly.

98.   CARTER

Starts to speak, then his head moves slowly to one side as
his gaze is arrested by something.

99.   PAN SHOT - CARTER'S POV

CAMERA MOVING PAST the edge of the bed to reveal a
crumpled telegram on the floor.

100. CARTER

Reaching down, he picks it up and looks at it. CAMERA
MOVES IN on his expression of total horror.

                    ROSS'S VOICE
                  (distantly, faintly)
               Carter.

                                    (CONTINUED)

100.   CONTINUED

His eyes raise, a look of dumb bafflement on his face.

                    ROSS'S VOICE
                       (closer)
        Carter.

He twitches, starts to glance around, looks back at the
telegram. Suddenly Ross's hand shoots INTO FRAME and
clamps on Carter's shoulder.

                    ROSS
        I'm talking to you.

Carter gasps in shock and starts to whirl.

101.   INT. SPACE SHIP - CABIN - ROSS AND CARTER

Both standing. Carter finishes his turn and gapes at Ross.

                    ROSS
        What's the matter with you?

Carter can't answer. He looks around in stunned confusion.

                    ROSS (CONT'D)
        What is the matter with you!?

                    CARTER
        I. . .I was - home.

                    ROSS
        What?

                    CARTER
        I was home.

                                    (CONTINUED)

101.   CONTINUED

                    ROSS
                (tightening)
        You were here.
                    (beat)
        You _are_ here.

                    CARTER
        No. No I swear I was. . .
                    (gasping)
        I saw Mary. She was -

He looks at his shaking hands, catching his breath.

                CARTER (CONT'D)
        There was a telegram.
                (looks at Ross, shakily)
        It said that I'd been killed.

Ross takes hold of Carter's arm and squeezes it hard, his
expression almost brutal.

                    ROSS
        You are alive.

                    CARTER
                (suddenly recalling)
        Those people I saw - Kramer; Mrs. Nolan.

102.   CLOSE SHOT - CARTER

                    CARTER
        They're dead.

103.   CARTER AND ROSS

> CARTER
> I just remembered that.

> ROSS
> Stop it, Carter.

> CARTER
> Kramer was killed in a hunting accident.
> Mrs. Nolan -
> ROSS
> Stop it!
> (cutting off Carter)
> It never happened, Carter! There's
> an explanation for this! I don't know
> what it is but we'll find it, Carter!
> We'll go over it again and again until we
> do! You! Me!
> (turns)
> Mason - !

He doesn't complete Mason's name, his voice strangling off
into dead silence. Carter looks in the same direction, reacts.
CAMERA PULLS AWAY from them until it MOVES
OVER Mason's bunk. Mason isn't in it.

104.   ROSS AND CARTER

Stunned. Ross starts turning quickly, looking around the small
cabin.

105.   FAST PAN SHOT - ROSS'S POV

Mason is not in the cabin.

106.   FULL SHOT - SHOWING ENTIRE CABIN

Carter and Ross standing in the b.g., Mason nowhere to be
seen.

                    ROSS
        Mason!
                    (pause)
        Mason!

                                        FADE OUT:

                    END OF ACT TWO

        FADE IN:

107.   INT. SPACE SHIP - CABIN - FULL SHOT - ROSS AND
        CARTER

Standing close together in the silent cabin, looking uneasily
toward the empty bunk.

108.   ROSS AND CARTER

                    CARTER
        Where is he?
                    (beat)
        Where did he go?

                    ROSS
                    (angrily)
        I don't know.

He gets an almost vengeful look on his face and walks over
to the empty bunk, CAMERA MOVING with him. He
looks down at the bunk. CAMERA PANS DOWN,
MOVES CLOSE on the blanket.

CUT TO:

109.   PICNIC AREA - CLOSE ON GRASS - DAY

O.s. can be heard SOUNDS of birds SINGING, the BAB-BLE of water. After several moments, Mason's hand moves INTO FRAME as he stirs in his sleep. CAMERA DRAWS BACK to reveal him lying on an expanse of thick grass. After several seconds, he turns onto his back and slowly, lids fluttering, opens his eyes. He does not comprehend, at first, what has happened. Then, abruptly, it hits him and he sits up fast, looking around in amazement.

110.   FULL SHOT - MASON

CAMERA SHOOTING OVER a charming, lily-pad covered pond. In the b.g. Mason sits, staring across the water in dumb astonishment.

111.   MASON

Turning his head, looking around, his eyes unblinking, incredulous.

112.   PAN SHOT - MASON'S POV

A beautiful, rustic scene - the pond surrounded by a growth of bushes, trees, turf. Birds SINGING constantly; an overall mood of tranquility. CAMERA STOPS on Mason, looking around, his expression one of awe. Now he looks down at the fishing pole propped beside him; picks it up and stares at it. Suddenly he drops it as there is a RUSTLING in the bushes o.s. and, starting, looks in that direction.

113.   POV SHOT - BUSHES

Someone approaching through them.

114.   MASON

Drawing back in uncomprehending dread despite the cheefulness of his surroundings. Now the rustling stops and Mason reacts in shock.

115.   JEANIE

Standing at the edge of the bushes, a pretty girl of about seven.

                              JEANIE
              Oh. At last. I thought I'd never find you.

116.   MASON

                              MASON
                            (stricken)
              Jeanie. . .

117.   MASON AND JEANIE

                              JEANIE
              I looked and looked.
                       (turning; calling)
              I found him!

She turns back, approaches Mason.

                         JEANIE (CONT'D)
              Lunch is ready, Daddy. And am
              I hungry after all that searching.

He doesn't move, staring at her as if he cannot accept the evidence of his sight.

                         JEANIE (CONT'D)
              What's the matter, Daddy?

                                          (CONTINUED)

117.   CONTINUED

Still, he can only gape at her. Then, realizing that she is
actually there, he reaches out trembling arms, barely able to
speak he is so overcome.

                    MASON
        Come 'ere.

Looking at him strangely Jeanie moves over to where he is
and drops to her knees beside him.

                    MASON
        What, Daddy?

He embraces her convulsively.

118.   TIGHT TWO SHOT - MASON AND JEANIE

Mason holding her tightly, cheek pressed to hers, eyes shut,
almost in tears.

                    MASON
        Jeanie. Jeanie.

                    JEANIE
        What is it, Daddy?

Mason draws back, looks at her as if he expects her to disap
pear at any moment.

                    MASON
        Is it you? Really?

                    JEANIE
            (alarmed)
        Daddy, what's wrong?

                                        (CONTINUED)

118. CONTINUED

                    MASON
                  (brokenly)
        Nothing. I'm just. . .glad to see you, that's all.

                    JEANIE
                  (not convinced)
        Oh.

                    MASON
                  (hoping against hope)
        That wasn't your. . .your Mother you
        were just calling.

She looks at him curiously, not understanding his behavior.

                    MASON (CONT'D)
                  (desperately)
        Jeanie, <u>was</u> it?

                    JEANIE
                  (confused)
        <u>Yes</u>, Daddy. You know -

She breaks off and looks at him in startlement as, with a
faint sob, he pushes to his feet and starts toward the bushes.
Suddenly, he stops, looks back.

                    MASON
        Where is she?

                    JEANIE
        Over by the - table, Daddy.

Turning quickly, Mason plunges into the bushes.

119.   MOVING SHOT - MASON

As he moves through the bushes, breathing hard, looking off
into the distance.

120.   EDGE OF BUSH CAMP

Mason comes pushing out into the open and stops panting,
looks around. He starts running again, CAMERA PULLING
AHEAD of him.

121.   thru 123.VARIOUS SHOTS

Showing Mason running through the woods, searching for his
wife. Stopping, looking around in rising panic. Running
again eyes searching in all directions.

124.   CLOSE SHOT - MASON

As he rakes to a halt beside a tree trunk, catching his breath
as he hears HUMMING o.s.

125.   POV SHOT - BUSHES

On the other side of them, the SOUND of Ruth HUMMING
softly; some nondescript tune.

126.   MASON

Starts forward, CAMERA DRAWING AHEAD of him
through the bushes. After a short while, he emerges from the
bushes, stops, reacting, as he sees -

127.   RUTH - MASON'S POV

Standing by a picnic table, setting down a plate of fried
chicken. She turns in surprise.

(CONTINUED)

127.   CONTINUED

                    RUTH
          <u>Bob</u>.
                    (smiling)
          You scared me, honey. Bursting out of the bushes
          like. . .

Her voice fades off as she sees the look on his face.

128.   MASON

Moving forward dazedly, CAMERA DRAWING AHEAD of
him as he approaches Ruth, unable to take his eyes from her.
CAMERA INCLUDES her now, STOPS.

                    RUTH
          Bob?
                    (beat; uneasily)
          What is it?

With a ragged breath, he embraces and clings to her, burying
his face in her hair.

                    MASON
                    (huskily)
          Oh, God. <u>God</u>.

                    RUTH
                    (concernedly)
          Sweetheart.

She begins to stroke his hair, disturbed by the way he is acting.

                    RUTH (CONT'D)
          What's wrong?

He draws back and looks at her with eyes that glisten with
tears.

                              (CONTINUED)

128.   CONTINUED

                        MASON
        Nothing.
                        (beat)
        Nothing - now.

                        RUTH
        Are you sure?

                        MASON
        Yes.
                        (pulling her close)
        Oh, yes.

He holds her tightly, eyes closed, a look of fervent gratification
on his face.

                        RUTH
                        (half-jokingly)
        All this just for lunch?

                        MASON
                        (a sobbing laugh)
        Yes.

He gets a little control of himself and looks at her again. She
brushes tears from his eyes, very touched by his behavior but
trying to cheer him up.

                        RUTH
        My goodness. So emotional over a
        little fried chicken.
                        (beat)
        Where's Jeanie?

                                        (CONTINUED)

128.   CONTINUED

                    MASON
          (keeping his eyes on her; pointing)
          Back there.

                    RUTH
          Were you asleep?
                    (as he fails to answer)
          Are you still asleep?

                    MASON
          If this is a dream - I hope I never wake up.

He holds her close again. After a moment, she sees something
o.s. and stiffens in his arms. Mason is not immediately
aware of it.

                 MASON (CONT'D)
          I hope I just go on dreaming and -

He breaks off, seeing the expression on her face. Abruptly,
he whirls.

129.   RUTH

At first we do not realize who it is as he stands in the deep
shade of a tree, an unidentifiable but definitely menacing figure. Then he steps into the sunlight.

                    ROSS
                 (threateningly)
          Let's go, Mason.

130.   MASON AND RUTH

Reacting to the sight of Mason.
                                        (CONTINUED)

130.   CONTINUED

> RUTH
> Bob, why is <u>he</u> here?

131. MASON, RUTH AND ROSS

Ross in f.g., back to CAMERA. Mason draws his wife back slowly so that he is standing between her and Ross. He does not understand why Ross is there but senses the threat of his presence.

> MASON
> Get out of here.

> ROSS
> Let's go, Mason.

> MASON
> Get away from us.

132.   ROSS

Starts forward.

> ROSS
> You're coming back with me.

133.   MASON, RUTH AND ROSS

> MASON
> (dumbly)
> Back?

> ROSS
> Where you belong - on the ship.

> RUTH
> (repelled)
> No, Bob.

(CONTINUED)

133.   CONTINUED

                        ROSS
                  (cutting in harshly)
         You're having an hallucination, Lieutenant.

Mason pushes his wife back out of the way, preparing to
defend himself.

                        MASON
         No. It's real.

                        ROSS
         It isn't. And you're leaving with me.

                        MASON
         No.

134.   MASON

Prepared to fight. He lunges forward.

                        MASON
         No.

135.   ROSS, MASON AND RUTH

Mason and Ross begin to grapple violently, the CAMERA
MOVING AROUND them, TURNING FASTER AND
FASTER.
                        ROSS
         You're coming back!

                        MASON
         I'm staying here!

                                        (CONTINUED)

135. CONTINUED

                    ROSS
You can't! I won't let you! You're coming back!
                    MASON
No!

                    ROSS
Yes! Back! Back! <u>Back</u>!

Suddenly, the CAMERA STOPS. The two men are standing in
the space ship cabin, Carter nearby. Mason looks around, his
nerves about to crack, a quavering noise of horror in his throat.

                    MASON
I don't want to be here.
              (beat)
I don't want to be here!

He tears free of Ross and staggers around the cabin.

                MASON (CONT'D)
Ruth!
              (starting to cry)
Ruth. . .Ruth.

Ross moves to him, grabs his arms.

                    ROSS
There was no Ruth. No Jeanie.

With a murderous snarl, Mason shoots out his hands to
Ross's throat and starts to choke him. Ross struggles with
him for a few moments, then slams a fist into Mason's stomach. Mason doubles over, gagging. Ross hauls him erect
and slams him brutally against a bulkhead. Reaching into
Mason's shirt pocket, Ross pulls out his billfold and opens
it, takes a newspaper clipping from it. This, he shoves into
Mason's face.

                              (CONTINUED)

135.   CONTINUED

> ROSS (CONT'D)
> What does it say, Mason?
> (beat)
> Look at it!

Mason focuses his eyes on the clipping, makes a faint, disbelieving noise.

136.   INSERT - CLIPPING

Showing a wirephoto of Ruth and Jeanie Mason. The headline of the article reads SPACE PILOT'S FAMILY DIES IN CAR CRASH. The wife and daughter of Spacepilot Robert Mason died early this morning when the car they were in -

137.   MASON AND ROSS

Mason gapes at the clipping, completely beyond comprehension.

> ROSS
> Now do you still insist that you were with them?
> (beat)
> You alive? - they dead?

Mason looks up blankly at Ross.

> MASON
> I was with them.
> (beat)
> I was, I was. And you took me away.

> ROSS
> It isn't true, Mason.

(CONTINUED)

137.   CONTINUED

                          CARTER
                       (breaking in)
        Isn't it?! You took me away from <u>my</u> wife,
        <u>my</u> home!

                           ROSS
                   (shakes his head; tensely)
        You were both here all the time.

                          CARTER
                     (pointing at Mason)
        He was gone!

                           ROSS
        No.
                         (beat)
        We just couldn't see him, that's all.

                          CARTER
        What are you talking about?

                           ROSS
                      (confidently)
        I know what it is now: that's what I'm
        talking about.

        He lets go of Mason who looks at the clipping again, then
        back at Ross.

                      ROSS (CONT'D)
        I was wrong. It has nothing to do with
        circumnavigating time - nothing at all.
                       (to Mason)
        You remember what you thought before
        you saw that ship over there?

                                              (CONTINUED)

137.   CONTINUED

Mason only stares at him. Ross points at him.

ROSS (CONT'D)
Alien contact, that's what you thought.
(beat)
And that's exactly what's happened to us.

MASON
(overlapping; bitterly)
But, Captain, there are no such things.

ROSS
(cutting in)
Listen to me! Neither of you were home.
(pointing o.s.)
And that ship over there isn't ours and those bodies
aren't ours.
(beat)
We've been tricked.

CARTER
(tightly)
By who?

ROSS
By whoever it is that lives on this planet -
and doesn't want anyone else to live here.
(as they stare at him)

ROSS (CONT'D)
Don't you understand?! We haven't seen
them but there are aliens here! But aliens
who aren't strong enough to kill us or chase
us away by force. So what can they do?
How can they keep their planet from being
colonized?

(CONTINUED)

137.   CONTINUED

> ROSS (CONT'D)
> (pause)

By mind-control, that's how. By picking our
brains and finding the death fear - and making
use of it by showing us our ship crashed and
us dead inside of it. Scaring us so much that
we didn't dare take off again. . .and, therefore,
haven't been able to make our report about
this planet.

> ROSS (CONT'D)
> (beat)

They even know we can't radio a report to
Earth because there's too much interference.

> MASON

You didn't believe there was interference before.

> ROSS
> (overlapping)

I believe it now.

> (beat)

Everything that's happened to us since we
landed on this planet has been a delusion!

> MASON

No. It happened. I was home, I -

> ROSS

It was a delusion!

> CARTER

Even Mason's disappearance?

(CONTINUED)

137.   CONTINUED

                              ROSS
          Why not? If they can make us believe
          we saw a crashed ship - saw our own
          bodies inside that ship. . .they can make
          us believe anything.

Carter turns toward the port.

                              CARTER
          It's not really there then, hanh?

                              ROSS
          You may see it - even touch it again.
                              (beat)
          That doesn't prove it's there.

                              MASON
          What's going to prove it isn't there, Captain.
                              (beat)
          What's going to prove that everything
          you've said is true?

138.   ROSS

                              ROSS
          I'll tell you what's going to prove it - Lieutenant
          Mason. Us. . .
                              (pointing upwards)
          - going up. . .and all the way back to Earth.
          Proving that there's been nothing holding
          us back but deluded fear.

139.   THE THREE

Ross smiles thinly, arrogantly and turns away, heading for
the control board.

(CONTINUED)

139.   CONTINUED

Mason and Carter watch him go, too startled to react.
Then, abruptly, Mason starts forward.

                    MASON
            Wait a minute.

140.   ANOTHER ANGLE

Ross in f.g., getting into the pilot's seat. Mason hurries up
as Ross begins turning on the controls.

                    MASON
            What if you're wrong?

                    ROSS
            I'm right.

                    MASON
            You thought you were right before.
                    (pause)
            You were ready to keep us here indefinitely
            you were so sure!

Ross doesn't answer and, suddenly, Mason reaches forward,
turns off the main switch and keeps his hand on it. Ross
turns on him, infuriated.

                    ROSS
            What do you think you're - ?

                    MASON
                    (cutting him off)
            Are you so arrogant that you'll take a chance
            on killing us just to make your point?!

                                    (CONTINUED)

140.   CONTINUED

Ross grabs Mason's hand and flings it off the switch.

                    ROSS
        I'm captain of this ship and you'll do as I say!

                CARTER'S VOICE
                    (quietly)
        You're not the captain of our lives.

They both look around.

141.   ANOTHER ANGLE - INCLUDING CARTER

Pointing a gun at Ross.

                    ROSS
                (controlled)
        Put it away.

                    CARTER
        You're not taking us up.

                    ROSS
        You want to stay here then? Starve?
        Freeze? Rot?!
                    (beat)
        Never see Earth again?!

Carter has no answer, a suspended moment of tension.
Then Mason's shoulders slump.

                    MASON
                (defeatedly)
        Put it away Mike. He's right.
        We can't just stay here.

                                    (CONTINUED)

141.   CONTINUED

Carter hesitates, then lowers the gun and Ross turns back to the controls. Mason moves into close f.g.

> MASON (CONT'D)
> (grimly)
> We have to go up.
> (beat)
> And may God have mercy on ours souls.

FADE OUT:

END ACT THREE

FADE IN:

142.   EXT. SPACE SHIP - NIGHT

Beginning to shudder as the rocket engines commence their warm-up phase.

143.   INT. SPACE SHIP CABIN - THE THREE MEN

Ross in f.g., working at the control board; Mason and Carter standing behind him, watching uneasily.

144.   CLOSE SHOT - MASON

Watching the captain.

145.   CLOSE SHOT - CARTER

Watching Ross.

146.   ROSS

Fingers moving deftly over the controls board. He re-checks the readings carefully.

147.   THE THREE MEN

Ross satisfied now.

                    ROSS
       All right.

He stands and the three men start for their foam rubber chairs.

148.   ANOTHER ANGLE

Foam rubber chairs in f.g. The three men come up to them
and take their places without talking, begin to strap themselves down.

149.   CLOSE PAN SHOT - THE THREE MEN

CAMERA MOVING PAST Carter, Mason, STOPPING ON
Ross. He finishes fastening the straps and looks over at the others.

150.   THE THREE MEN

                    ROSS
       Ready?

They look at him, then, without a word, recline on their chairs.

151.   CARTER

As his head leans back on the chair. He looks up at the over
head, face taut with premonition.

152.   MASON

Leaning back against the chair, staring upward apprehensively.

153.   ROSS

Leaning back in his chair. Once more, he glances at the
other two, sees that they are set.

                    ROSS
                  (tightly)
          All right, here we go.

CAMERA MOVES IN FAST on his right hand; beneath it
is a button on the arm of the chair. Ross's finger hesitates
above it, then depresses it.

154.   EXT. FIELD - CRASHED SHIP AND SPACE SHIP

The wreckage in f.g. CAMERA SHOOTING PAST it.
In the b.g. is the space ship, its rockets beginning to spew
out thunderous jets of flame.

155.   INT. SPACE SHIP CABIN - FULL SHOT - THE THREE
        MEN

The cabin shuddering violently.

156.   CLOSE SHOT - THE THREE MEN

Reclined on their chairs, bracing themselves for the worst.

157.   CARTER

Waiting tensely.

158.   MASON

Waiting.

159.   ROSS

Waiting.

160.   EXT. SPACE SHIP

After several moments, it begins to rise up slowly from the ground.

161.   INT. SPACE SHIP CABIN - THE THREE MEN

Being gradually depressed in their foam rubber chairs as the ship rises.

162.   CARTER

163.   MASON

164.   ROSS

Turning his head inchingly toward -

165.   THE CONTROL BOARD - ROSS'S POV

CAMERA ZOOMS IN on the altimeter. The needle moves past 200 - 300 - 500.

166.   CLOSE SHOT - ROSS

Staring at the altimeter as if willing the ship to rise.

167.   SPACE SHIP

It continues climbing, picking up velocity.

168.   INT. SPACE SHIP CABIN - ALTIMETER

The needle passes 1000 - 1250 - 1500.

169.   ROSS

Beginning to show some evidence of elation. He starts to say something to the others, then decides to wait.

170.   CARTER

Afraid to hope yet, still, hoping.

171.   MASON

Wondering if it is really true; that they are escaping.

172.   ALTIMETER

The needle passing 2250 - 2750.

173.   THE THREE MEN

Ross in f.g., looking toward the altimeter.

                    ROSS
        Three thousand.
                    (beat)
        Four.
                    (beat)
        Five.
                    (beat)
        Six.
                    (beat)
        Seven!
                    (beat)

                    CARTER
                    (jubilant)
        We're out!

He slumps in the chair and closes his eyes, sighs in relief.
Mason swallows dryly, wipes some perspiration from his
brow. Ross unstraps himself and stands. Mason undoes his
straps and follows Ross toward the control board.

174.   ANOTHER ANGLE

Control board in f.g. Ross comes up to the pilot's seat and
lowers himself onto it. Mason moves up behind him,
watches the Captain make knob adjustments.

                    ROSS
                (without turning)
Well?

                    MASON
                (glad to repent)
        You were right.
                (dryly)
        If I ever see anything glitter on that viewer
        again - I'll keep my big mouth shut.

175.   ROSS

Thinking hard.

                    ROSS
        I was right.

176.   ROSS AND CARTER

Abruptly, Ross pushes buttons, throws switches. Mason
stiffens, looking at Ross incredulously.

                    MASON
        What are you - ?
                (beat; appalled)
        What are you doing?

                    ROSS
        Landing.

                                    (CONTINUED)

176.   CONTINUED

In the b.g., Carter hears and starts over fast.

                    MASON
          What?!

                    ROSS
          Now that we know what it is - there's no
          reason why we shouldn't go back. Is there?

                    MASON
                 (incredulous)
          No reason?

                    CARTER
                  (arriving)
          Are you out of your mind?
                 (reaching for the controls)
          Captain, for God's sake - !

Ross shoves his hand away.

                    ROSS
          We have orders, Carter! Pick up speci-
          mens for analysis. We are going to pick
          them up.

                    CARTER
                 (lunging for Ross)
          You're not going to - !

Before he can reach Ross, the ship suddenly yaws wildly,
throwing Mason and Carter off balance.

177.   CARTER

Hitting the bulkhead, looking at Ross with a combination of
terror and fury.

>   CARTER
>   You did it!
>   (beat)
>   You <u>did</u> it!

178.   THE THREE MEN

The cabin tilted and shaking. Ross works desperately at the
controls.

>   CARTER
>   (panic-stricken)
>   You were right the first time! That <u>was</u>
>   us down there! We're going to crash!

>   ROSS
>   No!

>   CARTER

>   We're going to die!

>   ROSS
>   We're <u>not</u> going to die! I'm not going to <u>let</u> us die!

179.   SERIES OF SHOTS

Carter screaming as he is thrown about in the rocking cabin.
Mason, holding onto something for support, remembering
the vision he had before regarding the ship's crash. Ross,
holding onto his seat, working doggedly at the controls.

180.   ROSS

                    ROSS
        Auxiliary engines!

181.   CARTER

                    CARTER
        It's no use!

182.   ROSS

Lunges up in a fury and staggers across the deck, throws a
switch. Abruptly, the ship stops plunging, the rockets catch,
the cabin straightens out. Carter stands up, totally confused. Ross returns to the controls.

                    CARTER
        I don't understand.

                    ROSS
                 (cutting in)
        Shut up!
                  (beat)
        You're a coward, Carter! You haven't even
        got the guts to fight for your own life.

Carter starts to reply, then doesn't know what to say.

                    MASON
               (uncertainly)
        We're still going down?

                    ROSS
        You bet we're going down. And when we
        get there, you're going to see that that ship
        is gone - vanished.

                              (CONTINUED)

182.   CONTINUED

                    ROSS (CONT'D)
          Because it was never there in the first place.
                    (beat; curtly)
              Air spring.

Mason moves to the bulkhead switch and throws it - the
RUSH of AIR begins below.

                    ROSS
              Now get in your places.

Carter and Mason move almost meekly to their chairs and
sit on them.

183.   THE THREE MEN

Mason and Carter in f.g., sitting down. Ross in b.g. at the
control board.

                    CARTER
                    (dazedly)
          He's been right all the time.

                    CARTER (CONT'D)
                    (beat)
              Hasn't he?

                    MASON
              I don't know.

Ross gets up from the control board and comes over, seats
him self. A few moments later, the ship lands, the rockets
cut off and the cabin is motionless and silent. Ross gets up
and moves to the port. Carter and Mason follow.

184.   AT THE PORT

Ross, Carter, then Mason come up to it and look out. Ross turns on the spotlight.

185.   EXT. SPACE SHIP

As the spotlight flares on.

186.   INT. SPACE SHIP CABIN - THE THREE MEN

Looking out.

187.   POV SHOT - SPOTLIGHT BEAM

Illuminating the field. There is no ship in sight.

188.   INT. SPACE SHIP CABIN - THE THREE MEN

> ROSS
> (satisfied)

Well?

> MASON

How do we know we're facing in the right direction?

Before he has finished, Ross irritably turns on a mechanism to make the spotlight move.

189.   EXT. SPACE SHIP

The spotlight starts turning slowly.

190.   INT. SPACE SHIP CABIN - THE THREE MEN

Looking out through the port.

191.   POV SHOT - THE SPOTLIGHT BEAM

Moving slowly over the field.

192.   THE THREE MEN

Ross suddenly stiffens and turns off the spotlight mechanism. In the heavy silence, they look out with sickened
expressions.

193.   POV SHOT - CRASHED SHIP

Illuminated by the spotlight beam.

194.   INT. SPACE SHIP CABIN - THE THREE MEN

Looking out dumbly at the wreckage. Now Carter looks at
Ross, both hating and hurt.

                    CARTER
          Gone, Captain. Vanished?

                    ROSS
               (defensively)
          All right, it's still there. That doesn't
          mean -

                    CARTER
          I'll tell you what it means! It means
          you're wrong!

                    ROSS
          Hang on. There's an explanation for this.
          I don't know what it is yet but -

                    CARTER
          You'll never know!

                              (CONTINUED)

194.   CONTINUED

                    CARTER (CONT'D)
                       (tormented)
          Now we'll have to go up again. And this
          time we'll really crash. And be killed -
          and look just like those - those. . .

                    MASON
                    (lifelessly)
          No.

They look at him in uneasy surprise.

                    MASON
          We're not going to crash.

                    CARTER
          How do you know?

                    MASON
                    (dully)
          We're not going to crash because we
          already have crashed.

                    ROSS
                    (bristling)
          What are you talking about?

                    MASON
          Stop fighting it, Captain; you're all out of
          explanations. There's only one left -
          and you know what it is.

                    ROSS
                    (tightening)
          I know nothing of the kind.

(CONTINUED)

194.   CONTINUED

                    MASON
        Yes, you do.
                    (beat)
        Carter <u>was</u> home - and that telegram
        really was there. I was with my wife and
        my daughter. Because I'm <u>like</u> them now.

                    ROSS
                    (struggling)
        No.

                    MASON
        Accept it, Captain! Stop trying to prove
        that we're alive!

                    ROSS
        We <u>are</u> alive! I don't know what it is
        that's happening here but there's an answer
        somewhere - <u>somewhere</u>!

                    MASON
        I've given you the answer!

                    ROSS
        <u>I</u> don't <u>accept</u> <u>it</u>!

                    ROSS (CONT'D)
                    (tightly)
        We're going over this again. We're going
        to find an answer.

                    MASON
                    (agonized)
        Can't you see that that's what we've been <u>doing</u>?

                              (CONTINUED)

194.   CONTINUED

>   MASON (CONT'D)
>   Going over it! - <u>again</u> and <u>again</u>!
>   (pleading)
>   Let us die, Captain.

195.   ROSS

Tightening with resistance as he sees -

196.   MASON AND CARTER - ROSS'S POV

They are starting to fade; we can see through them.

>   MASON
>   (begging)
>   <u>Let</u> <u>go</u> <u>of</u> <u>us</u>.

197.   ROSS

Fighting it with all his will.

>   ROSS
>   No.
>   (enraged)
>   No! We're alive! <u>Alive</u>!
>   We're going over it again! You hear me?
>   (beat)
>   <u>We're</u>-<u>going</u>-<u>over</u>-<u>it</u>-<u>again</u>!

198.   CLOSE SHOT - ROSS

>   MASON'S VOICE
>   Captain.

Ross turns and rises, CAMERA DRAWING BACK to
reveal that he has just gotten up from the pilot's seat.

199.   UP ANGLE SHOT - MASON (SAME AS SHOT #3)

Looking down at the viewer. FOOTSTEPS on the deck.
Ross ENTERS FRAME and looks down at the viewer.

MASON
Something glittered.

ROSS
Put it on Reverse.

Mason reaches down and flicks a switch.

MASON
It was at two-five-five dash four-one-seven.

200.   ROSS

ROSS
(grunts)
I don't see anything.

SOUND CUTS OFF; we only see Ross's lips moving as he
talks, speaking; the dialogue from Shot #3.

SERLING'S NARRATION
Picture of a man who will not see anything he does not choose to see including
his own death.

CAMERA DRAWS BACK as Ross moves to the control
board and starts working on it. The ship begins to turn.

SERLING'S NARRATION
A man of such indomitable will that even
the two men beneath his command are
not allowed, by him, to see the truth.

(CONTINUED)

200.   CONTINUED

Carter comes through the doorway and asks (soundlessly) why they are turning. Action and dialogue continues as in Shot #9.

> SERLING'S NARRATION (CONT'D)
> Which truth is: that they are no longer
> among the living. That the movements
> they are now about to make - the words
> they are now about to speak - have all
> been made - and spoken - countless
> times before. And will be made - and
> spoken - countless times again. . .perhaps
> even unto eternity.

201.   EXT. SPACE SHIP

As it moves across the planet toward its place of landing.

> SERLING'S NARRATION
> Picture of a latter-day Flying Dutchman -
> sailing into the Twilight Zone.

FADE OUT:

THE END

Steel

Like "Nick of Time" and "Nightmare at 20,000 Feet," this episode remains high on Matheson's list as a successful interpretation of his script. In past interviews he has described it, in fact, as perhaps his favorite. Based on his 1956 short story (later included of course in *Collected Stories*), this tale of two losers—one human, one robot—who refuse to admit they are losers also coincidentally happened to deal with one of Serling's favorite sports: boxing.

"I remember when I wrote the short story I hadn't written prose in a long time, so what I did, I deliberately tried to take on a Hemingway style, which was absolutely minimalistic. I went on that way for four or five pages before finally I slipped back into my own style."

Matheson also had the rare advantage of sitting on the readings with the actors and director hired for that particular episode.

"I've always believed that it was very uncommon. It may still be uncommon—certainly for freelancers. Most shows are written by staff writers anyway, so they of course would be sitting in on the readings and the rehearsals. But back then, the television industry was almost entirely freelance. Whether this was done anywhere else, I don't know, but to me it certainly was remarkable.

"I remember them reading through it, Lee Marvin and Joe Mantell. I remember vividly walking with them to the set. And Lee Marvin was psyching himself into getting the feeling of it, even then. He was making crowd noises to himself, to work himself up into an involvement with the moment. He never did much television. I think this was before he was a star in films like *The Dirty Dozen* and *Hell in the Pacific*.

"It was very well done. Amazing how they cheated the sense of being in a crowded stadium, when obviously they had a mere handful of extras. Burt Granet, the producer, was very, very good to work with; I liked working with him a lot after Buck Houghton left the series. I liked both of them, but anyone would be a little uneasy after four seasons about getting a new producer. It worked out extremely well, though. He was a very nice man, very knowledgeable. It was very rewarding working with him. But I never worked with William Froug, who later replaced him. As soon as he came on—I was out. Probably not by my choice, either."

STEEL

PERFORMANCE DATE: 10/4/63

PRODUCER: BERT GRANET

DIRECTOR: DON WEIS

CAST:

STEEL KELLY: LEE MARVEN

POLE: JOE MANTELL

MAYNARD FLASH: CHUCK HICKS

BATTELING MAXO: TIP McCLURE

NOLAN: MERRITT BOHN

MAXWELL: FRANK LONDON

MAN'S VOICE: LARRY BARTON

FADE IN:

1.   EXT. MAYNARD STREET

A hot, summer afternoon. In the distance, a bus approaches,
pulls in toward the curb and stops near CAMERA.
The front door is opened and several passengers debark
before KELLY and POLE appear, rolling, what seems to be a
man covered by a cloth sack, draw-stringed at the ankles.
(No one gives the sight of this more than cursory interest)
As they lift the figure to the sidewalk, one of the two wheels
under its high-shoed right foot falls off. Pole scowls, holding
the covered "man" as Kelly, with a grimace, picks up the
wheel and pushes it back into place. Pulling out a crumpled
handkerchief, he mops at his sweat-streaked face and neck,
looking around. He removes his hat and wipes off the band.
Now he puts the hat back on and points at something o.s.
The two men push the covered figure toward CAMERA and
it blots out the screen.

                                              CUT TO:

2.   INT. CAFE - CLOSE ON WALL CALENDAR

The page for August, 1974. CAMERA PANS to show Kelly
and Pole entering with the covered figure. Several customers
watch with idle curiosity as they roll the figure into f.g.,
CAMERA WITHDRAWING to reveal an empty table with
four chairs. Kelly pulls out one of tile chairs and, with Pole,
pushes the figure against it. Reaching through a slit in back
of the covering, Kelly reels around and, with a groaning
squeak, the figure sits. Kelly winces.

                         KELLY
            Listen to 'im squeak.

                                         (CONTINUED)

2.   CONTINUED

POLE
(sitting down; apathetically)
What d'ya expect?

Kelly removes his suit coat and drapes it across the back of the chair beside that on which the figure sits. He plucks at his sweat-dampened shirt as he sits.

KELLY
We'll get 'im some oil paste soon as
we're paid off.

POLE
If we can find any.

KELLY
(bristling)
Why shouldn't we?

POLE
(falsely patient)
Because they don't make it any more,
that's why.

KELLY
Well, that's cra -

He breaks off and smiles at the WAITRESS as she comes up to the table.

POLE (CONT'D)
Couple beers, honey?

She turns away boredly and Kelly's smile fades. He turns back to Pole.

(CONTINUED)

2.   CONTINUED

> KELLY (CONT'D)
> That's crazy. There's still plenty o'
> B-twos around.

> POLE
> Name five.

Kelly looks at him worriedly, then turns his head to gaze at
the figure.

3.   ANOTHER ANGLE

The figure in close f.g. Pole can see, beneath the tautly
drawn cloth of the covering sack, the profile of a young
man. Kelly eyes him in concern.

> KELLY
> You think he'll be all right?

> POLE
> (smiling without amusement)
> If he don't get hit.

Kelly turns back angrily.

> POLE (CONT'D)
> No use glarin' at me. You know he's shot.

> KELLY
> (tightly)
> That ain't true. A little overhaul's all he needs.

(CONTINUED)

3.   CONTINUED

> POLE
> (sardonically)
> Yeah, a little three-four thousand dollar overhaul.
> With parts they don't make anymore.

They sit in silence as the waitress puts their bottles of beer in front of them and turns away. They each take a swallow.

> KELLY
> Oh, man, that tastes good.
> (pause; trying to sound amused)
> Way you talk, you'd think he was ready
> for the scrap heap.

> POLE
> Ain't he?

> KELLY
> (angrily)
> No! He ain't!

Pole blows out tired breath, Kelly looks at the figure affectionately.

> KELLY (CONT'D)
> Plenty o' fight left in him.
> (pause; looking back at Pole)
> Well, is he okay?

> POLE
> (wearily)
> Steel, I don't know. He needs work;
> you know that. The trigger spring in his
> left arm's been re-wired so many times
> it's just about had it.

(CONTINUED)

3.   CONTINUED

                POLE (CONT'D)
He's got no protection on that side;
his eye lens is cracked. The leg cables
are worn - they got no tension.
            (exhales hard)
Even his gyro's off.
            (beat)
Not to mention the oil paste he ain't got in him.

                KELLY
            (tautly)
We'll get im some.

                POLE
            (flaring)
Yeah, after the fight, after the fight!
What about durin' the fight?!
He'll be creakin' around that ring
like a - steam shovel! It'll be a miracle
if he goes two rounds.

                KELLY
            (swallows)
It's not that bad, Pole.

                POLE
            (cutting in)
It's worse. Wait till that crowd gets a load of
"Battling Maxo" from Philadelphia.
He'll be lucky to get car fare home much
less five hundred bucks.

                KELLY
            (firmly)
The contract is signed. They can't back out now.

                            (CONTINUED)

3.   CONTINUED

                    POLE
        That contract is for Battling Maxo.
        (gesturing scornfully toward the figure)
        Not this - steam shovel here.

                    KELLY
                (stubbornly)
        Maxo's gonna do all right.

                    POLE
        Against a B-seven?
        It's just a starter B-seven. It ain't got
        the kinks out yet.

Pole turns away with a disgusted noise. He looks at the
figure contemptuously.

                    POLE
        Battling Maxo.
                (beat)
        One-round Maxo-the battling steam shovel.

                    KELLY
                (furiously)
        Aw, shut up! You're always knockin' 'im.
        Well, he's been doin' ok for five years
        now and he'll keep doin' okay! So he
        needs some oil paste - and a little work.
        So what? With five hundred bucks, we
        can get him all the paste he needs. And a new
        trigger spring for his left arm and- and new leg
        cables and everything!

He falls back against the chair and glares at his bottle.
After a few moments, he turns and clumsily pats Maxo's
covered leg.
                                    (CONTINUED)

3.   CONTINUED

> KELLY (CONT'D)
> (smiling)
> You're gonna do all right, boy.
> (pause)
> You're gonna do all right.

He turns back to the table.

> SERLING'S VOICE
> Sports item, circa, 1974. Battling Maxo -
> B-2, light heavyweight, accompanied by his
> manager and handler, arrives in Maynard,
> Kansas, for a scheduled ten-round bout.

4.   SERLING

> SERLING
> Battling Maxo is a robot - or to be exact,
> an android. Definition: an automation
> resembling a human being. Only these
> automatons have been permitted in the
> ring since prize fighting was legally
> abolished in 1968.
> (beat)
> This is the story of that scheduled ten-round
> bout. More specifically, the story of two men
> shortly to face the remorseless truth that no
> law can be passed which will abolish cruelty or
> desperate need - nor, for that matter, blind,
> animal courage.
> (beat)
> Location for the facing of said truth: a small,
> smoke-filled arena just this side of
> the Twilight Zone.

FADE OUT

FIRST COMMERCIAL

FADE IN:

5.   EXT. ARENA - CLOSE ON POSTER - DAY

Maynard Flash (B-7 L.H.) vs. Battling Maxo (B-2, L.H.)
CAMERA DRAWS BACK to show that this is the third of
seven fights listed on the poster. O.s., the sound of Maxo
being rolled in is heard; then Kelly and Pole push him INTO
FRAME. CAMERA PANS to watch them heading for a side
door.

6.   INT. CORRIDOR

Gloomy and narrow. At the far end of it, the door is opened
and Kelly and Pole appear. They start lifting Maxo through
the doorway.

7.   CLOSE ON MAXO'S RIGHT FOOT

As the same wheel falls off again.

                    POLE'S VOICE
                     (disgusted)
          Oh, for - !

CAMERA WITHDRAWS to show Kelly picking up the wheel.

                        KELLY
          Tip 'im.

                        POLE
                      (sourly)
          What's the use!

                                        (CONTINUED)

7.   CONTINUED

> KELLY
> (tightly)
>
> Tip 'im.

Hissing out breath, Pole does as he's told and Kelly reinserts the wheel.

> KELLY (CONT'D)
>
> Put 'im down.

Pole does and Kelly stands. They start pushing Maxo along the corridor.

> KELLY (CONT'D)
>
> What's wrong with you anyway?
> After seven months, we finally get
> a bout and all you can do is complain.

> POLE
>
> Some bout. Maynard, Kansas; the
> prize-fighting center o' the nation.

> KELLY
>
> It's a start, ain't it? With what we earn,
> we can put Maxo back in shape.
> (beat)
> And if we win -

He breaks off as Pole groans and looks away.

> KELLY (CONT'D)
> (exasperated)
> I don't get you. He's our fighter, ain't he?
> What are you writin' 'im off for?

(CONTINUED)

7.   CONTINUED

                         POLE
          I'm a Class-A mechanic, Steel - not a
          day-dreamin' kid. We got a piece o'
          dead iron here.

                         KELLY
                      (stiffening)
          Shhh! Somebody'll hear ya.

                         POLE
                  (grimaces; more softly)
          Look. <u>Steel</u>. It's simple mechanics.
          Maxo'll be lucky to come out o' that
          ring with his head on.

                         KELLY
                       (angrily)
          Bull!
                  (beat tensely controlled)
          It's a <u>starter</u> B-seven. Full o' kinks - <u>full</u> of 'em.

                         POLE
                       (wearily)
          Sure, sure.

They reach a door on which a metal plate is fastened which
reads: <u>Manager</u>. Kelly knocks on it.

                    MAXWELL'S VOICE
                       Come in.

Kelly opens the door.

8.   INT. OFFICE

MAXWELL, seated at one of the two desks, looks around
as Kelly and Pole ENTER, pushing Maxo between them.

                    KELLY
                    (smiling)
        Mr. Nolan?

                    MAXWELL
        No, Maxwell. Nolan'll be back in a couple minutes.

                    KELLY
        Oh. Okay.
                    (smiling again)
        I'm Kelly - Battling Maxo's owner.

                    MAXWELL
        Oh, yeah.

                    KELLY
                    (pointing at Pole)
        This is Pole-my mechanic.

Maxwell nods at Pole and gestures toward the chairs.

                    MAXWELL
        Sit down. Nolan'll be right back.

                    KELLY
        Thanks.

He pushes Maxo against the wall and he and Pole take
chairs. Kelly smiles strainedly at Maxwell who has gone
back to his work.

                            (CONTINUED)

8.   CONTINUED

                    KELLY (CONT'D)
            You, uh, heard o' my fighter, Maxwell?

                        MAXWELL
                      (looking up)
        Mmmm?

                        KELLY
                   (pointing at Maxo)
            You heard about my fighter?

                        MAXWELL
        Nope.

                        KELLY
        He was almost light-heavyweight chapeen once.
                   (as Maxwell grunts)
        I was a light-heavyweight myself; before
        the law was passed, o' course. I used to
        be called "Steel" Kelly.
                   (beat; grinning)
        Called me that because I never got
        knocked down. Not once.

He keeps nodding , then, finally stops, swallows and draws
in a deep breath. Maxwell starts to go back to his work.

                    KELLY (CONT'D)
                      (seriously)
        Gonna be a great fight tonight.

Maxwell glances at him as Kelly gestures proudly toward
Maxo.

                              (CONTINUED)

8.   CONTINUED

> KELLY (CONT'D)
> My boy here knocked down Dimsy The
> Rock in '71. Maybe you heard about it.

> MAXWELL
> Nope.

> KELLY
> Oh. Uh-huh.

He nods, makes an important face.

> KELLY (CONT'D)
> It was in all the east coast papers.
> New York, Boston, Philly - that's where
> we're from.
> (clucks)
> Yeah, it got... a big spread. Biggest upset
> o' the year.

10.   ANOTHER ANGLE - KELLY, POLE AND MAXWELL

Kelly nodding and smiling; then, as he sees that Maxwell
has gone back to his work, slowly stopping. He sighs,
abruptly the door opens and NOLAN comes in; a fat,
balding man with a cigar in one corner of his mouth. Kelly
stands quickly.

> KELLY
> Mr. Nolan?
> (as Nolan grunts)
> I'm Kelly.

He extends his hand but Nolan ignores it.

(CONTINUED)

10.   CONTINUED

> NOLAN
> (unfriendly)
> Was wonderin' if you'd make it.
> (squints at MAXO)
> Your fighter in shape?

> KELLY
> Yes, sir, the best. My mechanic here
> took Maxo apart and put 'im back together
> just before we left Philly.

> NOLAN
> (gesturing toward Maxo)
> You're lucky to get a bout. We ain't used
> nothin' less than B-fours in more than two
> years now. The fighter we had got ruined
> in a car wreck though.

> KELLY
> (nodding)
> You got nothing to worry about, Mr. Nolan.
> My fighter's in top shape. He's the one
> knocked down Dimsy The Rock a few
> years ago. Maybe you -

> NOLAN
> (cutting in)
> I just want a good fight.

> KELLY
> You'll get it, Nolan: you'll get it.
> (as Nolan grunts, unconvinced)
> You, uh, got a ready room we could use?
> (gesturing toward Maxo)
> Like to check 'im over - make sure he's
> perfect.

(CONTINUED)

10.   CONTINUED

                         NOLAN
                     (interrupting)
         Third door down the corridor on the right
         hand side. Your bout's at nine.

                         KELLY
                        (nods)
         Okay.
                     (hesitates, smiles)
         Uh, about -

                         NOLAN
                    (cutting him off)
         You get your money after you deliver a fight.

Kelly's smile falters; he nods.

                         KELLY
         Okay.
         (opens the door; gestures awkwardly)
         See ya then.

He and Pole push Maxo out into the corridor.

11.   INT. CORRIDOR - ANGLE ON OFFICE DOOR

       As Kelly and Pole push Maxo out and shut the door, Nolan
       makes a noise inside the office as if to say - Christ, what
       have I gotten myself into this time? Maxwell snickers,
       Kelly's face tightens as he moves past CAMERA, he and
       Pole pushing Maxo OUT OF FRAME.

12.   INT. READY ROOM - ANGLE ON DOOR

Out in the corridor, we hear Maxo being pushed to the door.

                                        (CONTINUED)

12.   CONTINUED

Then the door is opened by Kelly who switches on the
overhead light. He and Pole push Maxo into the room.
Kelly shuts the door and removes the wheels from under
Maxo's shoes, Pole tilting Maxo as he does.

>KELLY
>(glancing up)
>I want you to check him over good now.

>POLE
>(disgustedly)
>What for?

>KELLY
>(glancing up)
>Did you hear me?

>POLE
>Yeah.

He starts to remove the covering as Kelly straightens up.

>KELLY
>He's gonna take that lousy B-seven.

>POLE
>Sure he is. With his teeth.

13.   ANOTHER ANGLE

Maxo just o.s.

>KELLY
>(uneasily)
>Wish we'd been able to get that oil paste.

(CONTINUED)

13.   CONTINUED

                    POLE
          I told you they wouldn't sell any here.
          Why should they? Maxo's probably
          the only B-two in a thousand miles.

                    KELLY
          Hurry up.

Blowing out a tired breath. Pole tosses the sack covering
on a bench standing against the wall. He removes his
wrinkled suit coat and tosses it on top of the sack.
CAMERA DRAWS BACK SLOWLY to reveal Maxo
garbed in a hooded robe, the hood tied so that only his eyes
show. Pole unties it and removes the robe. Except for his
rigid immobility, Maxo looks like a real man wearing
fighter's trunks. Pole starts working on his back with a
small prying tool he has taken from his pocket.

14.   INSERT - MAXO'S BACK

Pole prying along a seam in the "flesh" until a small plate
comes off, revealing a control board of buttons and
switches.. Pole's hand starts to raise this like a window.

15.   KELLY, POLE AND MAXO

Maxo in f.g., facing CAMERA so that we do not see what
Pole is doing to his back.

                    POLE
              (gesturing with his head)
          Gimme that table.

Kelly grunts and moves to a small table which he lifts and
carries back to Pole - who has removed a small, oil-cloth
packet of tools from inside Maxo's back.

                                    (CONTINUED)

15.   CONTINUED

As Kelly sets down the table, Pole unwraps the packet and lays the open array of pocketed tools on top of it. He takes what resembles a small ice pick from the tool packet and starts probing inside Maxo's back.

16.   INSERT - POLE'S HAND

Using the tool to prod and pick at the conglomeration of wires, coils, tubes, transistors, etc., behind the raised control board.

17.   KELLY, POLE AND MAXO

                    POLE
                (as he works)
    I hear Mawling's puttin' out a B-nine this year.

                    KELLY
                (disinterestedly)
    Yeah?

                    POLE
    Hyper-triggers in both arms and legs.
    All steeled aluminum. Triple gyro.
    Triple-twisted wiring. They say it'll be
    able to stand up after knockdowns, too.

                    KELLY
                (overlapping)
    Is he all right?

                    POLE
    Sure; he's great.

He pulls out a tiny, steel-caged tube and holds it up.

                                        (CONTINUED)

17.   CONTINUED

> POLE
> If this doesn't blow.

> KELLY
> (tightening)
> Why should it?

> POLE
> It's <u>sub</u>-<u>par</u>. I told you that eight months ago.

> KELLY
> We'll get 'im a new one after the bout.

> POLE
> There goes another seventy-five bucks
> down the drain.

> KELLY
> (stiffly)
> He's earnin' us five <u>hundred</u>, ain't he?

Pole grunts, returns the tube to its socket and starts to pull
down the control board.

18.   INSERT - POLE'S HAND

Pulling down the control board to its orginal position;
throwing a switch.

19.   KELLY, POLE AND MAXO

Maxo stirs. He begins to "breathe."

> KELLY
> Take it easy on that left arm.

(CONTINUED)

19.   CONTINUED

                          POLE
          If it don't work now, it won't work tonight.

                          KELLY
          Save it, I said.

Pole grimaces and jabs in one of the unseen buttons.
Maxo's left arm raises and begins move in little, circle
motions.

                          KELLY
          Set it so he don't counter punch.

Pole does so as Kelly moves in front of Maxo.

20.   MAXO'S EYES

Following Kelly's movement, somehow frightening in their
vacuous surveillance.

21.   KELLY, POLE AND MAXO

Kelly throws a right at Maxo's jaw and the android's arm
jumps up with a hitching motion to block the punch. Kelly
throws a left and Maxo's right arm jerks up squeakingly.
Pole winces.

                          POLE
          They'll hear him in the back row.

                          KELLY
          Try the rest.

                                        (CONTINUED)

21.   CONTINUED

> POLE
> (surprised)
> Steel, he's gonna get more than two
> punches thrown at his head.

> KELLY
> <u>Try</u> the <u>rest</u>, I said.

Pole grunts and reaches inside Maxo, jabbing another
button which activates the leg cable centers. Maxo begins
shifting around, feeling at the floor like a newly cured
cripple testing for stance.

> KELLY
> Put him on <u>Automatic</u>.

Pole pushes another button and Kelly retreats from the
android as it moves forward, shoulders rocking slowly, arms
raised in a defensive pose. Kelly feints a right and Maxo's
arm lurches up raggedly. Kelly starts shifting around the
floor and Maxo follows lumberlingly, changing direction
with jerking motions.

> POLE
> (sarcastically)
> Oh, he's beautiful. Just beautiful.

He throws the switch and Maxo freezes in mid-stride.
Kelly looks at Pole in frowning surprise.

> POLE
> Steel, we've gotta put him on defense.
> He'll get chopped to pieces if we let him move in.

(CONTINUED)

21.   CONTINUED

                         KELLY
                        (tightly)
        No.

                         POLE
        Oh, for - ! Will ya use your head?!
        He's a B-two. Steel! A B-two!
        He's gonna get slaughtered anyway!
        Let's save the pieces at least!

                         KELLY
        They want him on offensive. It's in the contract.

                         POLE
                      (turning away)
                    Oh, what's the use?

                         KELLY
        Test him some more.

                         POLE
                      (turning on him)
        What for? He's as good as he'll ever be!

                         KELLY
                      (overlapping)
        Will ya do what I say?

        Angrily, Pole jabs in a button and Maxo's left arm shoots
        out. There is a sudden SLIPPING noise inside it and the
        arm falls against Maxo's side with a dead clank.

                         KELLY
                      (horrified)
        What did you do?

                                          (CONTINUED)

21.   CONTINUED

Pole doesn't answer but pushes the button twice more.
The arm does not respond.

> KELLY
> I <u>told</u> you not to fool with that arm.
> (voice breaking)
> What's the matter with you?

Still Pole doesn't answer. Gritting his teeth, he starts prying
at the left shoulder plate.

> KELLY
> (voice low and shaking)
> So help me. If you broke it.

> POLE
> (whirling on him)
> If <u>I</u> broke it! Listen, you big, dumb Mick!
> This heap has been runnin' on borrowed
> time for three years now! Don't talk to
> <u>me</u> about breakages!

> KELLY
> (softly, deadly)
> Open it up.

Pole returns to prying at the plate.

> POLE
> (muttering)
> <u>Son</u>-of-a-

22.   INSERT - MAXO'S LEFT SHOULDER

The plate being pried off.

(CONTINUED)

22.   CONTINUED

> POLE'S VOICE
> You find another mechanic who could've
> kept this steam shovel together any better
> these last few years; you just find one.

He jerks off the plate and, reaching in, touches the trigger
spring. It breaks in half, part of it shooting OUT OF
FRAME.

23.   KELLY, POLE AND MAXO

In the heavy silence, we hear the spring half bouncing off
the wall and floor. Kelly stares at Maxo's shoulder with
horrified eyes.

> KELLY
> (shakily)
> Oh, God. Oh, dear God.

Pole starts to say something then doesn't. He looks at Kelly
without moving. After a while, Kelly turns to him slowly,
looking a little deranged.

> KELLY
> (hoarsely)
> Fix it.

> POLE
> (swallows)
> Steel, I -

> KELLY
> Fix it.

(CONTINUED)

23.   CONTINUED

                    POLE
        I can't. That spring's been ready to
        break for -

He stops, grimacing in pain as Kelly clamps rigid fingers on
his arm.

                    KELLY
        You broke it. Now fix it!

                    POLE
                 (teeth clenched)
        Let go o' me.

Kelly stares at him, then lets go, looking as if he is about to cry.

                    KELLY
        He's got t'be fixed. He's gotta be.

                    POLE
                 (distraught)
        Steel, he needs a new spring.

                    KELLY
        We'll get it then.

                    POLE
        They don't have 'em here! Don't you understand?
        They don't make 'em anymore!

                    KELLY
                 (breaking)
        Oh… Oh, God…

He stumbles to the bench and sinks down on it, covering his
face with both hands.

24.   CLOSE SHOT - POLE

Watching Kelly

25.   CLOSE SHOT - KELLY

Sitting motionless, hands across his face. After a while, he speaks, as if to himself.

                    KELLY
          If they don't watch 'em.

26.   KELLY AND POLE

                    POLE
      What?

Kelly lowers his hands and looks up.

                    KELLY
      If Maxwell and Nolan don't watch the bouts...

                    POLE
      What are you talkin' a-

He breaks off and stares at Kelly, aghast.

                    POLE
      Are you crazy?
              (pause; more loudly)
      Steel, you're out o' your mind!
      You can't do that!

                    KELLY
              (standing)
      We deliver a fight or we don't get paid.

                              (CONTINUED)

26.   CONTINUED

                    POLE
          Steel, come on.
                (beat; nervously)
          They'll never let ya. You can't make 'em
          think that you're-
                (grabs Kelly's arm)
          Steel, for God's sake!

                    KELLY
                    (softly)
          You'll help me.
                    (beat)
          Nobody knows what Maxo looks like.
          And only those two in the office saw.
          If they don't watch the bouts and, probably,
          they don't -

                    POLE
                (breaking in anguished)
          Steel!

                    KELLY
                (pulling his arm free)
          The crowd won't know. B-twos bleed and
          bruise just like the new ones.

                    POLE
                (grabs Kelly's arm again)
          Look; I can wire my sister; she'll send us
          the dough t' get back east.

     Steel shows no reaction.

                                        (CONTINUED)

26.   CONTINUED

POLE
Steel, I know a guy in Philly wants t'sell
a B-five cheap. We could scurry up the
cash and -
(beat; breaking)
Steel, for God's sake, use your head!
It's a B-seven! You'll be mangled!

Kelly pulls loose but Pole grabs him again.

POLE
I'm not gonna let you do it, Steel. I'll go to -

He breaks off with a shocked gasp as Kelly grabs him by
the shirt front and slams him against the wall.

27.   TIGHT TWO SHOT - KELLY AND POLE

KELLY
(murderously)
You'll help me.
(beat)
You'll help me - or I'll beat your brains
out on this wall.

POLE
(almost whispering)
You'll get killed, Steel.
(beat; almost haunted)
Then I will.

They stare at each other in deathly silence as we

FADE OUT:
END ACT ONE

FADE IN:

28.   INT. MAIN ARENA CORRIDOR - NIGHT

In b.g., the steps leading up to the arena from which we
hear SHOUTS, BOOS, CHEERS and the general din of a
prize fight audience. CAMERA DRAWS BACK down the
corridor, then PANS RIGHT to reveal the side corridor.

The door of the distant ready room opens and Pole leads out
Kelly who is wearing the robe, the hood tied so that only
his eyes show. They start toward the main corridor.

29.   MOVING SHOT - KELLY AND POLE

As they walk, the door to Nolan's o.s. office is opened.
Pole tenses but keeps guiding Kelly on. They move past
Nolan who checks his watch.

                    NOLAN
        Come on, come on, you're late.
                    (beat)
        Where's the owner?

                    POLE
        In the audience.

Nolan GRUNTS and walks off in the opposite direction.

                    POLE
        I should've told him.

                    KELLY
        I'd've killed ya if ya had.

They turn the corner and head toward the arena. A trickle
of sweat runs down Kelly's brow and, reaching up, he
fingers it off.

                                    (CONTINUED)

29.   CONTINUED

                    KELLY
          You're gonna have to towel me off
          between rounds.

                    POLE
                    (tenses)
          Between <u>what</u> rounds? You won't even last one.

                    KELLY
          Will you - ?

                    POLE
                    (breaking in; agitated)
          What do you think you're going up against -
          another fighter? You're going against a
          <u>machine</u>! - ya big dumb -

                    KELLY
                    (cutting in)
          Just do what I say.

                    POLE
                    (groaning)
          Oh...
                    (beat)
          If I towel ya off, they'll know, won't they?

                    KELLY
          They ain't seen a B-two in years; Nolan said so.
          If anybody asks, tell 'em it's an oil leak.

                    POLE
                    (hopelessly)
          Sure.

                              (CONTINUED)

29.   CONTINUED

They start up the steps and the noise of the arena
AUDIENCE gets louder. In a few moments, they are in the
arena, moving along the dark aisle.

MAN'S VOICE
Well, if it ain't Battling Maxo!

CROWD VOICES
Scrap Iron! Scrap Iron!

30.   ANGLE - FROM RING

Kelly and Pole come down the aisle and ascend the steps.
Kelly climbs through the ropes and sits down on the stool.
Pole removes the robe- on the back of which is printed
Battling Maxo - and the o.s. audience BOOS and HISSES.
Kelly's face tightens as he looks at -

31.   THE MAYNARD FLASH AND MECHANIC

The Maynard Flash sitting motionless on its stool, gloved
hands resting on its legs. It is blonde, its face that of an
impassive Adonis. Its body looks incredibly powerful.

32.   KELLY AND POLE

Kelly staring at the android in mute apprehension.
Pole leans over, pretending to examine an arm plate.
He speaks without moving his lips.

POLE
Don't do it Steel.
(pause)
Will ya -?

He breaks off and they both tighten as the o.s. bell is
CLANGED repeatedly.

33.   ANOTHER ANGLE - INCLUDING ANNOUNCER

Ducking between the rope strands, a microphone lowered to him as he moves to the center of the ring.

> ANNOUNCER
> Ladies and gentlemen! The third contest
> of the evening! A ten-round, light heavyweight
> bout! - featuring!
> (pointing at Kelly)
> -from Philadelphia, the B-two; Battling Maxo!

> CROWD VOICES
> 1. Rattling Maxo, you mean!
> 2. Get that junk pile out o' there!
> 3. Scrap Iron!

Plus assorted BOOS and HISSES.

> ANNOUNCER
> And his opponent - our own B-seven!
> (gesturing toward other corner)
> The Maynard Flash!

34.   THE MAYNARD FLASH AND MECHANIC

The mechanic pushes something in the android's left armpit and the B-seven jumps up and holds its arms over its head in the traditional gesture of victory. The crowd LAUGHS and CHEERS happily.

35.   KELLY AND POLE

Pole bending over again.

> POLE
> (sotto voice; pleading)
> This is your last chance, Steel.

(CONTINUED)

35.   CONTINUED

                          KELLY
                    (lips unmoving)
          Get out.

Pole looks at Kelly's immobile face a few moments more.

                          POLE
          For God's sake, stay away from him then.

He leaves the ring and removes the stool as Kelly stands,
looking at the B-seven.

36.   THE MAYNARD FLASH

      Standing in its corner, hitting its gloves together as if it
      were a real young boxer anxious to get the fight started.

37.   CLOSE UP- THE MAYNARD FLASH

      Eyes zeroed in on Kelly; cold, merciless eyes.

38.   CLOSE UP - KELLY

      Trying not to show the dread he feels. He winces as the
      bell RINGS and, raising his arms to a defensive pose,
      moves into the ring.

39.   THE MAYNARD FLASH

      Moving from its corner, arms raised, gloved hands making
      tiny, circling movements in front of it.

40.   KELLY AND THE MAYNARD FLASH-KELLY
      FEATURED

Kelly and the android approach each other. The B-seven's
left flicks out and Kelly blocks it, wincing as the rockhard
fist hits his glove. The fist shoots out again. Kelly jerks
back his head and eludes it, his own left shooting out to
bang against the android's nose. Kelly's jaw muscles
harden as the pain of impact flares in his wrist and lower
arm. The B-seven feints with a left and Kelly knocks it
aside. He cannot stop the right that blurs in after it and
grazes his left temple. He jerks away his head and the B-
seven throws a left that hits him over the ear. Kelly lurches
back, throwing a left that the android brushes off. Kelly
braces himself and hits the Flash's jaw with a right
uppercut. He reacts as a jolt of pain rips down his arm, the
android's head hardly budges. It shoots out a left that hits
Kelly on the right shoulder. Kelly backs off instinctively.
The audience BOOS.

                    MAN'S VOICE
              Get him a bicycle!

Remembering, Kelly braces himself and moves in again.

41.   POLE

                        POLE
                 (shakily; to himself)
              Stay away from him.

42.   KELLY AND THE MAYNARD FLASH - KELLY
      FEATURED

A left jars Kelly under the heart, the impact of it shuddering
through his frame, blanking his face.

                              (CONTINUED)

42.   CONTINUED

He throws a spasmodic left which bounces off the
B-seven's nose, drawing artificial blood, then staggers as a
hard right catches him high on the chest. He moves back.
The B-seven hits him on the chest again. Kelly loses
balance and steps back quickly to regain his equilibrium.
The crowd BOOS. The B-seven moves in and Kelly throws
a right that misses, the momentum of the blow throwing
him off-center. The android's left drives hard against his
upper right arm. As Kelly sucks in a teeth-clenched gasp of
pain, the B-seven shoots in a right that slams into Kelly's
stomach. The breath goes out of him. He side steps and,
for a moment or two, the android's radial eye lenses lose
track of him. Kelly moves out of range, sucking in air
through gritted teeth. The crowd ROARS and BOOS.

CROWD VOICES
1. Get that heap out o' there!
2. Scrap iron! Scrap iron!

Kelly swallows, braces himself and moves in again.

43.   POLE

Watching with fear-sickened eyes.

POLE
No.

44.   KELLY AND THE MAYNARD FLASH - KELLY
FEATURED

Kelly steps in close and throws a hard right at the B-seven's
body. The blow is deflected by the android's wrist. Kelly's
left is thrown off too and the Flash's left shoots in, driving
the breath out of Kelly again.

(CONTINUED)

44.   CONTINUED

He staggers back, the B-seven following. He keeps jabbing
but the android keeps deflecting the blows and counter-
jabbing with the same, precise motion. Kelly's head keeps
snapping back. Suddenly the B-seven hits him with a
violent right.

45.   KELLY

Staggering back against the ropes, nose and mouth trickling
blood.

46.   POLE

Watching in dazed silence.

47.   KELLY AND THE MAYNARD FLASH

Kelly raises his left arm as the B-seven moves in. The
android drives a violent right into Kelly's chest, a left to his
stomach. Kelly starts to double over. A savage right slams
off his skull, driving him back agains the ropes again. The
crowd SCREAMS.

48.   KELLY

Another blow smashes into his chest like a club. Sobbing,
he throws a wild left, missing. Another blow crashes
against his shoulder. He manages to partially deflect a left
to his jaw but another right concaves his stomach. He
doubles over. A hammering right drives him back against
the ropes. He stares up dumbly at the android.

49.   POV SHOT - THE MAYNARD FLASH

A blurred outline throwing in endless, piston-like blows.

50.   KELLY AND THE MAYNARD FLASH - KELLY
       FEATURED

       Blood running from his nose and mouth. With a desperate
       surge of energy, he throws a right as hard as he can.
       Something cracks in his wrist as he connects and a wave of
       pain sears his arm. His throat-locked cry is barely audible
       above the murderous ROAR of the crowd. His right arm
       falls, his left is bludgeoned aside. Now only inches
       separate him from the android.

51.   POLE

       Watching in horror.

52.   KELLY AND THE MAYNARD FLASH - KELLY
       FEATURED

       The B-seven raining blows on Kelly who lurches and
       staggers under their impact, his head snapping from side to
       side. Blood ribbons across his face. His arms hang at his
       sides like dead branches. He keeps getting slammed back
       against the ropes and bouncing forward only to be slammed
       back again. He draws in his head and hunches his
       shoulders to protect himself.

       CAMERA MOVES IN CLOSE on his pain-twisted face.
       After several seconds, a clubbing right sends him to the
       canvas, CAMERA DOWNPANNING with him, HOLDING
       on him. The crowd BOOS AND HISSES in furious
       dissatisfaction.

53.   FULL SHOT

       The announcer entering the ring to hold up the Maynard
       Flash's arm as Pole climbs through the ropes and moves
       hurriedly to Kelly.

54.   KELLY AND POLE

Pole kneels beside Kelly who stares at him groggily.

> POLE
> (lips unmoving)
> Can you get up?
> (beat)
> Steel, <u>can</u> <u>you</u> <u>get</u> <u>up</u>?

> ANNOUNCER'S VOICE
> (simultaneously)
> The winner-in two minutes, twenty seconds
> of the first round-The Maynard Flash!

The crowd CHEERS.

> KELLY
> (thickly)
> Get the robe.

> POLE
> What?

> KELLY
> (in agony)
> The robe, the robe.

Pole stands and hurries OUT OF FRAME as Kelly lies on
the canvas, trying not to black out. In a few moments, Pole
returns with the robe. He helps Kelly to his feet and covers
him, tying the hood on his head.

He guides Kelly through the ropes and down the ring steps.
CAMERA HOLDS. As Kelly and Pole move up the aisle
and disappear in the darkness, the crowd erupts with BOOS,
HISSES and CATCALLS. Cushions, programs, cups and
torn paper are flung into the air.

55.   MAIN CORRIDOR - SHOOTING TOWARD ARENA

Kelly comes down the steps with Pole. As they reach the corridor level, Kelly slips to one knee and Pole hauls him up, supporting him with both hands as he stumbles down the corridor.

56.   SIDE CORRIDOR - OUTSIDE READY ROOM

CAMERA SHOOTING toward the main corridor. Kelly and Pole turn the corner and approach, Kelly barely able to stay on his feet. They reach f.g., Pole opens the door and Kelly staggers into the ready room.

57.   READY ROOM - KELLY AND POLE

Kelly collapses on the floor as Pole turns on the light and shuts the door. Pole tries to get Kelly on the bench but cannot. Finally, he bunches up the sack covering and makes a pillow under Kelly's head.

> POLE
> (brokenly)
> You big dumb Mick, you.

He takes out his handkerchief and, opening the hood front, starts patting at the blood on Kelly's face. Kelly lifts his left hand and brushes Pole's hand away weakly. He says something unintelligible.

> POLE
> What?

> KELLY
> (tightly)
> Go - get - th' money.

(CONTINUED)

57.   CONTINUED

POLE
But you -

KELLY
Now!

Pole looks at him a few moments more, then nods and
leaves, moving OUT OF FRAME. The o.s. door OPENS
and CLOSES. Kelly lays motionless, breath wheezing in
his lungs. After a while, he turns his head, grimacing at the
pain and looks up at -

58.   MAXO - KELLY'S POV

Standing quietly in a corner.

59.   KELLY

Manages a twisted smile.

QUICK DISSLOVE TO:

60.   INT. READY ROOM - KELLY - MINUTES LATER

He opens his eyes as the o.s. door OPENS, CLOSES.
He looks up at -

61.   POLE

Walking over to Kelly and kneeling. He starts to pat at the
blood on Kelly's face, his expression somber.

KELLY
(a crusty whisper)
Ya get it?

(CONTINUED)

61.   CONTINUED

                    KELLY (CONT'D)
                      (pause)
        Well?

                        POLE
        Half of it.

Kelly stares at him blankly.

                        POLE
        He said he wouldn't pay 5 C's for a one-rounder.

                        KELLY
        What d'ya mean?

He tries to push up with his right hand and falls back with a
strangled cry. His head twists on the sack pillow, his eyes
shut tightly as he whines in agony. Pole looks at the hand
and grimaces.

                        POLE
        God…

                        KELLY
                    (opening his eyes)
        He can't do that. The contract doesn't say -

                        POLE
                    (cutting in)
        Steel, there's nothin' we can do. He's got
        a bunch o' toughs in there. He says we're
        lucky he don't have us run out o' town on
        a rail.

Kelly stares at him, chest laboring with breath. Finally, he
speaks.
                                    (CONTINUED)

61.   CONTINUED

                        KELLY
        Help me up.

Pole helps him to his feet and Kelly slumps down on the
bench. Pole sits beside him.

                        POLE
        We got t'get that wrist set.

                        KELLY
                    (obliviously)
        We'll go back by bus.

                        POLE
        What?

                        KELLY
                    (thickly, dazedly)
        We'll go all the way back by bus.
        That'll only cost us sixty-seven bucks-
        and leave us almost two hundred.
        We can get 'im a new - trigger spring
        and a - eyes lens and... oil paste, lots
        o' oil paste. He'll be good as new again.
                    (looks at Pole)
        Then we'll be all set. Maxo'll be in great
        shape again - and we can get us some
        decent bouts.
                    (pause)
        That's all he needs is a little work, hanh?
        New trigger spring. New eye lens.
        Oil paste. That'll shape 'im up. He'll
        show 'em what a - top B-two can do.
        Old Maxo'll show 'em. Right?

                                    (CONTINUED)

61.   CONTINUED

                    POLE
                (pause; softly)
        Sure, Steel.

62.   DOWN ANGLE SHOT - KELLY AND POLE

Pole puts his arm around Kelly's shoulders and listens,
nodding and smiling gently, as Kelly rambles on dazedly.

                SERLING'S VOICE
        Portrait of the losing side. Proof positive
        that you can't out-punch machinery.
        Proof, also, of something else. That, no
        matter what the future brings, men's
        capacity to rise to the occasion will
        remain unaltered; his potential for
        tenacity and optimism continues, as
        always, to out-fight, out-point and out-
        live any and all changes made by his
        society. For which three cheers and a
        unanimous decision-rendered from the
        Twilight Zone.

                                FADE OUT:

63.   TITLE BACK FOR END CREDITS

Nightmare at 20,000 Feet

One of the most chilling—and elaborate to produce— episodes was again based on a previously published story. (It originally was published in an anthology in 1961, and was later included in *Collected Stories*.) Once again, the most mundane exercises— looking out the window while on an airliner—can become something quite extraordinary—and terrifying—if you just put your imagination to work.

"I used to look out at the clouds while on airline flights, and I'd think, 'Gee, what if I saw a guy skiing through the clouds.' You know: it looks like you're going along these snowy fields. Then I altered it in my mind to someone being out on the wing. First I thought: 'Could it be a real person who was accidentally stuck out on the wing?' Then I thought, 'No, no—it *has* to be a gremlin.'

"William Shatner was just wonderful. In "Nightmare" he was so, so restrained. You could see him struggling to maintain his sanity, after just getting out of a sanitorium. He was wonderful, and I've said that many times. That and "Nick of Time" may well be my favorite *Twilight Zones*. I didn't care for the creature, or the actress who played his wife—but Shatner was marvelous. And the director was wonderful—at the time, who knew Richard Donner from anybody?

"I remember talking to director Jacques Tourneur later about how he would have done it. He would have let the gremlin been almost unseen except for covering him with a sort of sparkling dust that would have just shown its outline. Just bits and pieces of its features would be seen. It would have been interesting."

In a strange turn of Hollywood history, Matheson was approached decades later by Steven Spielberg to work on a new film he was producing. The assignment? To adapt this classic episode for his upcoming feature production *Twilight Zone: The Movie*, which was released in the summer of 1983. Coincidentally, the episode would star John Lithgow, the same actor who would appear in the *Amazing Stories* series episode adapted from Matheson's then unproduced original *The Twilight Zone* script, "The Doll." (See the Epilogue for further discussion of this "lost" script.) Did he find it strange to be reviving a classic television script into part of a multi-part, multi-writer feature screenplay?

"It <u>was</u> strange. Originally I was told it was going to be a ten or twelve minute filler, and I tried to work on it from that aspect. Then they said, 'No, it's going to be more full-length—we need a half hour. And Gregory Peck is going to play the main role.' You know—like the role he played in *Twelve O'Clock High*— so it could have been very effective. Then they gave the segment to George Miller, who is a very talented director, but he 'revised' it. He took out the idea of the guy recovering from a mental breakdown; it became just a nervous guy who nobody would believe.

"John Lithgow is a wonderful actor, but I thought he was a little over the top in his performance. He was already up to the level of "10" from the outset—so where could he go? But I loved the thing on the wing—I wish we had that in the original episode. Though the guy who was in that furry suit in my original *Twilight Zone* was just the way I described the gremlin in my script."

Already frustrated at often being thought of as someone forever going for an ironic or unhappy ending, Matheson still found himself "losing for winning" in another segment he adapted. It was a fresh interpretation of a classic short story—and equally famous *The Twilight Zone* episode—"It's a *Good* Life." A truly horrific story of a little boy with omnipotent psychic powers, the plot opens with a hopeless situation, and concludes just as hopelessly for the adult characters trapped in the hellish world created by this smirking monster. But Matheson just didn't want to go down that bleak road into utter darkness again.

"I was called to task in *Twilight Zone: The Movie* for putting a happy ending on Jerome Bixby's 'It's A *Good* Life.' But my reasoning was, it's too *easy* to have a downbeat ending. It's the easiest thing in the world! And I think writers in these genres who keep doing it are taking the easy way out. I thought, 'Well, can I maintain the integrity of the story, yet still give it a better ending?' And I tried. But the outcome was predictable: a lot of people said, 'Oh, you ruined a great ending!' Which was so downbeat, bleak, hopeless. Now, this worked great in the original short story, and it worked fine in the first *Twilight Zone* adaptation. But I just didn't want to do it again."

NIGHTMARE AT 20,000 FEET

PERFORMANCE DATE: 10/11/63

PRODUCER: BERT GRANET

DIRECTOR: RICHARD DONNER

CAST:

BOB WILSON: WILLIAM SHATNER

RUTH WILSON: CHRISTINE WHITE

GREMLIN: NICK CRAVAT

FLIGHT ENGINEER: EDWARD KEMMER

STEWARDESS: ASA MAYNOR

FADE IN:

1.   EXT. AIRPORT - NIGHT

2.   FULL SHOT - AIRLINER

A four-engine DC-7. Passengers boarding.

3.   INT. AIRLINER CABIN - ANGLE TOWARD DOOR

CAMERA SHOOTING OVER the backs of two seats
on the right side of the cabin, about halfway to the
front. Passengers are entering and being greeted by the
stewardess. Their names checked off on a clip-boarded
list by the copilot, after which they make their way to
various seats. (One of them is a uniformed State Police
officer.) Bob Wilson and his wife Ruth enter,
Bob carrying an overnight bag. Ruth waits for him to
give their names, then, seeing that he is too distracted,
does so herself. As they approach the foreground seats,
we see that he is very nervous, restraining it beneath a
tense veneer. Ruth, on the other hand, looks exhausted.
She stops beside the foreground seats and looks at
Bob, smiling.

                    RUTH
          These all right?

He nods jerkily, his smile a mere twitching of the lips.
He puts their overnight bag on the shelf and they shed their
topcoats.

Bob removing a newspaper and paperback book from one
of the pockets before putting the coat on the shelf beside
Ruth's. As he looks uneasily at the seats, one of the
entering passengers has to squeeze by him and Bob glances
at the man, then exchanges a look with Ruth.

                              (CONTINUED)

3.   CONTINUED

> RUTH
> You want me to sit by the - ?

> BOB
> (overlapping)
>
> No.

Hastily, he sits on the seat by the window and Ruth sinks down, tiredly, beside him. CAMERA MOVES IN on them. Bob smiles at her with effort, putting his hand over hers.

> BOB
> Don't worry, I'll be all right.
> (pause, looking round)
> I can face -

He breaks off, looking at the offscreen bulkhead.

> RUTH
> What is it?

He doesn't speak. Swallowing, he gestures slightly toward the bulkhead with his head. CAMERA DRAWS AROUND to reveal that he is sitting next to the emergency door.

> RUTH
> (not really understanding)
> The emergency door?

He continues looking at the door and Ruth closes her eyes a few moments as if bracing herself for what is coming, then opens them and manages a smile.

(CONTINUED)

3.   CONTINUED

                    RUTH
            (restrainedly cheerful)
        You want to move?

                    BOB
                (mutedly)
    No.

He takes his eyes from the door and looks at her with a
wavering smile.

                    BOB
        No, it - doesn't matter.
            (inhales shakingly)
        What's the difference where I sit anyway?
        It's not the seat, it's the airplane.

Ruth doesn't know what to say. She watches Bob take a
pack of cigarettes from his suitcoat pocket and drop one in
his nervousness. She bends over to pick it up.

                    BOB
                (quickly)
        That's all right.
            (as she hands it to him, tightly)
        Thank you.

He lights it and puffs out a cloud of smoke, makes a sound
of vague amusement.

                            (CONTINUED)

3.   CONTINUED

>   BOB
>   I don't act much like a cured man, do I?

>   RUTH
>   (pained)
>   Honey.
>   (taking his hand)
>   You are cured.
>   (beat)
>   Would Dr. Martin let you fly if you weren't?

>   BOB
>   (uncertainly)
>   I suppose not.

>   RUTH
>   Of course he wouldn't. If you weren't
>   well, he'd never let you fly home, it's
>   as simple as that.

>   BOB
>   (forcing a smile)
>   You make it sound that simple, anyway.

>   RUTH
>   It is, Bob. Just that simple.

He nods, trying to look convinced.

>   BOB
>   Yeah.
>   (pause, apologetically)
>   Here I am hogging the stage when
>   you're so tired.

                                    (CONTINUED)

3.   CONTINUED

> RUTH
> (smiling)

I'm all right.

> BOB

No, you look exhausted.

He gazes at her several moments more, then leans over and puts an arm around her, pressing his cheeks to hers.
CAMERA MOVES IN for a TIGHT TWO SHOT.

> BOB
> (brokenly)

I've missed you, baby. These last six months.

> RUTH

Shhh.
> (kisses his cheek)

It's all over now.
> (draws back to smile at him)

Mama's taking you home.

> BOB

It must have been awful for you.
Taking care of the kids; bearing the full responsibility.

> RUTH
> (cheerfully)

Everything's still intact.

> BOB
> (grimly, pause)

Except me.

(CONTINUED)

3.   CONTINUED

> RUTH
> (firmly)
> Now, I'm not going to let you -

She breaks off as the offscreen door CLANGS SHUT and, with a terrible gasp, Bob twists around to look in that direction, his face a mask of panic.

4.   CLOSE ON BOB AND RUTH

As Bob completes his turn and looks frightenedly toward -

5.   THE DOOR AREA

The copilot locking it shut, the stewardess starting to tell the nearest passengers to fasten their seat belts.

6.   BOB AND RUTH

Bob still looking toward the offscreen door.

> RUTH
> Honey?

He turns back quickly, manages a tremulous smile.

> BOB
> (trying to make a joke of it)
> Just a little - abject cowardice is all.

> RUTH
> (taking his hand)
> Shhh.

> STEWARDESS
> (as she passes)
> Seat belts, please.

(CONTINUED)

6.   CONTINUED

Bob presses his lips together and, averting his eyes, starts to fasten his seat belt. Ruth keeps glancing at him worriedly as she fastens hers. CAMERA MOVES IN on Wilson until he is in extreme closeup. He reacts as the offscreen engines are started, one by one, takes a last deep lungful of smoke and stamps out the cigarette in the ashtray.

> SERLING'S VOICE
> Portrait of a frightened man. Mr. Robert
> Wilson, thirty-seven, husband, father, and
> salesman on sick leave. Mr. Wilson has
> just been discharged from a sanitarium
> where he has spent the last six months
> recovering from a nervous breakdown,
> the onset of which took place on an
> evening not dissimilar to this one - on an
> airliner very much like the one in which
> Mr. Wilson is about to be flown home.

7.   SERLING

> SERLING
> The difference being that, on that evening
> half a year ago, Mr. Wilson's flight was
> terminated by the onslaught of his mental
> breakdown. Tonight he is traveling all the
> way to his appointed destination - which,
> contrary to Mr. Wilson's plan, happens to be
> the darkest corner of the Twilight Zone.

FADE OUT:

FIRST COMMERCIAL
FADE IN:

8.   EXT. SKY - AIRLINER - NIGHT

9.   INT. CABIN - FULL SHOT

Darkened except for the overhead aisle lights and the reading
light over Wilson's seat.

10.   BOB AND RUTH

The window curtains drawn. Ruth is asleep, Bob reading the
newspaper without interest, trying not to rustle the pages.
Finally, he lets his arms drop and the paper falls cracklingly
to his lap. Ruth starts a little and partly opens her eyes.

                    RUTH
                   (groggily)
        Honey?

Twitching slightly, Bob looks at her apologetically.

                    BOB
        I'm sorry.
                   (beat)
        Go to sleep.

                    RUTH
        I should stay awake with you.

                    BOB
        No, no. I don't want you to, sweetheart.
        Go to sleep now. I'm all right.

She sighs tiredly and closes her eyes again.

                    RUTH
                   (faintly)
        Can't you sleep?

                                        (CONTINUED)

10.   CONTINUED

                              BOB
                      (patting her hand)
              I will. Don't worry about me.

She becomes quiet and, after looking at her awhile, a tender
smile on his lips, he turns to the window and pushes aside
the curtains.

11.   ANOTHER ANGLE

CAMERA SHOOTING PAST Wilson, out through the
window. We can see the wing lights blinking, the flashes of
exhaust from the engine cowlings. After several moments,
lightning bleaches the sky.

12.   CLOSE-UP - BOB

Wincing at the lightning and averting his face. As darkness
falls again, he looks upward, scanning the sky uneasily.
Now he looks at the wing again, starts to turn to the front
after a while and does a mild double-take.

13.   EXT. WINDOW - CLOSE SHOT - BOB

The ROAR of the engines offscreen. He leans close to the
window, looking out, squints to see better.

14.   REVERSE SHOT - BOTH

CAMERA SHOOTING PAST him, revealing the dark wing
outside. Wilson presses his face against the glass, staring
intently. There is something large moving on the wing but
we cannot make out what it is.

15.   CLOSE-UP - BOB

Staring through the window, his expression verging on
incredulous dread.

16.   MED. SHOT - WING

Wilson's reflection seen in the window glass. Suddenly,
there is another flash of lightning and , in its momentary
glare, we see what appears to be an apelike man, crawling
on the wing.

17.   CLOSE SHOT - BOB

Recoiling against his seat, gaping at the wing in
stupefaction.

18.   POV SHOT - WING

Dark again. We can barely make out the crawling form
outside.

19.   BOB AND RUTH

Bob unable to function at first. Then, the expression of
stupefied horror printed on his face, he turns to Ruth and
reaches out to wake her, his lips stirring without sound.
Abruptly, he decides that she might become alarmed and
draws his hand back, looking around with rising
desperation. Now he catches sight of the button used to
summon the stewardess and starts to jab at it repeatedly,
looking through the window again.

He rises slightly, alternating between pained glances
through the window and across-the shoulder looks for the
stewardess who, after several moments, appears at the rear
of the cabin and moves quickly down the aisle.

(CONTINUED)

19.   CONTINUED

Wilson pushes up further and gestures for her to speed up.
The stewardess reaches him, her expression one of alarm.

> STEWARDESS
> (softly)
> What is it, Mr. -

Wilson points agitatedly at the wing.

> BOB
> (interrupting softly)
> There's a man out there!

> STEWARDESS
> (appalled)
> What?

Wilson drops back on the seat and presses back, still
pointing at the wing.

> BOB
> Look, look!
> (looking out)
> He's crawling on the - !

He breaks off in shock, leaning toward the window quickly.

20.   POV SHOT - WING

In a moment, a flash of lightning reveals that the man is no
longer there.

21.   CLOSE ON BOB

His dazed expression reflected on the window, also that of
the stewardess as she looks down at him blankly.
CAMERA DRAWS BACK as Wilson turns to look at her.

22.   REVERSE SHOT - BOB, RUTH, AND STEWARDESS

The stewardess pats her lips as if she means to speak, but
says nothing. An attempted smile momentarily distends her
features.

                          BOB
                 (barely able to speak)
        I-I-I'm - sorry. It - must have - been.. .

                         RUTH
                   (opening her eyes)
        Bob?

He glances at her in distracted alarm, then looks back at the
stewardess. Noting the shift of his gaze. Ruth twists
around and looks up at the stewardess who smiles at her
automatically.

                         RUTH
                    (still sleepy)
        What is it?

                      STEWARDESS
        Nothing, Mrs. Wilson.
                       (to Bob)
        May I get you anything?

                          BOB
                (anxious to get rid of her)
        A glass of water.

                      STEWARDESS
        Surely.

She turns away and Ruth looks back at Bob, blinking and
trying to wake up.

                                    (CONTINUED)

22.   CONTINUED

                    RUTH
        Is something wrong?

                    BOB
            No.
                (pause; trying to smile)
            No. I, uh. . .thought I saw something
            outside, that's all.

                    RUTH
            What?

                    BOB
            Nothing. I. . .
                (turning to close the curtains)
            - need a little sleep, I guess.

                    RUTH
                (pause)
            Are you all right?

                    BOB
            Yeah. I'm - fine.

Ruth looks groggily at her wristwatch and frowns in
concern, looks back at Bob.

                    RUTH
        Don't you think you'd better take a sleeping capsule now?

                    BOB
                (draws in a shaking breath, nods)
            Yeah. Yeah, I'll, uh -

                                    (CONTINUED)

22.   CONTINUED

He doesn't finish but watches as she retrieves her purse
from under the seat, opens it and takes out a tiny, plastic
container. Removing its cap, she shakes one of the capsules
into his palm as the stewardess returns with a paper cup full
of water. Bob avoids her eyes as he takes the cup from her.

                         BOB
                      (mutedly)
          Thank you.

                      STEWARDESS
          You're welcome.
                       (beat)
          Would you like a blanket?

                         BOB
          No, thank you.
                (remembering Ruth)
          Uh. . .honey?

                         RUTH
                 (to the stewardess)
          No, thank you.

The stewardess nods and moves away, glancing back
uneasily at Wilson, not certain whether she should ignore
him or not. Wilson washes down the capsule with some
water, holds out the cup to Ruth.

                         BOB
          Sip?

                         RUTH
          No, thank you, honey.
             (as the cabin lurches slightly)
          We must be moving into a storm.

(CONTINUED)

22.   CONTINUED

                         BOB
          I guess.

He finishes drinking the water, crumples the cup, and
disposes of it. He looks to the front, then after several
moments, back at Ruth.

                         RUTH
          You be all right now?

                         BOB
          Yes. Go back to sleep.

                         RUTH
          You call me if you need me.

                         BOB
          I will.

He turns on his side so that his back is to her. Ruth looks at
him for several seconds, then, unable to keep her eyes open,
closes them again and starts falling asleep.

23.   CLOSE-UP - BOB

Eyes closed, face held rigidly. Now he opens his eyes and
stares into his thoughts, clearly, he fears that he is suffering
a relapse.

CAMERA CIRCLES him SLOWLY until the window, with
its curtain drawn, is seen next to his face. Bob stares at it
awhile, tension building, then finally, on an impulse,
reaches up and pushes the curtain aside. Instantly, he
stiffens, his face distorted by shock. Inches away, separated
from him only by the thickness of the window, is the man's
face staring in at him.

                                        (CONTINUED)

23.   CONTINUED

It is a hideously malignant face, a face not human. Its skin
is grimy, its lips misshapen, cracked, forced apart by teeth
of a grotesque size and crookedness, its eyes small and
recessed, unblinking. All framed by shaggy, tangled hair
which sprouts, also, in furry tufts from the man's ears and
nose, in birdlike down across his cheeks. Wilson sits riven
to his seat, incapable of response, he cannot so much as
blink. Dull-eyed, hardly breathing, he returns the creatures
vacant stare.

24.   CLOSE-UP - BOB

As he suddenly closes his eyes and presses back against the
seat.

BOB
(whispering to himself)
It isn't there.
(pause, shakily)
It - isn't - there.

Bracing himself, he opens his eyes and turns them slowly to
the window. As a gagging inhalation fills his throat.
CAMERA WHIP PANS to the window. Not only is the
man there but he is grinning at Wilson.

25.   BOB AND RUTH

Wilson gaping at the offscreeen man. Now, keeping his
eyes on the man, he starts to reach back slowly to awaken
Ruth. He tries not to move his lips as he speaks.

BOB
Honey.

26.   THE MAN, BOB, AND RUTH

Bob and Ruth reflected on the window glass. Outside the window, the man is watching Bob with vacuous absorption.

27.   WILSON AND RUTH

Wilson aghast as he realizes that the man seems to know what he is trying to do. He puts his hand on Ruth's arm.

                    BOB
          Honey, wake up.

Ruth stirs in her sleep. Bob suddenly freezes, seeing -

28.   THE MAN

Turning his Caliban head to look toward the rear of the cabin.

29.   BOB

Jerking his head around to see -

30.   STEWARDESS

Approaching down the slightly bucking aisle.

31.   BOB AND THE MAN

Bob looking toward the stewardess in wild hope, then at the man. He stiffens as the man's gaze shifts to him, a smile of monstrous cunning appearing on his lips.

32.   BOB AND STEWARDESS

The window offscreen. Wilson whirls toward the approaching stewardess.

                                        (CONTINUED)

32.   CONTINUED

> BOB
> (with desperation)

Quickly.

He looks back to the window, his expression petrifying.
CAMERA PANS TO the window. The man is gone.

33.   BOB

Staring at the offscreen window, appalled. In background,
we see the lower half of the stewardess as she stops by
Ruth's chair.

> STEWARDESS
> (tensely)

Yes, Mr. Wilson.

Bob is afraid to turn to her. He looks sick and frightened.

> STEWARDESS

Can I help you, Mr. Wilson?

Bracing himself. Bob turns.

34.   ANOTHER ANGLE - BOB, RUTH, AND STEWARDESS

As he looks up at the stewardess, he knows, in an instant,
that she isn't going to believe him and clamps a vise on his
emotions.

> BOB
> (tightly)

Are we going into a storm?

> STEWARDESS
> (smiling with effort)

Just a small one. Nothing to worry about.

(CONTINUED)

34.   CONTINUED

He nods jerkily and, after an akward hesitation, the
stewardess smiles again, twitchingly, and moves down the
aisle, walking OUT OF FRAME. Wilson watches her go,
then slumps back against the seat.

35.   CLOSE SHOT - BOB

As his head falls against the seat back, his eyes staring
straight ahead, hauntedly.

                        BOB
                      (pause)
          Honey?
          (plaintively as he looks at her)
          Would you wake up, honey?

He breaks off before finishing and looks around quickly at
the window.

36.   POV SHOT - WING

With an arcing descent, the dark figure of the man comes
jumping down to it much like an ape dropping from a tree.
There is no visible impact, he lands fragilely, short, hairy
arms outstretched as if for balance. A flare of lightning
reveals him there, grinning triumphantly at Wilson.

37.   BOB

Staring at the man with uncertain fear and, now, a new
element, rising anger.

38.   POV SHOT - THE MAN

Barely visible in the darkness, located near the front of the
inboard engine.

39.   BOB

Trying hard to see what the man is doing.

40.   POV SHOT - THE MAN

The wing is chalked with lightning and we see that, like an inquisitive child, the man is squatting on the hitching wing edge, stretching out his left forefinger toward the whirling propeller.

41.   BOB

Watching in appalled fascination.

42.   POV SHOT - THE MAN

Moving his finger closer and closer to the blurring gyre of the propeller; he is, by now, imperfectly illuminated by the flash of the engine exhaust. A flare of lightning reveals him touching, then jerking his hand back from the propeller, his lips twitching in a soundless cry.

43.   BOB

Reacting with a sickened expression, certain that the man has lost his finger. Abruptly, his expression alters as he sees that the man is unharmed.

44.   POV SHOT - THE MAN

Seen, at first, only partially, then, as lightning flashes, completely, gnarled forefinger extended once more, the very picture of some monstrous infant trying to touch the spin of a fan blade. He jerks his hand back again and another flash of lightning reveals him putting the finger in his mouth as if to cool it. He looks across his shoulder now and grins moronically at Wilson.

45.   BOB

Reacting to this sensing that the man is playing a game
with him. Suddenly, he starts to draw back fearfully.

46.   ANOTHER ANGLE - INCLUDING WINDOW

The man is walking across the wing toward the window.
Just before he reaches it, Wilson sees the reflection of the
stewardess as she passes by in the aisle. He jerks his head
around in anguish, raising his left hand as if to signal her,
then, realizing the futility of it, lowers his hand and turns
back to the window, shrinking from the sight of the man,
just outside, leering in at him. The man grins hideously and
glances toward the engine and back at Wilson as if to say:
Wait till you see what I'm going to do now. He turns away
and Bob leans toward the window to watch.

47.   CLOSE-UP - BOB

Watching the man on the wing.

48.   POV SHOT - THE MAN

We cannot make out, immediately, what he is doing. Then,
in a flash of lightning, we see that he is settling himself
astride the inboard engine cowling like a man mounting a
bucking horse.

49.   BOB

Watching apprehensively.

50.   POV SHOT - THE MAN

In place now. A flash of lightning reveals him looking
across his shoulder at Wilson as if to make sure that Wilson
is watching. Seeing that he is, the man grins and turns back
to the engine.

51.   BOB

Staring through the window. A flare of lightning whitens
his face, making him grimace, then stiffen, horrified at what
the man is doing.

52.   CLOSE SHOT - THE MAN

Bent over the cowling, picking at the plates that sheathe the
engine, the glare of the exhaust reflected on his troll-like
face. CAMERA ZOOMS IN on his simian hand as the man
works his dark nails under the edge of the riveted seam and
starts to pull it up.

53.   CLOSE-UP - BOB

Watching in shocked horror. He looks around in frightened
desperation, then, realizing the helplessness of his position,
can only gaze through the window again, one finger pressed
to his trembling lips.

54.   THE MAN AND BOB

The man in foreground, working doggedly at the cowling
plate; in background, observing with impotent dread, Bob.

FADE OUT:

END ACT ONE

ACT TWO

FADE IN:

55.   EXT. AIRLINER - NIGHT

56.   THE MAN AND BOB

The man in foreground, working intently on the cowling plate; Bob in background, watching.

57.   BOB

Tensely indecisive, then, abruptly, deciding what he must do. CAMERA DRAWS BACK as he reaches over and shakes Ruth by the arm.

                    BOB
        Honey, wake up.

She twitches, stirs, begins to fall asleep again. Bob shakes her harder.

                    BOB
        Honey.

Ruth opens her eyes in startlement and looks at him, having trouble focusing. Bob looks through the window.

58.   POV SHOT - MAN

As a flash of lightning illuminates him, we see that he is looking across his shoulder at Bob, a malicious smile on his lips. Darkness. A second flash of lightning reveals that he is gone.

59.   BOB AND RUTH

Bob starting at the sight, then relaxing slightly.

                    RUTH
        What are you looking at?

                              (CONTINUED)

59.   CONTINUED

He turns to her hesitantly and she sits up, rubbing at her
eyes.

                          RUTH
          Bob?
                          (beat)
          Is it the storm? Does it bother - ?

                          BOB
                     (interrupting)
          No.
                     (bracing himself)
          You remember what I said before? About
          thinking that I saw something outside?

                          RUTH
                     (uneasily)
          Yes.

                          BOB
                     (taking a breath)
          Honey, there's a man out there.

Ruth stares at him, too shocked to respond.

                          BOB
                     (with rising agitation)
          I don't mean a man - a human being.
          I mean -
                     (beside himself)
          - I don't know what he is; maybe a -
          what did they call those things during the war?
                     (beat)
          You know - the pilots?
                     (pause; remembering)

                                        (CONTINUED)

59.   CONTINUED

> BOB (CONT'D)
> Gremlins, gremlins. You remember
> those stories in the papers -
> (breaks off, tensely)
> Honey, don't look at me like that.

> RUTH
> (faintly)
> Bob.

> BOB
> (overlapping, voice rising)
> I am not imagining it.

He breaks off as Ruth glances around startledly, indicating that
he'll wake up the other passengers.

> BOB
> (softly, tightly)
> I am not imagining it. He's out there.

Her gaze shifts automatically to the window.

> BOB
> Don't look; he isn't there now.
> (realizing what he's saying)
> He. . .jumps away whenever anyone might see him.
> (beat, weakly)
> Except me.
> (pause, almost rabidly)
> Honey, he's there.

Her lips stir but she can say nothing, she is so upset.

> BOB
> (shakily)
> Look, I - I fully realize what this sounds like.
> (abruptly, pitifully)
> Do I look insane?

(CONTINUED)

59.   CONTINUED

She clutches his hand and holds it tightly.

                    RUTH
        Honey, <u>no</u>.

                    BOB
        (regaining control; spelling it out)
    I know I had a mental breakdown.
    I know it looks, to you, as if the same
    thing's happening again - but it <u>isn't</u>!
    <u>I'm</u> <u>sure</u> <u>of</u> it!

The terrible thing is that he doesn't sound sure at all
because, increasingly, he is wondering if he really has
suffered a relapse. Putting into words what he has
witnessed makes the incredibility of the situation all the
more pointed to him; he has to fight hard to keep believing
that the man outside is not hallucinatory.

                    BOB
    <u>Look</u>, the reason I'm telling you -
    isn't just to worry you, you notice
    I didn't tell you before, because -

                    RUTH
                (overlapping)
        But I <u>want</u> you to tell me.

The tone of her voice makes him very aware of the fact that
she does, indeed, think he has had a relapse. His lips begin
to tremble, he presses them together, struggling for control.

                            (CONTINUED)

59.   CONTINUED

BOB
(with strained softness)
I didn't tell you before because I wasn't
sure if it was real or not.
(beat)
I am sure now. It's real. There is a man out there.
(losing confidence)
Or a - gremlin, or whatever he is -
(with a sudden, pained laugh, brokenly)
If I described him to you, you'd really
think I was gone.

She presses close to him suddenly, frightened, clinging to
him.

RUTH
(gently, lovingly)
Honey, no, no, it's all right.
(stroking his cheek)
It's all right, baby.

He closes his eyes, fighting, with all his strength, to hold
onto what he believes is true. After a few moments, he
takes hold of her wrists and draws her away from himself,
looking at her gravely.

BOB
I know your intentions are good.
I know you love me - and sympathize with me.

(tightening)
But don't patronize me, Ruth. I am not insane.

(CONTINUED)

59.   CONTINUED

                         RUTH
                    (protesting)
          Did I say -

                          BOB
             (interrupting; tautly pained)
          Does it have to be said? It's on your
          face, in your -
                  (breaks off; pause; tensely)
          For the last time -
                  (pointing at window)
          - that. . .creature's out there.
                  (swallows dryly)
          And the reason I'm telling you. . .
          is that he's starting to tamper with
          one of the engines.

She only stares at him; pained, frightened, concerned. His
face distorts with sudden fury.

                          BOB
                       (loudly)
          Look!

She grimaces and he controls himself.

                          BOB
          Look. . . honey. Think anything you want. Think that I
          belong in a straightjacket if it pleases you.

                         RUTH
                     (anguished)
          Pleases me - ?

(CONTINUED)

59.   CONTINUED

                    BOB
               (overlapping)
      All right, all right. I'm sorry.
      I didn't mean that. What I mean is -
      whatever you think about me -
      that I've lost my mind, <u>anything</u>!

He controls himself and continues.

                    BOB
      All I'm asking you to do is tell the
      pilots what I've said. Ask them to
      keep an eye on the wings.
               (looking at her)
      If they see nothing - fine. I'll - commit
      myself, I'll -
               (a deep shaking breath)
      But if they <u>do</u>.
                    (pause)
      Well?

She looks at him in distress, not knowing what to say.

                    BOB
             (appalled and frightened)
      Won't you even allow the possibility that -

                    RUTH
               (cutting in)
      <u>All</u> <u>right</u>.
                    (beat)
      I'll tell them.

                    BOB
I know it seems a lot to ask; it's as if I'm - asking you to
advertise your marriage to a lunatic but -

                              (CONTINUED)

59.   CONTINUED

He breaks off as she puts a hand on his.

RUTH
I'll tell them, honey. Just - sit tight!
I'll tell them.

She gets up and moves OUT OF FRAME. Bob watches her go without encouragement, he has the feeling that she is going to pretend to tell the pilots in order to pacify him.

60.   POV SHOT - RUTH

At the front of the cabin, glancing back at him worriedly, then knocking on the door to the pilot's compartment. In a moment it is opened by the copilot.

61.   BOB

Watching them, he glances aside as the stewardess hurries down the aisle to find out what Ruth is doing. As she passes Wilson, she glances at him with a combination of anger and fear. He watches as she moves OUT OF FRAME.

62.   POV SHOT - RUTH, COPILOT, AND STEWARDESS

Ruth talking to the copilot, the stewardess hurrying to join them.

63.   BOB

Watching them, then suddenly, looking toward the window as he catches sight of -

64.   THE MAN

Landing on the wing like some grotesque ballet dancer.
Immediately, he sets to work again, straddling the engine
casing with his thick, bare legs and picking up the plate.

65.   BOB

Watching. He stiffens suddenly, catching his breath, and
leaning toward the window as he sees -

66.   THE MAN

Slowly pulling up one edge of a plate.

67.   BOB

Reacting to the sight. Abruptly, he lunges to his feet,
signaling to the three in front.

                    BOB
          Here! Quickly!

68.   POV SHOT - RUTH, COPILOT, AND STEWARDESS

Jerking around to look at him. The copilot moves first,
pushing past the stewardess and lurching up the aisle. A
few of the passengers, awakened by Wilson's voice, look
around in sleepy alarm, the stewardess hastening to reassure
them.

69.   BOB
                    BOB
          Hurry!

He glances out the window in time to see -

70.   THE MAN

Leaping upward and out of sight.

71.   FULL SHOT - BOB AND COPILOT FEATURED

Ruth, in the background, returning quickly. The copilot
reaches Bob.

                    COPILOT
                    (sternly)
          What's going on?

                    BOB
          He's pulled up one of the cowling plates.

                    COPILOT
                    (obviously in the dark)
          He?

                    BOB
          Didn't my wife - ?
          (breaks off, understanding; quickly)
          There's a man outside! He just - !

                    COPILOT
                    (cutting in)
          Mister Wilson, keep your voice down.

                    BOB
                    (off-balance)
          I'm sorry - but -

Ruth comes up to them and he glances at her accusingly.

                    COPILOT
          I don't know what's going on here, but -

He breaks off as Bob turns to him angrily and points out the
window.

                                        (CONTINUED)

71.   CONTINUED

                           BOB
               Will you look?

                         COPILOT
              Mr. Wilson, I'm warning you -

Bob stares at him uncomprehendingly, then drops back into
the seat and points at the window with a palsied hand.

                           BOB
               In the name of - !
                    (beat; tensely)
               Will you please look?

Drawing in an agitated breath, the copilot leans over and
looks out. His gaze shifts coldly to Wilson.

                         COPILOT
              Well?

Bob stares at him a moment, not understanding, then,
abruptly, turns his head to look out.

72.   POV SHOT - ENGINE

In a flare of lightning we can see that the plate, which the
man had pulled up, is in its normal state.

73.   BACK TO SCENE

                           BOB
                    (stunned)
               Oh, now, wait. . .
                    (turns to copilot)
               I saw him pull that plate up.

(CONTINUED)

73.   CONTINUED

They stare at him. Ruth with numbed apprehension.

BOB
(teeth clenched)
I <u>saw</u> <u>him</u> <u>pull</u> <u>that</u> <u>plate</u> <u>up</u>.

Ruth sits beside him hurriedly and takes his hand, her
expression one of torment. Bob glances at her, then back at
the copilot.

BOB
(voice breaking)
Listen, I <u>saw</u> him!

COPILOT
(leaning over; confidentially)
Mr. Wilson, please. All right, you saw him. But remember,
there are other people aboard. We mustn't alarm them.

Bob is too shaken to understand at first.

BOB
You - you mean - you've seen him then?

COPILOT
(agreeing to anything)
Of course we have. But we don't want to frighten the
passengers, you can understand that.

Ruth looks at him, momentarily stunned.

BOB
(gratefully cooperative)
Of course, of course. I don't want to -

(CONTINUED)

73.   CONTINUED

Abruptly, it comes to him and he presses his lips into a
hard, thin line, looking at the copilot with malevolent eyes.

                    BOB
                  (coldly)
        I understand.

                    COPILOT
                  (mollifyingly)
        The thing we have to remember -

                    BOB
                  (cutting in)
        You can stop now.

                    RUTH
          (not exactly sure what's going on)
        Bob -

                    COPILOT
                  (simultaneously)
        Sir?

                    BOB
                  (shudders)
        Get out of here.

                    COPILOT
        Mr. Wilson, what - ?

                    BOB
        Will you stop?

He turns away and looks out at the wing, eyes like stones.

                                    (CONTINUED)

73.   CONTINUED

> RUTH
> Honey, what is it?

Before she can finish, Bob turns back to the copilot and glares at him.

> BOB
> I won't say another word.
> (cutting off the copilot)
> I'll see us crash first.

> RUTH
> Bob.

> COPILOT
> Mr. Wilson, try to understand our position.

He breaks off as Wilson twists away and stares out venomously through the window.

74.   BOB

Staring through the window, in it we see reflected Ruth and the copilot. After several moments of silence, the copilot puts his hand on Ruth's shoulder and gestures, with his head toward the rear of the cabin. Ruth hesitates, then, as the copilot looks insistent, rises. The plane is bucking sharply now and the copilot takes her arm to support her.

> RUTH
> (to Bob)
> I'll be right -

She stops as the copilot squeezes her arm, then, as she glances at him, shakes his head a little.

(CONTINUED)

74.   CONTINUED

Bob, observing all this in the window, tightens his mouth. As they move OUT OF FRAME, he suddenly covers his eyes with a shaky hand.

                    BOB
                (whispering)
        He did pull it up. He did!

After a few moments, he looks across his shoulder.

75.   POV SHOT - RUTH AND COPILOT

Talking at the rear of the pitching cabin. The copilot hands Ruth something.

76.   BOB

Turns back to the front and looks through the window again. The storm is getting more violent.

77.   POV SHOT - THE MAN

Landing on the wing, he stoops by the engine and grins at Wilson. Reaching down, he pulls up the plate without effort, starts peeling it back.

78.   BOB

Reacting in shock. He glances around as if for help, then realizing the hopelessness of it, looks out again.

79.   POV SHOT - THE MAN

The glow of the engine reflected on his bestial face as he starts to reach inside it.

80.   BOB

     Watching in frozen dread. Outside, the engine falters
momentarily, making him twitch, grimacing. He presses
against the window, staring.

81.   POV SHOT - MAN

     On his knees, poking a curious hand into the innards of the
engine. Again, it falters, sparking.

82.   BOB

     Turning from the window to look around. To his shocked
astonishment, no one has noticed: he makes a noise of
disbelieving panic. Abruptly, he looks toward the rear of
the cabin.

83.   ANOTHER ANGLE - INCLUDING RUTH

     Returning unevenly, a cup of water in her hand. Bob jerks
around to look through the window again.

84.   POV SHOT - MAN

     Looking toward Bob, then, with an awful grin, pressing the
plate back into position, standing and ascending OUT OF
FRAME like a marionette jerked upward off its stage.

85.   BOB

     Staring through the window. He tightens as Ruth sits down
beside him.

RUTH

    Bob,
        (as he looks at her tensely)
    Honey, I was going to tell him when you -

(CONTINUED)

85.   CONTINUED

                         BOB
                    (interrupting)
        Were you?

She swallows, hesitates, then holds out a capsule different
from the one she gave him earlier.

                         BOB
                      (tightly)
        For me?

                        RUTH
                   (close to tears)
        Please, Bob.

He looks at her, deliberating, then abruptly takes the
capsule and puts it in his mouth, drinks the water. He drops
the cup and turns on his side.

                        RUTH
        You'll sleep now, darling, and -

She breaks off as he stiffens when she rubs his arm. After a
while, still exhausted, she settles herself and closes her
eyes, holding onto his arm. Bob's eyes shift toward the
aisle, then suddenly close.

86.   DOWN ANGLE SHOT - BOB AND RUTH

In a moment, the copilot and stewardess ENTER FRAME,
coming from opposite directions, and pause by the seats, the
floor bucking beneath them. They converse in whispers.

                      COPILOT
                  (exhales, relieved)
        Boy.

                                        (CONTINUED)

86.   CONTINUED

                    STEWARDESS
        What did you do, have his wife give him one of those
        capsules?

                    COPILOT
                    (nod)
            He'll be out for hours.

                    STEWARDESS
                    (gratefully)
            Thank heaven for that. The way this
            storm is going.

They exchange a smile and move OUT OF FRAME, the
stewardess toward the back of the cabin, the copilot toward
the front. After several moments, Wilson looks around
cautiously.

87.   CLOSE ON BOB

        Removing the capsule from his mouth and pushing it into
        the holder behind the seat in front of him. He looks
        through the window with apprehension, staring as -

88.   THE MAN

        Lands on the wing and, with a grin at Bob, starts peeling
        back the cowling plate again.

89.   BOB

        Watching helplessly. Now he looks around, trying to think
        of something to do. Disengaging himself from Ruth, he
        stands and looks around further, stiffening as he sees -

90.   STATE POLICE OFFICER

Several seats down, located on the aisle across the way, he is asleep. CAMERA ZOOMS IN on his revolver in its button-down holster.

91.   BOB

Suffering from acute indecision. He leans toward the window, then realizes that he has no choice. He looks around to make sure no one is observing, then, bracing himself, eases past Ruth and into the aisle.

92.   UP ANGLE SHOT - STATE POLICE OFFICER AND BOB

The right side of the officer in foreground, Bob, in background, approaching stealthily along the pitching aisle. He reaches the officer and hesitates a moment, running a trembling hand across his mouth. Again, he braces himself and, bending over, reaches down for the pistol. He gets the holster flap unfastened and starts taking out the revolver. The officer stirs and Bob jerks back his hand, shrinking away. After a few moments, the officer subsides into heavy sleep once more and Bob regains the courage to go on. Moving with nerve-wracked slowness, he succeeds in withdrawing the revolver from its holster and, hastily, turns back toward his seat.

93.   CLOSE ON BOB

As he sinks back on his seat, glances worriedly at Ruth, then looks through the window. CAMERA DRAWS AROUND and he reacts, seeing that the glass is lashed by rain now. He squints through it, trying hard to see.

94.   POV SHOT - MAN

Illuminated by lightning, watching for Wilson's return.
Seeing him, he grins and leans over the engine, again,
pulling the cowling plate back a little more and preparing to
probe at the engine.

95.   BOB

Swallowing dryly, he begins to raise the pistol, then lowers
it, unable to aim.

                         BOB
                     (worriedly)
              I can't see. . .
                 (touching the window)
              It's too thick.

Close to total panic now, he looks out the window suddenly.

96.   POV SHOT - THE MAN

Seen in a flash of lightning, his hand inside the engine. He
is looking across his shoulder at Bob, grinning, an eruption
of sparks casting light across his animal features. The
engine smokes a little.

97.   BOB

A look of doomed horror on his face. Suddenly, motivated
by absolute desperation, he looks at -

98.   EMERGENCY DOOR HANDLE

A transparent plastic cover over it.

99.   BOB

Staring at the handle. Now he looks at the man and, in a
moment, makes his decision. With a sharp movement, he
pulls the plastic cover free and sets it down. He puts his
hand on the door handle and tests it; it does not move
downward but has upward play.

Abruptly, he sets the revolver in his lap and, leaning over,
starts to fasten Ruth's safety belt, then stops, uncertain.
After a moment, he hides the pistol and shakes Ruth's arm.

                        BOB
            Honey?
                (as she murmurs in her sleep)
            Would you get me a drink of water, please?
                (as she opens her eyes)
            Water? Please?

She looks at him groggily, then smiles and nods and
pushing to her feet, moves off weavingly down the bucking
aisle. As soon as she has gone, Bob fastens his seat belt
securely, glancing out at the man as he does. Now he
retrieves the pistol, takes hold of the door handle, and steels
himself. Abruptly, he glances across his shoulder.

100.   REVERSE SHOT - INCLUDING RUTH AND THE
        STEWARDESS

Ruth watching apprehensively as the stewardess comes
hurrying down the aisle, then freezes in her tracks, a look of
stupefied horror distending her features. She raises a hand
as if imploring Wilson, then suddenly cries out.

                    STEWARDESS
            Mr. Wilson, no!

101.   BOB

                              BOB
               Stand back!

Face tightening, he wrenches up the handle with his left
hand, with a hissing roar, the emergency door flies off.

102.   CLOSE SHOT - BOB

Enveloped by a monstrous suction, his head and shoulders
outside the cabin. For a moment, his eardrums almost
bursting from the thunder of the engines, his eyes near
blinded by arctic winds, he forgets everything but present
suffering. Then, remembering, he sees the man.

103.   POV SHOT - THE MAN

Walking across the wing, gnarled form leaning forward,
talonlike hands outstretched in eagerness.

104.   BOB

Aiming the revolver with all the strength he can muster and
starting to fire repeatedly, the detonations no more than
popping noises in the roaring violence of the air.

105.   POV SHOT - MAN

Flailing backward, then, suddenly, disappearing with the
appearance of a paper doll swept off by a gale.

106.   BOB

Despite physical agony, reacting with relief. Suddenly,
there is a bursting numbness in his brain. The pistol is
pulled from his failing grip by the wind and he passes out.
DARKNESS - and a cessation of all noise.

                                        (CONTINUED)

106.   CONTINUED

In several moments, we hear shuffling sounds, a faint swirl of unintelligible voices. Finally, light - and a gradual focusing in on -

107.   CEILING OF AIRLINE CABIN - BOB'S POV - NIGHT

Moving by over head. CAMERA REACHES the door where the stewardess and copilot look down, their expressions grave.

108.   CLOSE SHOT - BOB

Lying on a stretcher, being carried through the doorway of the airliner. He looks around, reacting with relief as he sees -

109.   RUTH AND AMBULANCE ATTENDANT - BOB'S POV

Ruth following the attendant, smiling down comfortingly at Bob.

110.   BOB

Smiling back at her weakly, then turning his head. The field level is reached.

>   MAN'S VOICE
>   (in background)
>   Nuttiest way o' tryin' to commit suicide
>   I ever heard of.

Bob stiffens and, twisting his head around, looks back toward the engine with which the gremlin was tampering. Seeing what he's looking for, he sighs, relaxes, and turns his head back once more. As the stretcher is carried across the field, Ruth comes INTO FRAME and takes his hand, walking beside the stretcher.

                                        (CONTINUED)

110.   CONTINUED

                    RUTH
        It's all right now.

                    BOB
        I know.
                (amused)
        But I'm the only one who does right now.

She looks confused for a moment, then lets it go and smiles at him again. CAMERA HOLDS as they move off, then, after a moment, starts PANNING UPWARD SLOWLY toward the wing, RETAINING Bob and Ruth and the ambulance attendants.

                SERLING'S VOICE
        The flight of Mr. Robert Wilson has
        ended now - a flight not only from point
        A to point B but, also, from the fear of
        recurring mental breakdown. Mr. Wilson
        has that fear no longer - though, for the
        moment, he is, as he has said, alone in his
        assurance. Happily, his conviction will
        not remain isolated too much longer.

CAMERA STOPS on the inboard engine. In background, we see Wilson being carried off, his wife beside him. In foreground, we see the engine plate pulled back, fire-blackened metal.

                SERLING'S VOICE
        For, happily, tangible manifestation is,
        very often, left as evidence of trespass -
        even from so intangible a quarter - as
        the Twilight Zone.

                                FADE OUT:
            THE END

Night Call

This melancholy tale of a unrequited love from beyond the grave was based on a short story first published in 1953 under the magazine editor's own title, "Sorry, Right Number." When Matheson later included it in his first *Shock!* collection, he changed the title back to his preferred "Long Distance Call." However the title had to be changed yet again when the story was produced, as the series had already aired an episode (by William Idelson and Charles Beaumont) with that very same title.

Matheson remains extremely pleased with this episode, which he counts among his three of four favorites of the entire series. The show was very effectively directed by Jacques Tourneur, a feature film director responsible for such classics as *Cat People* and *Curse of the Demon*. Matheson himself recommended the director to the show's producers."This was about as film noir as you can get. The premise, the shadowy look of night time, the darkened bedroom, the sudden, jarring ring of the telephone...it was noir to the *teeth*. And it must be repeated that Gladys Cooper was wonderful; she was a marvelous actress.

"And Jacques was a wonderful director. The producers were uneasy about hiring him. The feeling was Jacques was a motion picture director, and he would not be able to successfully accomplish such the short shooting schedule of a television show. Especially just a half-hour show. As I've mentioned a number of times, he was so organized. Looking at his script-book where all his notes were so meticulous—he knew ahead every single thing he was going to do. It's my understanding he shot the shortest shooting schedule of any *Twilight Zone* episode, which was 28 hours."

Anyone reading the original story and comparing it to the script will notice that Matheson took the rare step of changing the ending. But change in this instance had nothing to do with the wishes of Serling or the producers.

"It was my choice. Because you needed a little zapper at the end; a surprise ending. And my ending from my short story was not a zapper surprise ending, except for the fact of the ghostly voice saying 'I'll be right over.' And you visualize a corpse coming over to her house. But that really says nothing. To give the woman some sort of characterization, some sort of 'arc' as they say (I hate that word!), I created this new ending to make the surprise be that *she* was the one who was responsible for all this. Her own selfishness.

"I liked the new ending a lot better, actually. It was simple human nature which did this to her. I always prefer that kind of approach to fantasy or terror or whatever. She had done this to him while he was still alive, and, even dead, he still had the habit of doing exactly what she told him."

NIGHT CALL

PERFORMANCE DATE: 2/7/64

PRODUCER: BERT GRANET

DIRECTOR: JACQUES TOURNEUR

CAST:

MISS ELVA KEENE: GLADYS COOPER

MARGARET PHILLIPS: NORA MARLOWE

MISS FINCH: MARTINE BARTLETT

FADE IN:

1.   INT. ELVA KEENE'S HOUSE - FULL SHOT FROM
     WINDOW - NIGHT

     A violent storm in progress; thunder cannonading across the
     sky, lightning bleaching the night into moments of monstrous
     day. Miss Keene's darkened house is set by itself among a
     stand of wind-lashed trees; clearly, there are no immediate
     neighbors.

                                    DISSOLVE THROUGH TO:

2.   EXT. ELVA KEENE'S BEDROOM

     CAMERA MOVING TOWARD one of its curtain-blown
     windows. As lightning flares, we catch a momentary
     glimpse of the interior ELVA KEENE in b.g. on her bed.
     Nearby is her wheelchair.

     DISSOLVE THROUGH TO:

3.   INT. ELVA KEENE'S BEDROOM

     CAMERA MOVES TOWARD Miss Keene's bed. As it
     approaches, we see that she is in her fifties, frail and
     crippled. CAMERA CONTINUES MOVING IN on her
     until she is in CLOSE SHOT, then STOPS. She is trying,
     without success, to sleep, turning painfully from side to side,
     wincing uneasily at each new crash of LIGHTNING, each
     new leprous burst of LIGHTNING. Now she turns on her
     left side and closes her eyes; she is facing the bedside
     telephone now. The storm diminishes and Miss Elva sighs.
     Suddenly, the telephone RINGS. Miss Elva's eyes jerk open
     and the CAMERA WITHDRAWS to include the ringing
     telephone. Miss Elva pushes up on an elbow, her hand
     falters out and takes hold of the receiver.

4.   CLOSE-UP - MISS ELVA

As she draws the receiver to her ear.

MISS ELVA
Hello?

An extended roar of THUNDER shakes the night, making her twitch, grimacing.

MISS ELVA
I'm sorry, I didn't hear; the thunder. . .
(listens; frowns)
Hello?
(pause; tensely)
Who is on the line, please?

Nothing. Miss Elva's face tightens and, reaching out, she hangs up, slumps back against the pillow. She makes a whimpering noise and presses the palm of her right hand to her infirm back. The pain slackens a little and she labors over onto her right side, exhaling wearily. LIGHTNING flashes and she looks toward the window, wincing. Now she draws the covers to her chin and tries to fall asleep. In several moments, the telephone RINGS. Opening her eyes quickly, Miss Elva hesitates, then reaches out with a frown and lifts off the receiver, pulls it to herself.

MISS ELVA
(uncertainly)
Hello?
(pause; more loudly)
Hello?

She holds out the receiver and stares at it in apprehensive wrath, not sure what to do. She reaches out as if to hang up, then, abruptly, pulls the receiver back and listens intently for a betraying sound.

(CONTINUED)

4.   CONTINUED

There is none. The tension building in Miss Elva suddenly
erupts and, with a whine of aggravated distress, she reaches
out and slams down the receiver, then slumps against her
pillow, making faint noises of pain and self-pity.

SERLING'S VOICE
Miss Elva Keene lives alone on the
outskirts of Lenden Fleet in Maine.
Up until now, the pattern of Miss Keene's
existence has been that of lying in her
bed or sitting in her wheelchair; reading
books; listening to her radio; eating,
napping, taking medication - and waiting
for something different to happen.

5.   SERLING

SERLING
Miss Keene doesn't know it yet but her
period of waiting has just ended. For
something different is about to happen to
her - has, in fact, already begun to happen
via two most unaccountable telephone
calls in the middle of a stormy night.
Telephone calls routed directly through
the Twilight Zone.

FADE OUT:

FIRST COMMERCIAL

ACT ONE

FADE IN (HOLD 20 FEET FOR OPENING TITLES):

6.   EXT. ELVA KEENE HOUSE - FULL SHOT - MORNING

The storm over, the ground littered with leaves, twigs, branches, etc. Along the puddled dirt road comes the old coupe of nurse MARGARET PHILLIPS. She pulls up in front of the house's front gate, brakes, turns off the motor and gets out, carrying a small bag of groceries. She is a heavy-set, placid woman in her late forties, wearing a topcoat over her white uniform. CAMERA PANS with her as she trudges to the front porch, unlocks the door and enters.

7.   INT. LIVINGROOM

Margaret comes in and starts across the room, heading for the kitchen. She stops, hearing the cradle arm being TAPPED in the bedroom.

MISS ELVA'S VOICE
Hel-lo!

Turning, Margaret moves to the open bedroom doorway and looks in.

8.   POV SHOT - MISS ELVA

As she finishes tapping the telephone cradle arm impatiently and, listening, notices Margaret's presence, nods curtly.

9.   MISS ELVA AND MARGARET

Margaret in the b.g. doorway.

MARGARET
You're up early this morning.

(CONTINUED)

9.   CONTINUED

Miss Elva taps the cradle arm again, listens.

                    MISS ELVA
                (listens; frowns)
        What's the <u>matter</u> with her?

                    MARGARET
        No answer?

                    MISS ELVA
                    (stiffly)
        Obviously.

                    MARGARET
                  (unruffled)
        Well, I imagine they're pretty busy this
        morning - what with the storm and all.

Miss Elva grunts thinly, continues to tap the cradle arm.
Abruptly, the connection is made.

                    MISS ELVA
                (into the receiver)
        Miss Finch? This is Elva Keene speaking.

10.   ECU - MISS ELVA

                MISS FINCH'S VOICE
                  (over phone)
        Yes, Miss Keene. Can I help you?

                    MISS ELVA
                    (tightly)
        You can. Last night about - two a.m.,
        my telephone rang.

11.   MARGARET

Listening with mild curiosity.
                    MISS ELVA'S VOICE
        I answered it - but no one spoke. And I
        didn't hear any receiver being put down.

12.   ECU - MISS ELVA - TO BE INTERCUT WITH
       TELEPHONE SWITCHBOARD
                        MISS ELVA
            Just - silence.

                    MISS FINCH'S VOICE
            Well, Miss -

                        MISS ELVA
                        (interrupting)
        And the same thing happened again a few
        moments later.

                    MISS FINCH'S VOICE
                        (over phone)
        Well, I'll tell you, Miss Keene. That
        storm last night about ruined our service.
        We've been flooded with complaints
        about fallen wires and bad connections.
        I'd say you're pretty lucky that your
        telephone is working at all.

                        MISS ELVA
                        (displeased)
        Oh?
                        (beat)
        Would you say, then, that someone was
        trying to call me but that the connection
        was bad because of the storm?

                            (CONTINUED)

12.   CONTINUED

MISS FINCH'S VOICE
That's as good an explanation as any
right now, Miss Elva.
(beat)
I'm sorry. I wish I could be of more help
but -
(a harried laugh)
- the way things are right now.

MISS ELVA
(overlapping)
Is it likely to happen again?

MISS FINCH
Well, I couldn't say, Miss Elva. It might.
It depends on what's <u>causing</u> it to happen,
of course. If there's breakdown
somewhere that our crews haven't
repaired yet, well - yes, it might happen
again. If it does though, you just call me
and I'll have a special check run on it.
Will you do that?

MISS ELVA
(disliking the feeling of being patronized)
I will.

MISS FINCH'S VOICE
<u>Good</u>. I'll wait to hear from you then.
Goodbye, Miss Keene.

MISS ELVA
(thinly)
Goodbye.

(CONTINUED)

12.   CONTINUED

She hangs up and looks at the o.s. Margaret who is starting to leave the room.

                    MISS ELVA
          Margaret.

13.   MISS ELVA AND MARGARET

                    MARGARET
                  (turning back)
          Yes, Miss Keene?

                    MISS ELVA
          Did you call me last night?

                    MARGARET
                  (amused)
          At two in the morning?
                  (chuckles)
          No, Ma'am, not me.

14.   MISS ELVA

Looking toward the door, her expression an amalgam of dour resentment and self pity.

                    MISS ELVA
                  (to herself)
          You might have checked.
                  (beat; stiffly)
          But, then, I don't pay you for nights, do I?

                              DISSOLVE TO:

15.   INT. LIVINGROOM - ANGLE ON FRONT DOOR - DAY

Margaret out at the mailbox, removing three envelopes.
CAMERA PANS to Miss Elva sitting in her wheelchair,
knitting; nearby is a table with a telephone on it.
Margaret's FOOTSTEPS are heard crossing the o.s. porch.
The front door is CLOSED and Miss Elva looks up as
Margaret ENTERS FRAME, holding the three envelopes.

                    MARGARET
          Here's your mail, Miss Keene.

                    MISS ELVA
                     (cooly)
          Thank you.

She puts down her knitting, takes the envelopes and looks
at them, one by one, Margaret observing.

                    MISS ELVA
                    (grimly)
          An advertisement. Another
          advertisement.
                         (smiling bitterly)
          The light bill.
                         (sighs)
          How stimulating.

                    MARGARET
          You just heard from your sister a few
          days ago, didn't you?

Miss Elva looks up critically at the nurse.

                                        (CONTINUED)

15.   CONTINUED

>   MISS ELVA
> <u>Three</u> <u>weeks</u> <u>ago</u>, Margaret. Three weeks
> and two days to be exact.

>   MAGARET
> Oh; has it been that long?

>   MISS ELVA
> Yes; <u>that</u> long.
>   (pause; resentfully)
> Nobody cares whether I live or die.

>   MARGARET
> <u>Oh</u>; sure they do, Miss Keene.

Miss Elva looks at her somberly.

>   MISS ELVA
> You don't understand.
>   (beat)
> You have no idea what it's like to be alone.

>   MARGARET
>   (awkwardly)
> Oh. . .now, Miss Keene.

Miss Elva puts the three letters on the table beside the
telephone and returns to her knitting. Margaret moves OUT
OF FRAME. In a few moments, we hear the sound of
DISHWASHING in the kitchen; then, shortly afterward, the
telephone RINGS. Miss Elva looks at it quickly and, after a
moment's hesitation, picks up the receiver.

                                        (CONTINUED)

15.   CONTINUED
                        MISS ELVA
        Hello?

CAMERA MOVES IN QUICKLY on her face as she
realizes that another strange telephone call is being made to
her. She looks at the receiver; listens again.

                        MISS ELVA
                    (softly; tensely)
        Hello?

After a few moments, she puts her hand over the
mouthpiece and calls out.

                        MISS ELVA
        Margaret!

                    MARGARET'S VOICE
                      (in kitchen)
        Yes?

                        MISS ELVA
        Come here.
                        (beat)
        Quickly!

16.   ANOTHER ANGLE

The dining alcove in b.g., Miss Elva in f.g., listening to the
telephone receiver. In a few moments Margaret walks
briskly (for her) out of the dining alcove and crosses to
Miss Elva.

                        MARGARET
        What is it?

                                        (CONTINUED)

16.   CONTINUED

Miss Elva silences her with a look and holds out the
receiver. Margaret takes it, listens.

MARGARET
(pause)
There's nobody on the line, Miss Keene.

MISS ELVA
(grimacing; cutting in softly and urgently)
Just listen - listen! See if you can hear
the sound of a receiver being put down.

Margaret listens for a while longer, then shrugs.

MARGARET
Not a thing.

She hangs up.

MISS ELVA
Wait!
(subsides)
Oh, well, it doesn't matter. I'll call
Miss Finch and have them check on it. . .

MARGARET
You really think it's necessary?

MISS ELVA
(tightening)
Yes; I think it's necessary. Am I to have
calls like that coming in all the time!?

MARGARET
But, if it's a breakdown, Miss Keene, I'm sure they'll.

(CONTINUED)

16.   CONTINUED

Her voice trails off as Miss Elva picks up the telephone receiver and dials the operator. With a sigh and an upward glance, Margaret moves OUT OF FRAME. Miss Elva listens, waiting.

DISSOLVE TO:

17.   INT. BEDROOM - CLOCK - NIGHT

On the bedside table, illuminated by lamplight; it reads eight o'clock. A plate is put down in front of the clock, on a plate a peeled apple, two cookies, a glass of milk and a bottle of pills. CAMERA PANS past the lamp, a radio and the telephone to show Margaret, her topcoat over her uniform, puffing up the pillows, behind Miss Elva's back.

MARGARET
There we go. All comfy?

MISS ELVA
(withdrawn)
Thank you.

MARGARET
Don't you fret about those phone calls, now, Miss Keene.

MARGARET (CONT'D)
I'm sure that whatever the trouble was, the repairmen have fixed it by now.
(as Miss Elva remains silent)
Why don't you keep the receiver off the hook if it bothers you? Then whoever it is can't call you; although I'm sure nobody is.

(CONTINUED)

17.   CONTINUED

                    MISS ELVA
                    (stiffly)
        Thank you.

                    MARGARET
                    (smiles)
        Good night, Miss Keene. See you in the
        morning.

Margaret moves OUT OF FRAME and Miss Elva listens to
the fading sound of her FOOTSTEPS. The front door is
OPENED, CLOSED. In a few moments, the car door is
CLOSED and the motor STARTS. Miss Elva is so intent
on the sounds of nurse Phillips' departure that the ringing of
the telephone makes her twitch sharply. She jerks her head
around and looks at it, glances toward the door as if to call
nurse Phillips, then realizes that it is too late and looks back
at the telephone.

18.   TELEPHONE AND MISS ELVA

The phone in f.g.; Miss Elva in b.g., looking at it, fighting
the rise of apprehension in herself.

19.   CLOSE-UP - MISS ELVA

Staring at the o.s. RINGING telephone, not knowing what
to do.

20.   MISS ELVA AND TELEPHONE

Now she reaches out, then jerks her hand back. The phone
keeps ringing and, finally, bracing herself, she reaches out
and picks up the receiver, listens tensely. There is no
sound. Moments pass. Miss Elva grits her teeth; she makes
a move as if to hang up. As she does, there is a faint sound
from the receiver and she jerks it back to her ear.

                                    (CONTINUED)

20.   CONTINUED

MISS ELVA

Hello?

CAMERA MOVES IN until her face is in E.C.U. Her face
tightens as she listens to the SOUND. It might be a
murmuring. It might, also, be a dull humming - or a sound
of faint rustling; there is no way of being certain the sound
is so soft, so undefined. It alters from a sort of whining
vibration - to an escape of air - to a bubbling sibilance.

MISS ELVA
(faintly)

What. . .?

Soon the sounds cease and there is only the silence again.
Miss Elva makes a noise of confusion and alarm, then
catches her breath as the SOUNDS begin once more, this
time a little more loudly. She shudders, listening, the
receiver pressed to her ear, breath quickening, unreasoning
dread rising like a tide in her. The sounds cannot possibly
be caused by a human being, it seems - and, yet, there is
something about them; some inflection, some undeniable
arrangement of -

MISS ELVA

Who's there?
(beat; brokenly)
Who's on the line?

As if in answer, the eerie sounds increase in pitch and
volume. Miss Elva's lips shake and a whine begins to
hover in her throat. But she cannot put down the telephone;
the sounds grip her in, almost, a hypnotic daze.

(CONTINUED)

20.   CONTINUED

                    MISS ELVA
        Who is it?
                    (beat)
        Who's there? Hello!

Again, the sounds increase in pitch and volume.

                    MISS ELVA
                    (fiercely)
        Hello!

                    VOICE
                    (toneless; hideous)
        H-e-l-l-o. . .

Miss Elva makes a gagging noise, the receiver dropping
from her hand and falling OUT OF FRAME. CAMERA
HOLDS momentarily on her staring face, then
DOWNPANS SLOWLY to the receiver. The telephone
base is further in on the table now; the receiver swings back
and forth on its wire. CAMERA MOVES IN on it. As it
swings IN and OUT OF FRAME, we hear fragments of the
unearthly voice.

                    VOICE
        H-e-l-l-o-o-o-o. . .

                                    FADE OUT:

                END OF ACT ONE

FADE IN:

21.   INT. BEDROOM - SERIES OF ECU'S - MISS ELVA -
MORNING - TO BE INTERCUT WITH SWITCHBOARD

Listening to the operator's voice over the telephone.

> MISS FINCH'S VOICE
> Are you sure it was someone saying
> hello, Miss Keene? It could have been -

> MISS ELVA
> (interrupting)
> I tell you it was someone: The same one
> who kept listening to me say hello over
> and over again without answering back!
> The same one who made those horrible
> noises!

> MISS FINCH'S VOICE
> You have no idea though whether it was a
> man or a woman.

> MISS ELVA
> I've already told you! There's no way of
> knowing! It could be either one!

> MISS FINCH'S VOICE
> And you're positive it wasn't someone on
> your party line?

> MISS ELVA
> (rigidly)
> Don't you think I know the people on my
> party line?

(CONTINUED)

21.   CONTINUED

> MISS FINCH'S VOICE
> (placatingly)
> Of couse, Miss Keene; of couse. Well,
> I'll. . .have a man check your line as soon
> as possible. The crews are pretty busy
> right now but -

> MISS ELVA
> (cutting in)
> What am I to do if this - person calls
> again?

> MISS FINCH'S VOICE
> Hang up on them, Miss Keene.

> MISS ELVA
> But whoever it is just keeps on calling!

> MISS FINCH'S VOICE
> (affability failing)
> Well. . .why don't you try to find out who
> it is; whether it's a man or a woman? Try
> to get their name if you can. If you do
> that, why, we can take immediate action,
> you see.

> MISS ELVA
> (tensely)
> Yes.
> (pause)
> Yes.

22.   MED. SHOT - MISS ELVA AND MARGARET

Margaret standing beside the bed. Miss Elva hangs up and
falls back against the pillows.

                    MARGARET
        What did she say?

                    MISS ELVA
        Nothing.
                    (beat)
        It's obvious that she doesn't believe a
        word I told her.

                    MARGARET
        Oh, now -

                    MISS ELVA
                    (interrupting)
        As far as she's concerned, I'm just a
        nervous old - biddy falling prey to my
        imagination!
                    (cutting Margaret off)
        Well, she'll find out differently. I'll just
        keep calling her and calling her until she
        does.

                                        DISSOLVE TO:

23.   INT. LIVINGROOM - MISS ELVA - DAY

Sitting in her wheelchair, eating a sandwich; on the table is
a plate with a glass of milk and two cookies on it. O.s. is
the sound of nurse Phillips SNORING. Miss Elva looks at
her.

24.   MARGARET

Lying asleep on the sofa, a movie magazine open on her chest.

25.   MISS ELVA

She is taking a bite of her sandwich when the telephone
RINGS. She looks at it fearfully; puts down the sandwich.
She looks toward nurse Phillips, then, after a few moments,
panicking, takes off the receiver and, without listening,
holds down the cradle arm to break the connection. After
several moments, she hangs up. She starts to draw back her
hand, then, abruptly, reaches out, lifts off the receiver and
dumps it on the table. She turns away from it and picks up
her sandwich again. She starts to bite it, hesitates, looks at
the receiver.

MISS ELVA
(to herself)
If I don't let them call. . .I may never find
out who it is.

After several moments, she hangs up the receiver once
more, jerking back her hand with a gasp as, immediately,
the telephone RINGS.

Miss Elva gapes at it frightenedly, then, bracing herself,
picks up the receiver. She draws in a deep, ragged breath
and puts it to her ear.

MISS ELVA
Hello?

26.   ECU - MISS ELVA

VOICE
(on phone; hollow; inanimate)
Hel-lo?

(CONTINUED)

26.   CONTINUED

                    MISS ELVA
                    (swallows)
         Who is this?

                    VOICE
         Hel-lo?

                    MISS ELVA
         Who's calling, please?

                    VOICE
         Hel-lo?

                    MISS ELVA
         Who's calling, please?

                    VOICE
         Hel-lo?

                    MISS ELVA
                    (fear rising)
         Can you hear me?

                    VOICE
         Hel-lo?

                    MISS ELVA
                    (voice breaking)
         Please - !

                    VOICE
         Hel-lo?

27.   CLOSE SHOT - MISS ELVA

Lunging out her hand, she slams down the receiver with a
hoarse sob and bends forward, trying to catch her breath.
Abruptly, she jerks up her head.

                    MISS ELVA
          Margaret!

28.   MARGARET

Grunting in her sleep and twitching slightly.

                MISS ELVA'S VOICE

          Margaret!

Margaret opens her eyes and looks around groggily.

29.   MISS ELVA

Shaking uncontrollably. O.s., Margaret stands and starts to
walk across the room. Miss Elva tries to control herself,
pressing hands to her fevered cheeks. Margaret ENTERS
FRAME.

                    MARGARET
          What is it?

                    MISS ELVA
          It's a man who's been calling.

                    MARGARET
                 (still waking up)
          How do you know?

                              (CONTINUED)

29.   CONTINUED

                    MISS ELVA
          Because he just called me!

                    MARGARET
          What does he want?

                    MISS ELVA
          I don't know. He just keeps saying hello
          - over and over again. That's all he says -
                    (voice cracking progressively)
          Hello. . .hello. . .hello.

                    MARGARET
                    (interrupting)
          Now you've got to stop this, Miss Keene.
          You're working yourself into a state over -

She breaks off awkwardly. A beat; then -

                    MISS ELVA
                    (almost rabidly)
          Over nothing?

                    MARGARET
          I didn't say that, Miss Keene.

                    MISS ELVA
                    (overlapping)
          You were going to say it!

                    MARGARET
          Now, Miss Keene, I was not. I think I
          better put you in your bed so you can -

                                        (CONTINUED)

29.   CONTINUED

MISS ELVA
(overlapping; close to frenzy now)
I don't <u>want</u> to be put in my bed: I want
to know who this terrible man is who
keeps calling!

MARGARET
Now what did miss Finch tell you?
(beat)
She told you it probably was a bad
connection, didn't she?

MISS ELVA
It is <u>not</u> the connection! It's a <u>man</u>!

MARGARET
I didn't say it wasn't Miss Keene. But if
he keeps on saying hello, then, obviously,
he can't hear you - <u>because</u> <u>of</u> <u>a</u> <u>bad</u>
<u>connection</u>.

MISS ELVA
(shaking her head)
No. He heard me. I know he heard me.

MARGARET
(patiently)
Then why don't you hang <u>up</u> on him,
Miss Elva? You don't have to listen.
Just hang up. Is that so hard to do?

MISS ELVA
Over - and <u>over</u>. Hello. Hello. Hello.

(CONTINUED)

29.   CONTINUED

She breaks off, twitching, as Margaret lifts the receiver and
sets it down on the table.

>   MARGARET
>   There. Now nobody can call you. Right?
>   Leave it that way. Then, if you want to
>   make a call, all you have to do is hold
>   down the arm a second. Isn't that right
>   Miss Keene?
>   (beat)
>   Miss Keene?

>   MISS ELVA
>   (frightened)
>   Why is he calling me? Why?

                                        DISSOLVE TO:

30.   INT. MISS ELVA'S BEDROOM - FULL SHOT - NIGHT

Dark and still - except for the faint HOWL on the bedside
phone. It grows louder as the CAMERA MOVES IN
toward the bed, STOPPING on a CLOSE-UP of Miss Elva
who is lying on her back, staring at the ceiling. Obviously,
she cannot sleep. After a few moments, she turns her head
to look at the telephone.

31.   POV SHOT - TELEPHONE

The receiver lying beside the base, HOWLING as a
receiver will when left off the cradle arm too long.

32.   MISS ELVA

Turns her head back and stares at the ceiling again. After a while, the noise aggravates her so that she pushes fingers into her ears, grimacing. She draws in long, shaking breaths, intent on sleep; but nothing will blot away the sound. Tension builds steadily in her. Abruptly, her hand slaps around on the bed until she locates her woolen bedjacket. Turning on the lamp, she wraps the receiver up in the jacket, swathing it in as many turns as possible. Then she turns off the lamp and falls back against her pillow, breathing hard. Moments pass. At first, she hears nothing. Then, little by little, the HOWLING noise becomes audible again; then, gradually, more than audible. She fights against it, getting more and more taut.
Finally, she can take it no longer and, reaching out with talon-like fingers, she unwraps the receiver, dropping it in her haste. Pulling it up by its wire, she hangs up.
The silence, albeit menacing, makes her sigh with grateful relief. She sinks back on her pillow, groaning weakly.
In a few moments, the telephone RINGS.

33.   ECU MISS ELVA

Her breath snuffs off. The o.s. RINGING permeates the darkness, surrounding her with a cloud of ear-lancing vibration. She reaches out to put the receiver on the table, then jerks back her hand. She tenses herself and reaches out cautiously for the RINGING telephone, CAMERA DRAWING AWAY from the movement of her hand, STOPPING as the hand hovers above the receiver in close f.g. Abruptly, Miss Elva picks up the receiver, sets it down and reaches for the cradle arm. Her hand freezes as the mans VOICE starts to speak.

34.   ECU MISS ELVA

Listening to the o.s. sound of the man's VOICE on the telephone, the words not distinguishable. They repeat several times before Miss Elva, holding herself in tight check, draws the receiver to her ear.

                    VOICE
                (dully; pitifully)
        Where are you? I want to talk to you.

Claws of ice clamp down on Miss Elva's breath-shuddering chest. She lies petrified, unable to cut off the sound of the man's dull, expressionless voice.

                    VOICE
        Where are you? I want to talk to you.

A sound fills Miss Elva's throat, thin and fluttering.

                    VOICE
        Where Are you? I want to talk to you.

                    MISS ELVA
    No. No.

                    VOICE
        Where are you? I want to talk to you.

                    MISS ELVA
                (screaming)
        Leave me alone!
                (beat)
        Leave me alone!

She presses down the cradle arm tautly, then drops the receiver. In a few moments, the HOWLING begins again. Miss Elva lies staring and immobile, listnening to it.

                                        CUT TO:

35.   INT. BEDROOM - CLOSE SHOT - MISS ELVA - DAY
(EARLY MORNING)

MISS ELVA
(wildly)
I tell you I won't have it!

CAMERA PULLS BACK to reveal her sitting inflexibly on
the bed, releasing her frightened anger into the telephone
receiver.

MISS ELVA
I've explained all that! Yes; he just waits
for me to hang up so he can call!

MISS FINCH
Why don't you leave the receiver off - ?

MISS ELVA
I left the receiver off all night! I can't do
it anymore! - the noise keeps me awake!
I haven't had a bit of sleep in twenty-four
hours!

MISS FINCH
Well, Miss Keene, you could have the
telephone disconnected -

MISS ELVA
I am an invalid, Miss Finch! I have to
have a bedside telephone in case of
emergency!
(shakily)
Now I want this line checked, do you
hear? I want this terrible thing stopped!

36.   ECU - MISS ELVA - TO BE INTERCUT WITH
SWITCHBOARD

> MISS FINCH'S VOICE
> (distressed)
> All right! Miss Keene. I'll put a man on
> it; right away.

> MISS ELVA
> (relieved)
> Thank you; thank you. Will you call me
> as soon as you find out anything?

> MISS FINCH'S VOICE
> Yes, Miss Keene. Of course.

> MISS ELVA
> (beat; fearfully)
> You will see to it, won't you?

> MISS FINCH'S VOICE
> First thing, Miss Keene. Don't you worry now.

> MISS ELVA
> Thank you.

She hangs up and leans back against the pillow, closes her
eyes.

DISSOLVE TO:

37.   INT. LIVINGROOM - WALL CLOCK - DAY

Three-twenty. CAMERA PANS to show Miss Elva and
Margaret playing a game of cards. Miss Elva keeps looking
at the clock impatiently.

(CONTINUED)

37.   CONTINUED

> MARGARET
>
> Your play.

> MISS ELVA
>
> What? Oh. . .

She plays a card, stares worriedly into her thoughts.
Margaret plays a card and Miss Elva looks at it, deliberates,
then plays one of her own. She looks at the clock again.

> MISS ELVA
> (tautly)
> What is the matter with that girl? She
> promised faithfully that a man would
> check on it today - and here the afternoon
> is almost over.

> MARGARET
>
> Maybe he doesn't have to check on it
> here, Miss Elva.

Miss Elva stares at Margaret, unconvinced.

> MARGARET (CONT'D)
>
> Your play.

Miss Elva looks at her cards. Abruptly, the phone RINGS,
making her hand twitch so hard that several of the cards
skid across the table. She looks at the phone in
apprehensive dread.

> MARGARET
>
> You want me to answer it?

(CONTINUED)

37.   CONTINUED

Miss Elva looks at her for several moments before nodding
jerkily. Margaret picks up the receiver.

>   MARGARET
>   Hello?
>   (listens)
>   No, this is Margaret Phillips. Here's
>   Miss Keene.

He holds out the receiver to Miss Elva.

>   MARGARET
>   It's Miss Finch.

With a quick, anxious breath, Miss Elva takes the receiver
from Margaret.

38.   ECU - MISS ELVA - TO BE INTERCUT WITH
       SWITCHBOARD

>   MISS ELVA
>   Yes?

>   MISS FINCH'S VOICE
>   (embarrassedly)
>   Uh. . .about those calls you say you've been
>   receiving, Miss Keene.

>   MISS ELVA
>   (beat; stunned)
>   <u>Say</u> I've been -

(CONTINUED)

38.   CONTINUED

                    MISS FINCH'S VOICE
                        (cutting in)
            We sent a man out to trace them. I have
            his report here.

                    MISS ELVA
                        (mutedly)
        And?

                    MISS FINCH'S VOICE
            He says he traced the difficulty to a fallen
            wire on the edge of town.

                    MSS ELVA
                    (not understanding)
        Fallen-wire?

                    MISS FINCH'S VOICE
                        (unhappily)
        Yes, Miss Keene.

39.   MISS ELVA AND MARGARET

                    MISS ELVA
                        (tensely)
        Are you telling me that there were no calls?

Margaret frowns uneasily.

40.   ECU - MISS ELVA

                    MISS FINCH'S VOICE
                        (apologetically)
            There's no way anyone could have called
            from that location, Miss Keene.

                                    (CONTINUED)

40.   CONTINUED

                    MISS ELVA
                   (overlapping)
        I tell you a man called me!
           (as Miss Finch remains silent)
        There must be a phone there! There must
        be some way for him to call me!

                MISS FINCH'S VOICE
        Miss Keene, the wire is lying on the
        ground; tomorrow our crew will put - it
        back up and you won't be -

                    MISS ELVA
                    (rigidly)
        There must be some way he could call
        me.

                MISS FINCH'S VOICE
                (patience failing)
        But, there is no one out there.

                    MISS ELVA
        Out where? - where?!

                MISS FINCH'S VOICE
                (beat; softly)
        Miss Keene, it's the cemetery.

Miss Elva reacts to this almost in slow motion, drawing the
receiver from her head to stare at it in appalled,
unbelieving horror.

                MARGARET'S VOICE
        What is it, Miss Keene?

                                    (CONTINUED)

40.   CONTINUED

Miss Elva's fingers seem to uncurl of their own accord and
the receiver drops OUT OF FRAME. She stares at her
open palm which begins to tremble more and more
violently until she presses it to her head. Lips parted, her
expression one of dumb shock, she stares at Margaret.

                    MARGARET'S VOICE
              What is it?
                         (beat)
              What's wrong, Miss Keene?

                                              CUT TO:

41.   EXT. COUNTRY ROAD - DAY

Margaret Phillips' coupe moves along the road, occupied by
the nurse and Miss Elva.

42.   POV - MOVING SHOT - CEMETARY

The coupe is starting to pass it. It shows signs of storm
damage; fallen limbs and branches, etc.

43.   INT. COUPE - MISS ELVA AND MARGARET

The car comes to a halt. Miss Elva in f.g., dressed, sitting
tautly erect and staring ahead, her hands gripped together
on her lap. Margaret, in b.g., glances over at her.

                    MARGARET
              I wish you'd tell me why you want to
              come out here, Miss Keene.
                         (beat)

                                      (CONTINUED)

43.   CONTINUED

MARGARET (CONT'D)
This isn't good for you. If you hadn't
made such a to-do about it, I'd have
never taken you in the first place.
(beat)
What can there possibly be out here for
you to see?

Miss Elva slowly turns her face toward CAMERA, her
expression one of rigid containment as she looks at -

44.   CLOSE SHOT - MISS ELVA

Staring at the o.s. cemetery which is reflected on the
window.

45.   EXT. CEMETARY - CLOSE ON GATE POST PLAQUE

Reading; Valleyview Cemetery. CAMERA PANS to show
the coupe parked and nurse Phillips just completing the
transfer of Miss Elva from the car to the wheelchair.

46.   MISS ELVA AND MARGARET

Margaret finishes tucking a blanket around Miss Elva's legs
and, straightening up, looks inquiringly at her. Miss Elva is
gazing fixedly at something o.s.

MARGARET
(finally)
Miss Keene?

Miss Elva twitches and looks at Margaret, then back o.s.

(CONTINUED)

46.   CONTINUED

MISS ELVA
Over there.

A worried Margaret gets behind the wheelchair and begins
to push. Just as Miss Elva moves into CLOSE SHOT, the
CAMERA starts to DRAW AHEAD of her. Her gaze rises
uneasily.

47.   POV SHOT - TELEPHONE POLE

A wire is hanging from it. CAMERA DOWNPANS along
its drooping arc.

48.   MOVING CLOSE SHOT - MISS ELVA

Just able to hold herself under control as her eyes follow the
wire.

49.   PAN SHOT - WIRE

CAMERA MOVING SLOWLY along its length, following
it across the grass. Its end lies on top of a grave.
CAMERA UP PANS quickly to reveal the time-worn
gravestone: BRIAN DOUGLAS/1905-1932.

50.   CLOSE ON MISS ELVA

With a gasp of dread and anguish, she clutches a hand
across her eyes and, unable to contain the tension any
longer, releases it in sobbing tears.

MARGARET'S VOICE
Miss Keene!

(CONTINUED)

50.   CONTINUED

>   MISS ELVA
>   It's him!

CAMERA DRAWS AROUND to include Margaret as she
leans over worriedly to look at Miss Elva in concern.

>   MARGARET
>   Miss Keene, what's the matter?

>   MISS ELVA
>   (brokenly)
>   It's him. Brian.

>   MARGARET
>   Who? What are you talking about?

>   MISS ELVA
>   (overlapping)
>   Brian!
>   (beat)
>   My fiancé.

>   MARGARET
>   (stupefied)
>   Your - ?

>   MISS ELVA
>   He died a week before we were to be
>   married.

CAMERA MOVES IN SLOWLY on her haunted face until
it is in ECU.

(CONTINUED)

50.   CONTINUED

>   MISS ELVA
> We were in a car together. I insisted on
> driving. I was always - <u>insisting</u> on
> things, telling him what I wanted;
> dominating him. He always did what I
> said; always.
>   (pause; painfully)
> I lost control of the car - steered it right
> into a tree. Brian went through the
> windshield.
>   (eyes closing)
> He was cut to pieces.
>   (beat)
> I was crippled.
>   (pause; tensely)
> And now he's trying to reach me.

After a while, her expression begins to alter slowly,
changing to one of, almost, happiness, albeit a deranged
kind of happiness. She opens her eyes, a faint smile
quivering on her lips as she looks at the gravestone.

>   MISS ELVA
>   (seeing it differently now)
> Now he's trying to reach me.

51.   ANGLE OVER GRAVESTONE - MISS ELVA AND
       MARGARET

Margaret looking at her uneasily.

>   MISS ELVA
>   (with an eerie tone)
> I can talk to him.
>   (pause)
> <u>I</u> <u>won't</u> <u>be</u> <u>lonely</u> <u>any</u> <u>more</u>.

                                        DISSOLVE TO:

52.   INT. BEDROOM - MISS ELVA AND MARGARET -
       NIGHT

Miss Elva in a state of tautly repressed exhilaration which is
turning into anger due to Margaret's frustrating presence.

                    MARGARET
                    (worriedly)
        Miss Keene, I can't leave you like this.

                    MISS ELVA
                (overlapping; tensely)
        I'll be all right, Margaret. Good night.
                    (cutting her off)
        Good night, Margaret.

Margaret starts to speak, then gives up and moves toward
the door. There, she stops and looks back.

                    MARGARET
        You call me if you need me now.

                    MISS ELVA
                    (overlapping)
        Yes; I will.

                    MARGARET
        I'll be home all -

                    MISS ELVA
                    (interrupting)
        Yes, Margaret; yes. Good night.

Margaret looks at her, disturbed. Again, she starts to speak,
then decides there is no point to it and, sighing, leaves.

55.   CLOSE UP - MISS ELVA

Waiting tensely, breath quickening; as she listens to the o.s.
SOUND of Margaret closing the front door, then, afterward,
the car door. The car MOTOR starts and the coupe is
driven away. Miss Elva looks eagerly at the telephone,
then, after a while, lifts it off the table and sets it on her lap.
Her breathing continues to be erratic as she stares at the
phone, almost willing it to ring. Moments pass but the
telephone doesn't ring. Miss Elva's hand twitches
empathically with her urge to pick up the receiver and talk
to Brian. Finally, the suspense is too much for her and she
picks up the receiver quickly.

                    MISS ELVA
          Brian?
                    (pause)
          Brian, are you there?
            (as she hears only the DIAL TONE)
          Can you hear me, Brian? It's Elva.
                    (beat)
          Elva.

She winces as the HOWLING sound commences on the
telephone. Abruptly, she hangs up and stares at the
receiver, her anxiety increasing by the moment. She starts
to make infinitesimal sobbing noises in her throat.
Abruptly, she picks up the receiver again.

                    MISS ELVA
               (more desperately)
          Brian?
                    (beat)
          Where are you?
                 (beat; tightly)
          Where are you, Brian? Can't you hear me?

                                   (CONTINUED)

55.   CONTINUED

She listens intently. After a while, the HOWLING starts
again. She grimaces, starts to hang up again, then,
suddenly, jerks the receiver to her ear again the CAMERA
MOVING IN until her face is in ECU. The howling has
ceased; there is, instead, complete silence on the phone.

                    MISS ELVA
          (with appropriate pauses; excitedly)
          Brian? Are you there? Brian? If you're
          there, please talk to me. It's Elva. Elva.
          You can talk to me now. I didn't know it
          was you. I thought. . .Brian, please talk
          to me. I know you're there. It's Elva -
          Elva! Talk to me, Brian! Please! Talk to
          me!

                    VOICE
          You. . .said. . .leave you alone.

Miss Elva's face stiffens with shocked dread.

                    VOICE
          I. . .always do. . .what you say.

Miss Elva listens but there is no more.

                    MISS ELVA
          Oh, but I - didn't mean. . .Brian, I didn't
          mean that -

She breaks off as the dial tone starts to BUZZ again.

                    MISS ELVA
          No Brian! Brian, don't go! Don't leave
          me! I didn't know it was you! I didn't
          mean to say - !

                              (CONTINUED)

55.   CONTINUED

She breaks off as the HOWLING starts on the receiver.

> MISS ELVA
> (in total agony)
> BRIAN!!

She begins to cry dementedly as the CAMERA DRAWS BACK from her, ACROSS the bedroom and OUT THROUGH the window.

> SERLING'S VOICE
> According to the Bible, God created the
> Heaven and the earth. It is man's
> prerogative - and woman's - to create
> their own particular and private hell.
> Case in point: Miss Elva Keene who, in
> every sense, has made her own bed and,
> now, must lie in it - sadder but wiser by
> dint of a rather painful lesson in
> responsibility - transmitted from the
> Twilight Zone.

FADE OUT:

THE END

54.   TITLE BACK FOR END CREDITS

Spur of the Moment

Looking back over his contributions to the series, Matheson believes that the final season had more favorites of his than any other season.

As fate would have it, however, the only original script he wrote for the fifth season also was to be his very last. Not that he had ever purposely intended it to be. But a new producer, William Froug, had stepped in to replace Bert Granet, and Matheson and Froug had creatively never seen eye to eye. This lack of mutual appreciation had been going on for several years, back to the time when he and Charles Beaumont had first decided to collaborate on scripts for other television series.

"We were so inundated with requests for meetings and everything else, we had decided to collaborate. So for a long time we worked on a number of shows together: *Have Gun Will Travel, Wanted: Dead or Alive, Philip Marlowe.* I offered to write the first drafts of the scripts if he would go out and take the meetings, because I didn't like being bothered to go to all these meetings.

"But it backfired in a number of cases. Particularly with William Froug, who I think was producing *Philip Marlowe* at the time. He became convinced I was the poor country cousin that Beaumont was carrying. So when he got control of *The Twilight Zone* in its last year, I believe he was the one who canceled one of my previously accepted scripts. Which in hindsight I'm glad he did, because years later it was done for *Amazing Stories,* and there it really turned out beautifully.

"I can only surmise—it was during that time that Beaumont was taking all the meetings—that Froug assumed I was really not that capable as a writer. I don't why he felt that way about my work, but that's how it was. If Bert Granet had stayed as producer, I probably would have written a couple of others. I mean, Granet was the one who chose 'The Doll.' But as I've said, I'm just as glad Froug dumped it, because it turned out really beautifully years later." (See Epilogue.)

Once again, the concept of time travel was behind the original inspiration for this script, in which following the path of true love does not necessarily insure a happy ending. Matheson is endlessly intrigued by the theme. "The enigma of time, and what you can do with it, the games you can play as a writer are always interesting. The idea came to me by concentrating on one figure in the story, and then ending up with the same situation repeated, only now your emphasis is on the other figure."

Once again, there's a very effective zapper at the end, one which obliterates any hope of there being a traditional happy ending. For here the main character does ultimately choose the man of her dreams, and wakes up twenty years later to realize her choice was a nightmare.

"I'm sure that happens to a lot of people," Matheson confesses. "Probably more people than not go by the heart rather than the head. Which is perfectly understandable at that age. And they often make terrible mistakes. But who could expect a young person to calculatedly figure out which of two suitors was the best one?"

And the not so subtle irony hidden in that title?

Matheson freely admits, "I love that title! She married on the 'spur of the moment,' really. She married from emotion. And there was also the spurs of the person riding the horse...there were multiple and hidden meanings in that title, which is something I like to do. Titles are very important, and it's really nice if you can get a good one. As a writer, I prefer to have the title occur to me instantly—even sometimes before I do the story. It colors how I approach the story, and I feel much more comfortable."

In hindsight, Matheson is fairly satisfied with the way his last episode for the show finally turned out. "The only part that really bothered me was that, at the beginning—the opening scene—I felt that they should not have showed a close-up of Diana Hyland's face as the forty-three year-old woman. Because I thought—and maybe I was wrong—that it would give away the whole thing."

And now, reflecting on a television series which has since become an icon of popular culture around the world, his episodes rerun endlessly, how does he sum up the experience?

"It was a wonderful experience, and it makes me wish that at the time I knew what was going to happen to us." Matheson sighs wistfully. "We were just a bunch of guys writing a bunch of scripts, trying to make them as good as we could in a field that we were supposedly expert at."

SPUR OF THE MOMENT

PERFORMANCE DATE: 2/21/64

PRODUCER: BERT GRANET

DIRECTOR: ELLIOT SILVERSTEIN

CAST:

ANN HENDERSON: DIANA HYLAND

ROBERT BLAKE: ROBERT HOGAN

DAVID MITCHELL: ROGER DAVIS

MR. HENDERSON: PHILIP OBER

MRS. HENDERSON: MARSHA HUNT

REYNOLDS: JACK RAINE

FADE IN:

1.   EXT. COUNTRY MANSION - DAY

ANNE MARIE HENDERSON, 18 and lovely, emerges from the house and crosses to where the GROOM is waiting with her saddled horse. Smiling distractedly at the groom, she mounts and rides off.

2.   EXT. ESTATE GROUNDS – SERIES OF SHOTS

Riding through the beautiful countryside, lost in thought.

3.   LONG SHOT - ANNE

Approaching CAMERA, she slows her horse to a walk; as she reaches f.g., CAMERA DRAWS AHEAD of her. After several moments, she pulls her mount up, looking o.s. in consternation. As, suddenly she becomes aware of

4.   POV SHOT – WOMAN ON HORSEBACK

Posed on a ridge ahead, looking down at Anne; a woman in her early forties. CAMERA ZOOMS IN on her frighteningly malignant features.

5.   ANNE

Staring at the woman apprehensively, her mount shifting and nickering in alarm. She starts to back off instinctively.

6.   POV SHOT - WOMAN

Abruptly, she whips her horse forward, driving it down the rise, CAMERA PANNING to reveal that she is riding straight at Anne.

ANNE

Frozen with stricken indecision; then, in an instant, jerking her horse around and galloping away in dread. Shortly afterward, the woman rides INTO FRAME pursuing her.

8. CLOSE MOVING SHOT - ANNE

Face twisted by fear as she flees from the woman. Now she looks across her shoulder.

9. POV SHOT - WOMAN

Whipping her horse mercilessly as she gallops after Anne in a manner that indicates intent to kill or maim. She is shouting something but is too far off to be heard.

10. MOVING SHOT - ANNE

Looking toward the front again, and, driven to desperation by rising panic, whipping her horse. CAMERA DRAWS AROUND to include the woman following in b.g., still shouting, then MOVES IN until Anne is in CLOSE-UP. Her expression strained as she flees the o.s. woman.

> SERLING'S VOICE
> This is the face of terror:
> Anne Marie Henderson, eighteen years
> of age – her young, ingenous existence
> suddenly marred by a savage and wholly
> unanticipated pursuit.

11. SERLING

> SERLING
> Miss Henderson has no idea whatever as
> to the motive for this pursuit; worse, not

11.   CONTINUED

the vaguest notion regarding the identity
of her pursuer. Soon enough she will be
given the solution to this two-fold
mystery but in a manner far beyond her
present capacity to understand; a manner
enigmatically bizarre in terms of time and
space. Which is to say: an answer from
the Twilight Zone.

FADE OUT:

FIRST COMMERICAL

FADE IN: (HOLD 20 FEET FOR OPENING TITLES)

12.   EXT. MANSION - DAY

A Rolls-Royce parked in front of it. CAMERA PANS to
show Anne as she rides her horse up at full speed and jumps
to the ground, letting the horse run off, untended, while she
dashes for the house, still terrified. (NOTE: The year is
1940 but within the bounds of accuracy, nothing should be
seen which might not, also, identify the period as the
present.)

13.   INT. LIVING ROOM – MR. HENDERSON

In his middle forties, well-dressed and distinguished
looking; a pipe between his lips. He is standing at the
french doors, back turned to CAMERA. O.s., Mrs.
Henderson and Robert Blake are CHATTING.

HENDERSON
What in the name of - ?

MRS. HENDERSON'S VOICE
What is it?

(CONTINUED)

13.   CONTINUED

Mr. Henderson turns toward CAMERA.

MR. HENDERSON
(disturbed)
Anne just came riding back as though the
devil himself were chasing her.

14.   MRS. HENDERSON AND ROBERT BLAKE

Mrs. Henderson, an attractive matron in her early forties,
Blake, a good-looking man in his middle twenties. They
are sitting on a sofa together, looking toward the o.s.
Henderson.

MRS. HENDERSON
(concerned)
Really?

They both look toward the front hall, Robert standing.

ROBERT
(worriedly)
I wonder what's wrong.

15.   FRONT HALL – ANGLE THROUGH DOORSIDE
WINDOW

The car not visible at this angle.   Anne comes dashing up
the porch steps and races to the door, CAMERA PANNING
as she enters the house, closing the door by leaning back
against it in gasping exhaustion, her expression one of
haunted dread. After several moments, Robert speaks o.s.

ROBERT'S VOICE
Anne?

(CONTINUED)

15.   CONTINUED

She twitches, gasping as she looks toward the living room.
Seeing who it is, her expression alters to one of tearful
anguish.

> ANNE
> (piteously)
Bob...

She hesitates momentarily, as if uncertain whether to seek
his particular comfort; then distress overrides uncertainty
and she starts running toward him, CAMERA
WITHDRAWING as she does to reveal that the hall has
been lavishly decorated for a party. CAMERA STOPS as
Anne throws herself against Robert and he puts his arms
around her. Mrs. Henderson emerges from the room,
followed by her husband.

> ROBERT
> (alarmed, but trying to soothe Anne)
> Hey...hey; what's the matter?

She cannot answer, clinging to him, letting out her fear in
great, racking sobs.

> ROBERT (CONT'D)
> (sounding more disturbed)
Anne.

Mrs. Henderson comes close to Anne and looks at her
uneasily.

> MRS. HENDERSON
> Darling, what is it?

Henderson takes hold of his daughter's arm.

(CONTINUED)

15.   CONTINUED

> MR. HENDERSON
> What happened, baby?

> ANNE
> (barely able to speak)
> There was a w-w-woman out there!

> MRS HENDERSON
> (confused)
> Woman?

> MR. HENDERSON
> What woman?

> ANNE
> (disjointedly)
> I-I don't know! I never saw her before.
> (sobs)
> It was horrible!

> ROBERT
> (tensely)
> What did she do?

> ANNE
> She chased me! She was on horseback
> too – and she chased me as hard as she
> could!

> ANNE (CONT'D)
> (beat; brokenly)
> I-I think if she'd caught me, she w-would
> have killed me!

(CONTINUED)

15.   CONTINUED

> MRS HENDERSON
> (appalled)
>
> What?

> ANNE
> The way she looked at me!

> MR. HENDERSON
> (suddenly all business)
> Where was this?

> ANNE
> I-I don't –

> MR. HENDERSON
> (overlapping urgently)
> Try to remember.

> MRS. HENDERSON
> John, don't you think we'd better -?

> MR. HENDERSON
> (ignoring his wife)
> Was it where you usually ride? Out
> beyond the meadow?

> ANNE
> I-I-I think...
> (nods)
> Yes.

Mr. Henderson pats his daughter's arm.

(CONTINUED)

15.   CONTINUED

> MR. HENDERSON
> (crisply assuring)
> All right, baby. I'll take care of it.

He moves back into the living room, a man who knows
exactly how to proceed in any emergency.

> ROBERT
> (patting Anne's back)
> Shhh. It's all over now, honey.
> Everything's going to be all right.

> MRS. HENDERSON
> Poor darling. What a <u>fright</u> you must have
> had.

Anne makes an effort to get herself under control, Robert
drying her eyes with his handkerchief.

> ROBERT
> (gently)
> There we go. All over now.

He steers her toward the living room.

> ROBERT (CONT'D)
> Come on.

> ANNE
> It was so frightening. She just...<u>rode</u> at
> me – with such a look of...<u>hatred</u>.

(CONTINUED)

15.   CONTINUED

MRS. HENDERSON
(upset)
I don't understand.
(pause)
You've never seen her before?

ANNE
(pained)
No.

16.   INT. LIVING ROOM

Mr. Henderson in f.g., talking into the telephone. In b.g., Robert leads in Anne, Mrs. Henderson walking close beside her. They settle her on the sofa, sitting on each side of her to comfort her with words and touches.

MR. HENDERSON
(into phone)
Take the gardener with you; it's possible that she's insane.
(beat)
Yes. When you find her, bring her to the house immediately.
(beat)
Immediately.

He presses down the button, then dials the operator, waits a moment.

MR. HENDERSON (CONT'D)
(a quiet order)
Get me the police.

17.   ANOTHER ANGLE

Anne, Robert and Mrs. Henderson in f.g.; in b.g., Mr.
Henderson at the telephone. (Also in b.g., French doors
leading to a terrace.)

                    ROBERT
        Better now?

                     ANNE
                (nods feebly)
        I'll be all right.
                (catching breath)
        It was just so...unexpected. One second,
        I'm alone; the next -
                (gesturing upward)
        -there she was...up on a hill – glaring
        at me.
                (voice breaking)
        Then she – started down the hill –
        whipping her horse.

Mrs. Henderson puts her cheek to Anne's.

                MRS. HENDERSON
                (interrupting gently)
        Shh, darling. You don't have to tell us
        about it anymore. Try to forget it.

                     ANNE
        I can't.
                (beat)
        I just don't understand. Who is she?
        Why did she chase me like that?

(CONTINUED)

17.   CONTINUED

> ROBERT
> (assuringly)
> We'll find out. I'm sure your father's
> calling the police right now.

> ANNE
> I can't imagine where she came from.

> ROBERT
> (trying to cheer her; with a grin)
> Maybe it was a warning, huh?

SUBDUED DIALOGUE FOR SCENE 17

> MR. HENDERSON
> (into phone)
> This is John Henderson up at the Spires.
> My daughter Anne was just attacked by a
> woman on horseback.
> (listens; answers)
> On our property. My daughter was out
> riding when she came across this woman -
> (breaks off; answers)
> On the meadow. It runs roughly parallel
> to the old Granite Road – there's a gate
> just past the cross-road you can –
> (breaks off; answers)
> Yes, that's right!
> (listens; answers stiffly)
> No; my daughter was able to outride her
> – which is, of course, beside the point.
> I've sent two of my staff out to find her
> but I will, naturally, wish her arrested
> when and if she's -
> (breaks off; listens; answers)

(CONTINUED)

17.   CONTINUED

> MR. HENDERSON (CONT'D)
> Thank you. As soon as possible if you will.

> ANNE
> (distractedly)

Warning!

> ROBERT

Mm-hmm.
> (teasing)
> You're sure you're telling us everything?

> ANNE
> (confused)

What?

> ROBERT
> You're sure she wasn't carrying a sign in
> her hand that read: <u>Cancel</u> <u>that</u>
> <u>engagement</u> <u>party</u> (?) <u>Don't</u> <u>marry</u> <u>that</u>
> <u>investment banker</u> <u>from</u> <u>New York</u> (?)
> <u>Yours</u> <u>truly,</u> <u>Fate.</u> (?)

> ANNE
> (tightly)
> Please don't joke about it, Bob; it wasn't
> funny.

> BOB
> (gently)
> I'm sorry, Anne, I was only trying to
> cheer you up.

They all look around at Mr. Henderson who has replaced
the telephone receiver and walked into f.g.

(CONTINUED)

17.   CONTINUED

> MR. HENDERSON
> All set; we'll find her.
> (smiles)
> Feeling better?

> ANNE
> (nodding with a smile)
> Yes, father.

> MR. HENDERSON
> Good.
> (to Robert)
> Wouldn't do to have a red-eyed fiance at
> the party tonight, would it?

> ROBERT
> (mock serious)
> Certainly wouldn't

18.   ANOTHER ANGLE

Mr. Henderson settles in a nearby chair and commences to
re-light his pipe.

> MR. HENDERSON
> Tell us about this woman now. You have
> no idea, at all, who she might be?

> ANNE
> No, Daddy.

> MRS. HENDERSON
> She must have ridden onto our property by mistake.

(CONTINUED)

18.   CONTINUED

>   MR. HENDERSON
>   (critically)
>   Mistake?

>   ROBERT
>   That's right, Mrs. Henderson. If she were
>   on the property by mistake, why should
>   she attack Anne?

Mrs. Henderson looks distressed as she recognizes the truth of this.

>   MR. HENDERSON
>   (to Anne)
>   Did she shout at you?

>   ANNE
>   Yes, but – she was too far away; I didn't
>   hear what she was saying.
>   (pause)
>   I know she wanted to kill me though.

>   ROBERT
>   You're just assuming that, honey.

>   ANNE
>   (shaking her head)
>   No.
>   (beat)
>   She wanted to kill me.

They all look around as there is a KNOCK on the o.s. front door, Anne gasping with renewed dread.

(CONTINUED)

18.   CONTINUED

> MR. HENDERSON
> (amused)
> I doubt if she followed you all the way
> home, baby.

> ANNE
> (irrational with fear)
> What if she did?

> MR. HENDERSON
> Let's hope she did; save us the trouble of
> looking for her.
> (beat)
> Now where, exactly, did this happen?

Anne is looking worriedly toward the hall.

> MR. HENDERSON (CONT'D)
> Anne?

> ANNE
> (looking at him)
> Aren't you going to look?

> MR. HENDERSON
> (smiling cooly)
> Whoever it is, Reynolds will let them in.

> ANNE
> I know but –

> MR. HENDERSON
> Come on now, baby, where did it happen?

> ANNE
> Well; it was –

(CONTINUED)

18.   CONTINUED

She breaks off as, o.s., the sound of Reynolds'
FOOTSTEPS is heard.

                    MR. HENDERSON
        Yes?

                        ANNE
        Uh…beyond the meadow, out near that –
        fallen oak; you know. Where the –
        stream –

She breaks off as the o.s. front door is opened. VOICES are
heard indistinguishably, those of David and Reynolds, the
butler. Anne looks worriedly in that direction.

ON STAGE ACTION

                        ROBERT
        No mysterious woman, I'm afraid.
                (beat, drily)
        Unless she's a baritone.

                        ANNE
                (catching her breath)
        That sounds like -

OFFSTAGE DIALOGUE

                    REYNOLDS' VOICE
        Yes, Mr. Mitchell?

                    DAVID'S VOICE
        I want to see Miss Henderson.

                                    (CONTINUED)

18.   CONTINUED

REYNOLDS' VOICE
I'm sorry sir, but Mr. Henderson has
given strict orders that I'm not to -

DAVID'S VOICE
(flaring)
I said I want to see Miss Henderson!

ANNE
(stunned)
David.

Stiffening, Mr. Henderson stands abruptly and heads for the
front hall. Robert stands to follow but Mr. Henderson
waves him back.

MR. HENDERSON
I'll take care of it.

ANNE
(pleadingly)
Father...?

He pays no attention but moves out of the room without
hesitation.

MRS. HENDERSON
Oh, dear.
(to Anne)
I thought everything was ended.

ANNE
(unconvincingly)
It is, Mother. I didn't know he was –
(coming here.)

She breaks off as Robert looks at her; she avoids meeting
his eyes.

(CONTINUED)

18.   CONTINUED

> ROBERT
> Anne?

As if meaning to forestall discussion, Anne stands and moves toward the hall.

> MRS. HENDERSON
> (fearfully)
> Now, Anne, you stay away from him.

> ANNE
> (distractedly)
> I will, Mother.

Mrs. Henderson and Robert look at each other, she with embarrassed apology, he with an attempted smile. He stands and follows Anne.

19.   INT. FRONT HALL – ANGLE ON FRONT DOOR

David is trying to push past Reynolds. He is a young, darkly handsome man.

> DAVID
> Get out of my way.

> REYNOLDS
> I'm sorry, Mr. Mitchell, but I'm not at
> liberty to admit you.

David looks toward Mr. Henderson as the older man ENTERS FRAME determinedly, gesturing, with his head, for Reynolds to leave.

(CONTINUED)

19.   (CONTINUED)

>   MR. HENDERSON
>   All right, Reynolds.

Reynolds retreats discreetly as Mr. Henderson takes his place and blocks David's path.

>   MR. HENDERSON (CONT'D)
>   (coldly)
>   You're not welcome in this house,
>   Mr. Mitchell.

>   DAVID
>   (tensely)
>   I came to see Anne.

>   MR. HENDERSON
>   She doesn't care to see you.

>   DAVID
>   Are you making all her decisions now?!

Mr. Henderson starts to close the door but David pushes it back open.

20.   ANGLE ON LIVING ROOM DOORWAY – ANNE
       AND ROBERT

Anne looking strickenly toward David. Robert looks at her and, noting her expression, reacts disturbedly.

21.   MR. HENDERSON AND DAVID

>   MR. HENDERSON
>   (restraining his anger with effort)
>   Would you rather I called the police?

>   (CONTINUED)

21.   CONTINUED

                    DAVID
        Call who you will! I'm here to see Anne!

He starts by Mr. Henderson who clamps a hand rigidly over his
wrist.

                MR. HENDERSON
        What does it take to convince you, Mr.
        Mitchell? Prosecution?

                    DAVID
                  (quietly)
        Just a few words from your daughter, Mr.
        Henderson.

Henderson glares at him, then, abruptly, flings down David's
wrist.

                MR. HENDERSON
        Hear them then; if that's the only way we can
        be rid of you.

22.   INT. LIVING ROOM

Anne turns back in distress, starts moving across the room.

                    ROBERT
        Anne.

She pays no attention and he moves after her, grabbing her arm.

                ROBERT (CONT'D)
        Anne.
                  (quietly)
        It is over between you and him; isn't it?

                                    (CONTINUED)

22.   CONTINUED

> ANNE
>
> Yes, Robert. I just don't want to see him,
> that's all.

She breaks off and they both look around as David comes
in, followed by Mr. Henderson. Paying no attention to
Robert, David walks up to Anne.

> DAVID
>
> It's not too late, Anne.

> ANNE
> (averting her face)
> David, please...

> DAVID
>
> It's not too late, Anne.

> ROBERT
> (tautly)
> Only a blind man could convince himself
> of that.

> DAVID
> (glaring at Robert)
> I wasn't talking to you.

> ROBERT
> (rigidly calm)
> That's right; I was talking to you.

> DAVID (CONT'D)
> (gripping her arms; pleadingly)
> We belong together, Anne; you know
> that.

(CONTINUED)

22.   CONTINUED

> DAVID (CONT'D)
> Don't let your father force you into this.
> Don't make this mistake with your life!
> Break your engagement.

> ANNE
> (mutedly)
> I can't, David.

> DAVID
> (overlapping)
> You broke ours!

Robert starts toward him, then holds himself as Mr.
Henderson restrains him, still keeping his eye on his watch.

> DAVID (CONT'D)
> (pleading again)
> Please, Anne – marry me.
> (beat)
> We always knew that we'd be married;
> even when we were children.
> (beat; passionately)
> You belong with me, Anne!

> ANNE
> (sorrowfully)
> Oh, David...don't.

Mr. Henderson lowers his watch.

> MR HENDERSON
> (pause; quietly)
> Time...Mr. Mitchell.
> (looking up)
> Get out.

(CONTINUED)

22.   CONTINUED

>   DAVID
>   (tensing)
>   I'm not through yet.

>   MR. HENDERSON
>   (casually)
>   You're through.

He starts toward the phone and walks OUT OF FRAME.
David, suddenly desperate, grabs Anne, trying to embrace her.

>   DAVID
>   Anne!

Robert has had enough. Moving forward quickly he grabs
David's arm and wrenches him away from Anne. Whirling,
David smashes a fist into Robert's jaw, knocking him
backward to the floor. Mrs. Henderson gasps in shock,
rising to her feet.

David glares, almost frenziedly, toward Robert, starting for
him; then, as Anne lurches for the door, turns back and
clutches at her arm.

>   DAVID (CONT'D)
>   Anne!

>   ANNE
>   (begging)
>   Please!

>   MR. HENDERSON
>   (tightly)
>   Hold steady, Mr. Mitchell.

They look around, reacting.

>   (CONTINUED)

22.   CONTINUED

                        ANNE
        Father, no!

23.   MR. HENDERSON

    Standing by the telephone table – its top drawer pulled out
    – a pistol in his hand.

                    MR. HENDERSON
            I think you will leave now.

24.   ANOTHER ANGLE - EVERYONE

    Mrs. Henderson helping Robert to his feet. David starts to
    say something but Mr. Henderson cuts him off.

                    MR. HENDERSON
            Don't think for a moment, Mr. Mitchell,
            that I won't use this.
                    (teeth clenching)
            To the contrary.

                        ANNE
                    (pitifully)
            Don't hurt him, Father.

                    DAVID
                    (to Anne)
            You want this?
                    (beat; with a bitter smile)
            To let your Father break us up at the
            point of a gun.

    Before he has finished, Anne whirls with a sob and runs for
    hallway. Mrs. Henderson starts after her. David suddenly
    runs for the hall as well. Mr. Henderson runs after him.

                    MR. HENDERSON
        Mitchell!

25.   INT. FRONT HALL

Anne rushes from the living room, crying, crosses the hall
and hurries up the staircase, the bannister railing of which is
close f.g. Mrs. Henderson follows. David comes out of the
living room and runs to the railing, looking up.

                        DAVID
                       (agonized)
          Anne!

Mr. Henderson, then Robert, runs from the living room,
Henderson prepared to fire when he sees that David is
motionless at the bannister railing, head bowed in grief. He
walks over to him, breathing hard.

                    MR. HENDERSON
          And now, if you will have the common
          courtesy and sense to leave this house...

David looks at him and Robert, a glimmer of tears in his
eyes. Turning away, he moves to the door, CAMERA
PANNING to follow his despairing exit.

26.   MR. HENDERSON AND ROBERT

Mr. Henderson lowers the pistol as the o.s. door CLOSES.

                        ROBERT
                       (sighs)
          You know, I – almost feel sorry for him.

                    MR. HENDERSON
                (looking at Robert; drily)
          But not quite, anh?

                                        (CONTINUED)

26.   CONTINUED

                    ROBERT
                  (fingering his jaw)
        Not quite.

Mr. Henderson smiles and puts his arm around the
shoulders of his prospective son-in-law.

                    MR. HENDERSON
        I think a good stiff drink is in order right
        now, don't you?

                    ROBERT
                  (grinning wryly)
        Amen.

They start for the living room and enter it, CAMERA
HOLDING, then PANNING SLOWLY toward the front
door. CAMERA STOPS, then begins to MOVE TOWARD
the door...

27.   DISSOLVING THROUGH

Several times until, finally CAMERA STOPS close by the
window through which we first saw Anne enter the house.
(CAMERA ANGLE is, once more, such that we do not
realize that now the car is no longer parked outside.) In
several moments, the strange woman comes riding up to the
house, dismounts, and ignoring the horse, moves toward the
house. She crosses the porch, CAMERA PANNING as she
opens the door and enters into CLOSEUP, closing the door
exactly as Anne did earlier – by leaning back against it. On
her hard, dissipated face, the same expression of haunted
dread.

                                        FADE OUT:
                  END OF ACT ONE

FADE IN:

28.   INT. FRONT HALL –CLOSE SHOT – WOMAN - DAY

Leaning against the door, a look of angry torment on her
face. After a while, she pushes away from the door and
walks slowly across the hall, CAMERA WITHDRAWING
to reveal that this is not the same hall we have seen in the
first act. There are no decorations now and there is, about
its appearance, an air of careless deterioration; some of the
more expensive furnishings are gone. CAMERA PANS to
follow the woman's weary movement to the living room.

29.   INT. LIVING ROOM – ANGLE FROM TELEPHONE
       TABLE

(The same angle as the scene in which Mr. Henderson was
seen in f.g. at the telephone.) The interior of this room is,
also, different; gone to seed. The woman enters and moves
to the table on which sits a tray with glasses and a decanter
of whiskey. Removing the top of the decanter, the woman
pours herself a long drink and swallows half of it in a single
gulp, grimacing at the taste. Now she opens a cigarette box
and removes one, lights it with a lighter, then moves to the
window. As she finishes the whiskey, there are slow
FOOTSTEPS o.s. She doesn't turn as they stop in the
living room doorway. A few moments pass; then –

                    MRS. HENDERSON'S VOICE
          Anne?

The woman closes her eyes, teeth gritted, as if she wishes to
avoid any discussion. Then, with a sigh, she opens her eyes
and turns.

                    ANNE
          What?

30.   MRS. HENDERSON

In her late sixties now; old, tired and sadly disillusioned.

> MRS. HENDERSON
> That lawyer phoned again.

31.   TWO SHOT – ANNE AND MRS. HENDERSON

Anne in b.g., looking at her mother. Now she moves for the whiskey decanter.

> MRS. HENDERSON
> Did you hear me? I said that lawyer
> phoned again.

> ANNE
> (disgustedly)
> Who gives a...?

32.   ANOTHER ANGLE

Reaching the table and pouring herself more whiskey.

> MRS. HENDERSON
> (tightly)
> Will that help?

> ANNE
> (snapping)
> Yes! It'll help.
> (pause; defeatedly)
> If I drink enough of it.

Mrs. Henderson watches in pained disapproval as Anne gulps down the whiskey with no sign of enjoying it but rather with the sole desire to get drunk. Anne grimaces, holds up the glass to look at it.

(CONTINUED)

32.   CONTINUED

                    ANNE (CONT'D)
                    (sardonically)
          Ambrosia.

                    MRS. HENDERSON
                    (tightly)
          They're going to take the house away
          from us, Anne.

                    ANNE
                    (disinterestedly)
          Are they really?

                    MRS. HENDERSON
          Yes.

                    ANNE
                    (sourly)
          They can have it.

                    MRS. HENDERSON
                    (approaching)
          That's all it means to you?

                    ANNE
                    (interrupting)
          That's all.

                    MRS. HENDERSON
                    (persisting)
          The home you were raised in?

                    ANNE
          Raised?

                                        (CONTINUED)

Richard Matheson

32.   CONTINUED

                    ANNE (CONT'D)
                        (beat)
            You mean <u>lowered</u>. Spoiled. Squeezed to
            death with a velvet glove.

                  MRS. HENDERSON
                      (offended)
              Are we starting that again?

                       ANNE
            We <u>started</u> it the day I was born.
                   (contemptuously)
            Father, dear, Father.

                  MRS. HENDERSON
                    (a brief anger)
            I won't hear you debase his memory.

        Anne laughs bitterly.

                       ANNE
                    (sarcastically)
              Debase his memory.
                       (beat)
              How cornball can you get?

                  MRS. HENDERSON
                    (injured again)
            How can you talk like that about your
            own father? – who gave you everything.
            Everything.

                       ANNE
            That's right – <u>gave</u> me everything. I
            never had to <u>earn</u> a bit of it.
                                        (CONTINUED)

32.   CONTINUED

> ANNE (CONT'D)
> Never had to work for anything in my life.
>> (bitterly)
> Never had to bother acquiring such useless traits as judgement – discrimination.
>>> (a somber laugh)
> Who needs 'em?
>>> (raising her glass)
> Cheers.

She drinks, wincing at the taste.

> MRS. HENDERSON
> You blame your father for - ?

> ANNE
>> (cutting in savagely)
> Yes! I blame my father!
>> (pause; tightly)
> Oh, he was so strong, wasn't he? So efficient, so meticulous. I was his baby. Sixteen, seventeen, <u>eighteen</u> years of age and I was his <u>baby</u>!
>> (turning away)
> With all the keen insights of a baby; all the capacity to understand – the ability to judge.

She stares moodily into her glass.

> ANNE (CONT'D)
> (beat; broodingly)
> So I made a mistake. A little mistake.

(CONTINUED)

32.   CONTINUED

> ANNE (CONT'D)
> (beat; sarcastically casual)
> Just enough to ruin my life.

Mrs. Henderson's intuitively generous nature responds to this and she puts her hand on Anne's arm. Anne pulls away and pours herself more whiskey.

> MRS. HENDERSON
> Anne, don't.

> ANNE
> Ah; how wonderful. I'm finally being disciplined...at the age of forty-three.

> MRS. HENDERSON
> (pause)
> What about the house, Anne?

> ANNE
> I don't care about the house, Mother.

> MRS. HENDERSON
> (distraught)
> Well, I care!

> ANNE
> (pause; somberly)
> That's your misfortune. And none of my own.

She drinks, turns and eyes her mother solemnly.

> ANNE (CONT'D)
> Do you know what I saw today?
> (pause)
> Do you?

(CONTINUED)

32.   CONTINUED

                    MRS. HENDERSON
        I –

                         ANNE
                    (overlapping)
        I saw a ghost, Mother.
                         (pause)
        My own.

                    MRS. HENDERSON
                    (uneasily)
        What?

                         ANNE
                    (interrupting)
        Intriguing, isn't it? To be haunted by
        one's own self.

    She turns away, her voice breaking.

                    ANNE (CONT'D)
        Positively intriguing.

                    MRS. HENDERSON
                    (confused)
        What are you talking about?

33.   ANOTHER ANGLE

    Anne in close f.g., gazing through the french doors with a
    lost expression; her mother in b.g. watching her.

                         ANNE
        I'm talking about ghosts, Mother.
        Phantoms, Visitations.

                              (CONTINUED)

33.   CONTINUED

> ANNE (CONT'D)
> (bitterly)
> Reminders from the past and the future.
> (pause)
> I was out riding – where I always go, out
> beyond the meadow. I was on a ridge when
> I saw this young girl riding toward me.

34.   ANNE

As she turns to face her mother.

> ANNE

Me.

35.   ANNE AND MRS. HENDERSON

> ANNE
> (pause)
> Me, Mother. As I looked at eighteen.
> (beat)
> You remember the day of my engagement
> party? June 13, 1941? I even remember
> the date. Do you recall how I came in,
> terrified, because a woman had attacked
> me? And Father had them search for her
> – in vain?
> (beat)
> I was that woman, Mother.
> (beat)
> I am that woman.

She takes a drink.

(CONTINUED)

35.   CONTINUED

> ANNE (CONT'D)
> (hauntedly amused)
> And you want to hear something funny?
> Something –
> (tormenting herself)
> <u>marvelously</u> funny?

36.   ECU - ANNE

> ANNE
> (whispering)
> <u>It's not the only time I've seen her</u>.

37.   ANNE AND MOTHER

> ANNE
> Isn't that bizarre? I keep seeing her again
> and again – keep seeing myself – just on
> that day, that – <u>one, particular day</u>.
> (she laughs weakly; a sick demented laugh)
> You know the expression- "Go chase
> yourself?" That's what I've been doing –
> <u>chasing myself</u>; trying to -

Abruptly, she begins to cry and turns away from her mother,
moving to the fireplace.

38.   ANNE AND MRS. HENDERSON

Anne in close f.g., at the fireplace; her mother in b.g.,
looking at her, partly in sympathy, partly in fright.

> ANNE
> You remember what Bob said that day?

(CONTINUED)

38.   CONTINUED

> ANNE (CONT'D)
> (pause)
> Maybe it's a warning, he said.
> (beat)
> He thought he was joking. But it <u>was</u> a
> warning. <u>I</u> <u>was</u> <u>warning</u> <u>myself</u> - not to
> marry the wrong man.
> (pause; bleakly)
> But I married him anyway; didn't I? And
> now I've paid the price. I've become the
> grotesque phantom that frightened that
> poor child-like girl half to death twenty-
> five years ago. A sterile, alcoholic
> phantom – married to a man who's run
> our estate into ruin.

39.   UP ANGLE SHOT – ANNE AND PAINTING OVER
MANTEL

Showing her as she was at eighteen.

> ANNE
> If only I'd known that I was being
> warned!
> DAVID'S VOICE
> (sourly drunk)
> Warned of what?

Anne turns quickly. CAMERA WHIP PANS to show David
in the doorway – an older, terribly dissolute looking David,
sloppily dressed, unshaven.

40.   FULL SHOT – THE THREE

Almost a tableau.

(CONTINUED)

40.   CONTINUED

                        DAVID
          Well?

With an agonized sob, Anne lunges to the french doors and, shoving them open, rushes outside.

                   DAVID (CONT'D)
                   (to Mrs. Henderson)
          What's the matter with her?

41.   CLOSE-UP - DAVID

                        DAVID
                      (cruelly)
          Can it be she doesn't _love_ me anymore?

42.   EXT. HOUSE - ANNE

Dashing to where her horse stands and mounting it quickly, riding off.

43.   SERIES OF SHOTS - ANNE

Riding across the countryside at full gallop, blinded by anguish.

44.   EXT. RIDGE - ANNE

Slowing her horse down, she walks it up the ridge, the tension relieved somewhat, by her wild gallop. As she reaches the peak of the ridge, she freezes, pulling in the reins convulsively as she sees-

45.   THE YOUNGER ANNE – POV FROM PEAK OF RIDGE

Approaching on horseback along the bridle path far below.
Suddenly she draws up, seeing the "strange woman" ahead.

46.   THE OLDER ANNE

Face contorted into the malignant expression we saw in
Shot #4 as she reacts in furious hatred to the cruelty of this
renewed visitation. Abruptly, she whips her horse down the
ridge, CAMERA PANNING to show her riding toward the
young girl below who after momentary hesitation, jerks her
horse around and gallops off.

47.   CLOSE MOVING SHOT – THE OLDER ANNE

Her immediate fury now converted to desperate anxiety as
she pursues what may be her last hope.

                         ANNE
                    (hysterically)
         Wait! Wait!
                         (beat)
         Don't run!
                 (beat; voice breaking)
         Don't run away from me! Please come
         back!
                 (beat; extendedly)
         COME BACK!

CAMERA HOLDS on her tormented face as she rides in
hapless pursuit of yesterday.

                    SERLING'S VOICE
         This is the face of terror: Anne Marie
         Mitchell, forty-three years of age – her
         desolate existence once more afflicted by
         the hope of altering her past mistake –

                                        (CONTINUED)

47.   CONTINUED

    SERLING'S VOICE (CONT'D)
  a hope which is, unfortunately, doomed to
  disappointment.

48.   LONG MOVING SHOT – THE CHASE

Seen in the distance, CAMERA PASSING BEHIND f.g.
trees and bushes.

    SERLING'S VOICE
  For warnings from the future to the past
  must be taken in the past. Today may
  change tomorrow – but once today is
  gone, tomorrow can only look back – in
  satisfaction – or, as in the case of Anne
  Marie Mitchell, in regret; and in sorrow
  that the warning was ignored.

CAMERA PANS UP to the sky.

    SERLING'S VOICE (CONT'D)
  Said warning, as of now, stamped NOT
  ACCEPTED and stored away in the dead
  file – in the recording office of
  The Twilight Zone.

        FADE OUT:

    THE END

EPILOGUE

"BUTTON, BUTTON"

When *The Twilight Zone* series was revived in the mid-Eighties, only a single story by Richard Matheson was produced. It was telecast on March 7, 1986 and starred Mare Winningham and Brad Davis. Yet if he could have employed a time machine of his own device, Matheson probably would have insured the episode was never aired during his own lifetime.

"The first *Twilight Zone* series was by far the best one. The revived series was a little *too* ambitious, and I think by trying to do something new and bigger they lost the flavor. Some of them were well done, some of them weren't. When they did my story 'Button, Button' though, I thought they did an abominable job."

The history behind this episode is a convoluted one, to say the least. According to Alan Brennert in his "Introduction" to *New Stories from The Twilight Zone*, Matheson had originally written that story as a script for the original series, then rewrote it as a short story for *Playboy*, then rewrote it *again* as a one hour script for the revived *The Twilight Zone*. And Brennert freely admits in print that they botched the job. Even so, Matheson doesn't recall the sequence of events that way—at all.

"No—I hadn't ever written 'Button, Button' at that time. My first memory of it is as a short story. I had never submitted the idea to the original *Twilight Zone* since it was written years after. And I didn't even write the script from it for the new *Twilight Zone*. I just don't recall. Maybe I did, but they loused it up. Whatever the case, they *did* louse it up.

"He may have been thinking of 'Duel.' I tried to sell that idea to a number of shows and they all said, "No, there's not enough story here." So I figured I'd better write it as a short story first, which I did, and that appeared in *Playboy*." (Besides the *New Stories from The Twilight Zone* anthology, 'Button, Button' would also later be included in *Collected Stories*.) "I had also submitted the idea which eventually became the story 'Prey'—which Dan Curtis later made as part of *Trilogy of Terror*—I had originally submitted *that* to the original *Twilight Zone*. But they didn't go for it; I guess it would have been slightly derivative of the episode with Agnes Moorehead, 'The Invaders.'"

Ultimately, Matheson was so displeased with the changes made to his story he demanded his pseudonym "Logan Swanson" replace his own name in the credits.

"Good old Logan Swanson!" he now recalls with an affectionate chuckle. "I always wanted to write a short story about a writer sitting in a fancy restaurant, and this seedy guy in rags comes in and sits at his table. And his eyes are all red, and he hasn't slept for days, and it turns out to be the writer's pen-name—who is miserable because he got stuck with all the stuff the successful author didn't like."

"THE DOLL"

The other "lost" *Twilight Zone* script by Matheson is of course "The Doll," which was purchased for the original series, but not produced until years later as a segment of *Amazing Stories*. It aired on May 4, 1986 and starred John Lithgow and Annie Helm. Steven Spielberg, who was producing the series, invited Matheson to contribute, which coincidentally debuted the same season as the revived *The Twilight Zone* in the fall of 1985.

"I told the producers about the old script, and they read it and loved it. I think they approached the owners of *The Twilight Zone* and asked if I could have the rights back to the script. So they gave it to us and it was done for *Amazing Stories*. It turned out great! My recollection is that John Lithgow won an Emmy for his role.

"This all goes back to my 'non-relationship' with producer William Froug, who never cared for my writing. 'The Doll' situation is ample evidence of that. They had an entire script, but Froug just didn't like it. Fortunately, *Amazing Stories* was later able to get the rights to it. I made a few improvements to the script—I hope—but it was pretty much the same script, because there was no short story to adapt." (Fans on the lookout for "The Doll" should be pleased to know that it was eventually included in one of the several multi-part "TV-movies" compiled from the series.)

Never imagining that it would ever eventually be produced, Matheson had allowed the original script to be published in the June 1982 issue of *Rod Serling's The Twilight Zone Magazine*. It's quite remarkable the script was ever produced at all, as Matheson had once claimed the story would be rudely dismissed as "too sentimental" once the original *The Twilight Zone* went off the air. "Fortunately, Spielberg and his creative people were as inclined to sentiment as they were the scary stuff."

Apparently they were not alone in seeing the lasting value in the story: Matheson received a nomination from the Writers Guild of America for outstanding teleplay for "The Doll."

And so, with only a small delay of a few decades, this memorable "lost" script ultimately provided a perfectly suitable happy ending for Richard Matheson.

Both in—and out—of *The Twilight Zone*.

APPENDIX
Suggested Further Reading
And Viewing

Beyond the fact that the phrase "the twilight zone" has become part of our everyday language, the television series has been preserved in our popular culture in a number of mediums. These include several books about the series, three biographies of Rod Serling, an official magazine, at least two comic book series, a graphic novel, audiocassettes, board games, soundtrack albums, computer games, a trivia collection, and on and on. Herein, a brief overview of the more vital books—and videocassettes of episodes—available to fans of the series.

* Bloch, Robert. *Twilight Zone: The Movie.* New York: Warner Books, 1983. (A novelization of the motion picture, authored by a world-famous writer of horror and suspense—who, curiously and regrettably—never wrote for the original series.)

* Engel, Joel. *Rod Serling: The Dreams and Nightmares of Life in The Twilight Zone.* Chicago: Contemporary Books, 1989.
(A biography of Rod Serling.)

* Gibson, Walter. *Rod Serling's The Twilight Zone.* New York: Grossett & Dunlap, 1963. (A collection of "13 New Stories from the Supernatural Especially Written for Young People." At the time of its publication, a very popular hardcover edition of original stories.

Curiously, none were adapted from any episode in the series, yet the collection was fully authorized by Rod Serling, nonetheless.)

* Gibson, Walter. *Rod Serling's The Twilight Zone Revisited.* New York: Grossett & Dunlap, 1964. ("Thirteen New and Unforgettable Explorations into the Realm of the Supernatural." Another authorized collection of original short stories, most noteworthy for the fact that two—"The Purple Testament" and "The 16-Millimeter Shrine"—were actually based on episodes penned by Serling. Also, for no clear reason, the paperback editions from the same publisher are each shorn a few of the stories, and were then inexplicably no longer packaged as "juveniles.")

* Greenberg, Martin H., Matheson, Richard, and Waugh, Charles (editors). *The Twilight Zone: The Original Stories.* New York: Avon Books, 1985. (The definitive collection—with one exception not included due to reasons of copyright—of all the short stories purchased by the series for adaptation into episodes. Naturally, the anthology contains the six original stories written by Matheson. The obvious exclusion is the "lost" story "And Now I'm Waiting," the basis for the episode "A World of His Own." Matheson himself also includes a warmly nostalgic introduction.)

* Greenberg, Martin H. (editor). *New Stories from The Twilight Zone.* New York: MJF Books (reprint edition as *The New Twilight Zone*), 1991. (An anthology of "21 Tales by the Greatest Sci-Fi and Dark Fantasy Writers of Our Time." In spite of the somewhat misleading title, this collection refers to the revived series of the Eighties. It contains the original Matheson story "Button, Button.")

* Sander, Gordon F. *Serling: The Rise and Twilight of Television's Last Angry Man.* New York, Dutton, 1992.
(A biography of Rod Serling.)

* Schumer, Arlen. *Visions from The Twilight Zone.* San Francisco: Chronicle Books, 1991. A wonderful, if difficult to summarize examination of the series. Schumer is an award-winning designer, who formatted his book to try and duplicate, in print and with

graphics, the experience the show presented in the same spirit as a viewer might undergo in watching it on a black and white television. For example, the typeface of the book is the very same typeface used on the opening and closing credits of the series itself! Unique, delightfully obsessive, and highly enjoyable once you realize you're not meant to simply "read" it as much as lose yourself between its covers.

* Serling, Rod. *Stories From the Twilight Zone.* New York: Bantam Books, 1960. (Collects six scripts from the series, adapted into short story form. Curiously, this is the only volume of the trio to note the original broadcast dates and to include Serling's closing narration to each episode.)

* —*More Stories From The Twilight Zone.* New York: Bantam Books, 1961. (Collects seven more stories adapted from the series.)

* —*New Stories From The Twilight Zone.* New York: Bantam Books, 1962. (Collects six more stories adapted from the series. Since their initial publication, these three collections have been reissued by publishers in various omnibus editions, beginning with a Science Fiction Book Club edition in 1963.)

* Serling, Carol (editor). *Journeys to The Twilight Zone.* New York, DAW Books, 1993. (An anthology collecting new stories created in the spirit of the original series, edited by the widow of Rod Serling. Also includes a classic story adaptation from the original series by Rod Serling.)

* —*Return to The Twilight Zone.* New York, DAW Books, 1994. (An anthology collecting new stories created in the spirit of the original series. Again includes a story adaptation from the original series by Rod Serling.)

* —*Adventures in The Twilight Zone.* New York: DAW Books, 1995. (Third in the series of new stories created in the spirit of the original series.)

* Wolfe, Peter. *In the Zone: The Twilight World of Rod Serling.* Kentucky: Bowling Green State Univ., 1997. (A biography of Rod Serling.)

* Zicree, Mark Scott. *The Twilight Zone Companion.* New York, Bantam Books, 1982. (Quite simply, *the* definitive guide to the series, the result of five years of exhaustive research by the author. A must-have for anyone with any interest in the series; quite simply one of the best examinations of a television show that has ever been done. A "Revised and Expanded Thirtieth Anniversary Edition" was published in 1989, covering the motion picture and the revived series.)

Finally, three important associational items:

* *"Rod Serling's The Twilight Zone Magazine."*
Published from 1981 to 1989, this nationally distributed glossy magazine not only first serialized Zicree's book, it has since become an incomparable research tool for anyone attempting to grasp the lasting impact the series has had on our popular culture.

In many ways, RSTZM remains the greatest American magazine in contemporary history to deal with dark fantasy and horror in the mass media. Beyond serving as a barometer of anything *fantastique* that was happening in the mass media, the graphic arts, and literature, it featured new stories by the field's greatest living practitioners: Stephen King, Peter Straub, Anne Rice, Dean Koontz. The magazine also saw fit to publish the early fiction of such new masters as Joe R. Lansdale, David J. Schow, Chet Williamson, Dan Simmons and not surprisingly, Richard Matheson's son Richard Christian Matheson.

Each issue also reprinted the script from an individual episode from the original series. Naturally, the majority of these featured the work of Rod Serling. His widow, Carol Serling, served as associate publisher and "guiding spirit" to the publication throughout its entire run.

While Richard Matheson contributed a few scripts and stories, all previously unpublished; most notably the tale "And Now I'm Waiting." (Presently still uncollected.) The magazine also published for the first time the original script for "The Doll."

For no sensible reason, no American publisher has yet seen fit to issue a "best of" retrospective of any of the material from this incredible and virtually irreplaceable periodical.

* *"The Best of Rod Serling's The Twilight Zone."* (VCD 47233) Varase Sarabande: The Original Television Scores.
Originally offered in a series of vinyl records in the Eighties, selections from the five albums in the series were later reissued (to date) on this one CD. Containing the unforgettable opening and closing theme to the series—of course!—the collection is also notable for presenting Jerry Goldsmith's wonderfully eerie score to "The Invaders."

* Videocassettes/DVD.
Numerous episodes—two episodes to a cassette for the most part—of the series are currently available, the only authorized edition being *"Twilight Zone: The Collector's Edition"* from Columbia House. The same company with the popular record and movie clubs, the Matheson episodes are of course included here in this exclusively mail-order "club." From time to time, however, various episodes may be found for sale in the larger video stores nationwide. The full series is now available on DVD from Image Entertainment. Each disc contains three episodes, some with special features. IE has also released a Special Edition *"40th Anniversary Gift Pack"* on DVD containing nineteen episodes (three of the Matheson episodes) on six dics. And finally, also from IE, *"More Treasures of the Twilight Zone"* with three episodes, rare footage of creator Rod Serling interviewd in 1959 by Mike Wallace and "Inside the Twilight Zone," including info on Rod Serling, a history of the series, reviews of each episode, cast info and a season-by-season commentary. The series itself is currently exclusively broadcast in America on the Sci-Fi Channel.

About The Author

Born in Allendale, New Jersey in 1926, Richard Burton Matheson has been rightly called "one of the world's most diverse and respected writers of imaginative fiction."

For his fantastic novels, screenplays, teleplays, and short stories, he has won the Bram Stoker Award, the Hugo, Golden Spur, the Edgar, World Fantasy, and Writer's Guild Awards, among others. He has been named a Grand Master by both the World Fantasy and Horror Writers Association.

Among his classic novels are *I Am Legend, The Shrinking Man, Hell House,* and *Bid Time Return.* (All of which he also adapted into feature films.) In the Sixties, he also wrote a series of successful interpretations of Edgar Allan Poe for director Roger Corman. Some of his most acclaimed movies-for-television are *Duel, The Night Stalker* (later made into the series *Kolchak: The Night Stalker*), *The Morning After, Trilogy of Terror,* and *The Dreamer of Oz.*

In 1989, his multiple award-winning *Collected Stories* was published. In 1997, three of his earliest suspense novels were collected in the omnibus edition entitled simply *Noir. Hunger and Thirst,* his first written novel, was finally published in 2000.

He resides in Los Angeles, California.

About The Editor

Stanley Wiater is a widely published cineteratologist and observer of popular culture. He has interviewed more horror and dark suspense authors and filmmakers than any other contemporary writer. His first compilation, *Dark Dreamers: Conversations with the Masters of Horror*, won the Bram Stoker Award from the Horror Writers Association in 1990. A companion volume, *Dark Visions: Conversations with the Masters of the Horror Film*, was a Bram Stoker Award finalist. *Comic Book Rebels: Conversations with the Creators of the New Comics,* co-authored with Stephen R. Bissette, was both an Eisner Award and Harvey Award nominee. His latest compilation, *Dark Thoughts: On Writing, Advice and Commentary from Fifty Masters of Fear and Suspense,*won the Bram Stoker Award in 1997.

Wiater's first published short story was the sole winner of a competition judged by Stephen King. He has also edited the acclaimed original anthologies *Night Visions 7* and *After The Darkness.* In 1993 he was Master of Ceremonies at the World Horror Convention, where Richard Matheson was honored as Grand Master. (And where the initial idea for this present collection was first suggested.) He is currently the writer and host of a television series, *Dark Dreamers,* inspired by his interview books.

He can be reached via his website at: www.stanleywiater.com.

Other Titles Coming By Richard Matheson!

Signed Limited Edition of
STIR OF ECHOES
Includes Matheson's
COMPLETE screenplay

COMING IN 2003
THE COLLECTED STORIES OF RICHARD MATHESON VOL. 1
Edited by Stanley Wiater

ABU AND THE 7 MARVELS
Previously unpublished children's novel
lavishly illustrated by William Stout
ISBN 1-887368-49-3

DARKER PLACES
Two previously unpublished dark novellas
and one short story

A PRIMER OF REALITY
An approach to the meaning of life

COME FYGURES, COME SHADOWES
Previously unpublished novel

RICHARD MATHESON'S THE TWILIGHT ZONE SCRIPTS VOL. 1
Now available! ISBN 1-887-3684-26

Order your favorite
RICHARD MATHESON titles
from our online bookstore and check out
our website for more from Gauntlet Press!

Free chapbooks of an unpublished Matheson short story are available with
selected titles, as well as CD readings from Matheson classics
SOMEWHERE IN TIME, THE SHRINKING MAN
and his previously unpublished first novel HUNGER AND THIRST

www.gauntletpress.com
Shopping Cart and Secure Server
for your convenience and protection.